Class No. 362.7	Book No. 13203

Author	IWANIEC, Dorata AND HILL, Malcolm. (Eds.)
Title	Child welfare policy and practice: Issues and lessons emerging from current practice.

This book must be returned on or before the date shown above

North Trafford College of FE

Talbot Road Stretford Manchester

Tel: 0161 886 7012

of related interest

Residential Child Care
International Perspectives on Links with Families and Peers
Edited by Mono Chakrabarti and Malcolm Hill
ISBN 1 85302 687 5 pb

Making an Impact – Children and Domestic Violence
A Reader
Marianne Hester, Chris Pearson and Nicola Harwin
ISBN 1 85302 844 4 pb

Children and Domestic Violence
Action Towards Prevention
Caroline McGee
ISBN 1 85302 827 4 pb

Domestic Violence
Guidelines for Research-Informed Practice
Edited by John P. Vincent and Ernest N. Jouriles
ISBN 1 85302 854 1 pb

Family Support
Direction From Diversity
Edited by John Canavan, Pat Dolan and John Pinkerton
ISBN 1 85302 850 9 pb

Children in Need and Voluntary Sector Services
The Northern Ireland Approach
Kerry O'Halloran, Arthur Williamson and Goretti Horgan
ISBN 1 85302 712 X pb

Permanent Family Placement for Children of Minority Ethnic Origin
June Thoburn, Liz Norford and Steven Parvez Rashid
ISBN 1 85302 875 4 pb

Effective Ways of Working with Children and their Families
Edited by Malcolm Hill
ISBN 1 85302 619 0 pb

Child Welfare Services
Developments in Law, Policy, Practice and Research
Edited by Malcolm Hill and Jane Aldgate
ISBN 1 85302 316 7 pb

Social Work with Children and Families
Getting into Practice
Ian Butler and Gwenda Roberts
ISBN 1 85302 365 5 pb

Child Welfare Policy and Practice

Issues and Lessons Emerging from Current Research

Edited by Dorota Iwaniec and Malcolm Hill

Jessica Kingsley Publishers
London and Philadelphia

First published in the United Kingdom in 2000 by
Jessica Kingsley Publishers Ltd,
116 Pentonville Road, London
N1 9JB, England
and
325 Chestnut Street,
Philadelphia, PA 19106, USA.

www.jkp.com

© Copyright 2000 Jessica Kingsley Publishers

Library of Congress Cataloging in Publication Data
Child welfare policy and practice : issues and lessons emerging from current
  research / edited by Dorota Iwaniec and Malcolm Hill
      p.   cm.
Includes bibliographical references and index.
ISBN 1-85302-812-6 (alk. paper)
1. Child welfare--Government policy--Great Britain. I. Iwaniec, Dorota. II. Hill,
Malcolm.
HV751.A6C586   1999
362.7'0941--dc21   99-41627
                                                                             CIP

British Library Cataloguing in Publication Data
Child welfare policy and practice : issues and lessons emerging from current research
  1. Child welfare - Great Britain 2. Child welfare - Government policy - Great
  Britain
I. Iwaniec, Dorota. II. Hill, Malcolm
362.7'0941
ISBN 1 85302 812 6

ISBN 1 85302 812 6

Printed and Bound in Great Britain by
Athenaeum Press, Gateshead, Tyne and Wear

Contents

Part I Services for Children in the Community

Part II Looked-after Children

Part III Child Protection

List of Figures

List of Tables

Issues Emerging from Child Care Research: Post-implementation of the Children Act 1989

Dorota Iwaniec and Malcolm Hill

Law, policy and research

In his foreword to the book *Child Care Research Policy and Practice*, Sir William Utting (1989) stated:

> Being professional imposes, among other requirements, the responsibility of keeping up-to-date with the professional development in existing knowledge and improving skills in one's chosen craft. Conscientious application to the lessons of relevant research is an essential part of this process. (p.6)

Social work as a profession has never experienced so many changes or seen so many new developments in policy and practice as in the last decade. These changes were particularly important and took place at considerable speed in the field of child and family welfare. The renaissance in child care policy and practice has been dictated by political factors, societal pressures and general dissatisfaction with how cases of presumed child abuse were dealt with. A fundamental review was required to strike a balance between protection and prevention; to address a lack of involvement by parents in decision-making about their children; and to ascertain why there was a growing number of children entering the care system. It was also recognised that children's feelings and wishes were seldom taken into consideration. Within this context, the Children Act 1989 became law in England and Wales, and six years later the Children (Scotland) Act 1995 and Children (Northern Ireland) Order 1995 were introduced. Following the implementation of the Children Act, the Government commissioned 20 major research projects to monitor its effectiveness and to generate new knowledge. An extensive research programme indicated a growing awareness of the value, necessity and importance of research. Not only has central government policy become more concerned with its empirical base, but social work practice too has been urged and enabled to become more research-minded (Cheetham *et al.* 1992; Shaw 1996; Iwaniec and Pinkerton 1998). In child welfare, as in medicine, criminal justice and other spheres, increasing attention has been given to 'evidence-based practice' and 'what works?', although varied views are held about what can or should constitute appropriate evidence (Hill 1999a). For example, Shaw (1999) distinguished four paradigmatic approaches to evaluation: positivism, postpositivism, critical evaluation and constructivist evaluation. Each may have merits, depending on the circumstances. Concerns with rigour need to be accompanied by relevance and reflection on personal or structural influences on research agendas, data production and interpretation.

Legislation brought about a new philosophy and new directions regarding child care law, policy and practice in the United Kingdom. These fundamental changes also created demands for clear, well-thought-out rules, procedures, regulations, and so on, based on sound research. Indeed, the need for new approaches to service delivery and the accumulation of knowledge deriving from such research (rather than ideologies and doctrines) became apparent. Implementing positively such extensive and complex legislation demanded rigorous and systematic evaluation of what was effective and what needed to be changed or modified. For all these reasons, the contributions of social researchers to the formulation of well- informed policies and practice cannot be underestimated. This book presents material from current and recent research illustrating most of the key developments in child welfare. The studies were conducted in Scotland and Northern Ireland but they reflect policy and practice across the UK and indeed elsewhere.

Child protection and family support

The relationship between policy and research has not been a simple one-way process. The 1990s witnessed a refocusing of policy and practice with the aim of developing more informal family support as an alternative to investigative intervention. This both informed and was reinforced by the programme of research reviewed in *Messages from Research* (Department of Health 1995). Within formal child protection arrangements, attempts have increasingly been made to work openly and where possible jointly with parents. Research has broadly supported this trend, while clarifying some of the difficulties (Thoburn, Lewis and Shemmings 1995; Marsh and Peel 1998). Many parents continue to experience confusion and alienation

(Corby and Millar 1997). Children too often feel their needs and wishes are neglected within an adult-oriented service, though when they are listened and spoken to sympathetically this is much appreciated (Farmer 1993; McGee and Westcott 1996).

Further research has been stimulated because concepts introduced by child care legislation had to be defined, and information gathered and analysed in order to evaluate the newly implemented changes. Such key concepts as *children in need, needs assessment, family support* and *significant harm*, which are central to legislation in all parts of the UK, are very complex and so required extensive research to assess how they work (Hill and Aldgate 1996).

Family support has been given a new legislative mandate and directives throughout the UK. The philosophy behind the Children Act 1989 in England and Wales, and the equivalent statutes in Scotland and Northern Ireland (1995), rests on the belief that children are generally best looked after within the family, with both parents playing a full part and without resort to legal proceedings. That belief is reflected in:

- the new concept of parental responsibility
- the local authority's duty to provide support for children in their families
- the local authority's duty to return a child looked after by them to the family unless this is against his/her interests.

Such requirements, if they are to have any real meaning, put tremendous responsibility on social workers and resource managers to conduct skilled assessments of needs and to provide interventions based on recognised needs in order to facilitate and produce the necessary change in the child's parents and the conditions of his/her home life.

It became very clear that in order to care for vulnerable children and families new services and resources would have to be created to meet the needs of children and the obligations of the legislation. Equally, it became apparent that effectiveness of service delivery in terms of outcomes would have to be evaluated and monitored for value for money and benefit to the service users.

Although family support is probably the primary policy matter facing child welfare as we enter the twenty-first century, there is still considerable confusion and debate over what is meant by the concept and whether the principle advocated by the Act actually works in practice. The extensive literature on the subject, based on both theoretical and empirical work, has promoted, described and evaluated family support but at the same time questioned the government's commitment to provide the resources to make it work (Tunstill 1998).

These issues are evident in the wealth of research studies in the UK which have described and evaluated child welfare and family support using qualitative or mixed methodologies (Gibbons, Thorpe and Wilkinson 1990; Thoburn *et al.* 1995; Thoburn, Wilding and Watson 1997; Higgins, Pinkerton and Devine 1998a). Family support as a means of prevention is nothing new and was widely used before the Children Act 1989 (Phelan 1983; Smith 1987; De'Ath 1988). A wide range of services is available to assist families on an open-access or more targeted basis. Many of these are directed at families with young children, so older children and their parents may find it harder to access support. A range of various family support initiatives has also been evaluated over the past decades such as HomeStart (Van der Eyken 1982; Frost 1996) and Newpin (Oakley and Roberts 1996). The study by Gibbons *et al.* (1990) indicated that families benefited when there was a choice of formal and informal services in their area. Long-term gains for disadvantaged children appear to be best when they participate in structured programmes with an active learning curriculum for an extended period (McDonald and Roberts 1995). On the other hand, many parents value the support provided in family centres, which on the whole tend to be less formalised but more participative (Hawthorne-Kirk 1995).

Although current family support research is showing some signs of narrowing and becoming more focused (McAuley 1999) there remains in the UK literature a dearth of studies which evidence the effectiveness of family support services or interventions by examining the outcomes for children and families. Attempting to address this gap has led to further debate on how such effectiveness can best be evaluated, as summarised by Hill (1999b).

Steering a pragmatic course through such debate suggests that in the search for 'what works' in family support, a number of research issues remain to be tackled. There has to be much more rigorous evaluation to identify what works better for which children and what problems. There is a need to conduct rigorous qualitative case studies in order to understand and explore in greater detail how interventions are experienced by both workers and service users. Finally, there is the issue of finite resources, requiring a much more detailed understanding of the real costs of family support not just to government departments but also to informal carers and communities (Beecham 1999). The achievement of this requires the development, specifically in relation to family support, of a much more sensitive and sophisticated social care economics (Beecham and Knapp 1995).

The need to provide services to prevent abuse occurring in the first place or prevent it recurring has always been considered and claimed as a primary objective of social services child care teams. On closer examination, however, only cases of actual physical or sexual abuse receive prompt attention and are allocated for assessment and intervention, while referrals of physical neglect and emotional abuse are often left unassessed. Wilding and Thoburn's (1997) study found that although physical neglect was the largest category of child maltreatment, such cases were the lowest in resource allocation for family support. Equally, emotional maltreatment is seldom investigated in spite of the serious effects it has on children's development and behaviour (Iwaniec 1997; Doyle 1997; Glaser and Prior 1997).

The problem of when and how to intervene in cases of emotional and physical neglect, including failure-to-thrive, was grossly overlooked prior to the Children Act and has continued to be marginalised in post-Act policy and practice. Managers and practitioners alike are still preoccupied with the cases of sexual and physical abuse, leaving little time and few resources to deal with the growing number of children in need of family support and, in some instances, protection. Neglected children and neglectful families do not appear often on the social services' priority lists (although they clearly come under the category of children in need) and even when they do they are dealt with briefly as a response to crises which are then patched up, and left without proper assessment of needs and ongoing support (Iwaniec and Herbert 1999).

There seem to be two main influences on current policy and practice. The first one is scarcity of the resources necessary to engage fully in preventative work, and the second is targeting cases where risk of abuse seems to be greater and evidence of such abuse is more obvious and explicit. Additionally, neglect referrals are not seen as urgent cases and are therefore put to the bottom of the pile. All-embracing deprivation, emotional vacuum and lack of attention are not seen as immediate significant harm and therefore do not warrant action for protection or need assessed family support.

According to the requirements of the Children Act 1989 social services were expected to deliver on family support while maintaining a high level of child protection work, but in collaboration with other agencies such as health and education, each participating in the provision of services to ensure child health, education and welfare. In reality there has been little collaboration, leaving the burden largely to social services. The Audit Commission report *Seen But Not Heard* (1994) examined the co-ordination of community child health and social services for children in need in England and Wales, and found that changes demanded by new legislation required major adjustments in the way health and personal social services agencies discharged their responsibilities and collaborated to promote child health and well-being. Social services and local authority health services were recommended to:

- ensure that children are given opportunities to establish strong attachment and a stable relationship with their carers without disruption for the duration of childhood
- provide services which meet specific objectives of children and family needs
- check outcomes to verify the effectiveness of services
- work jointly to provide an integrated range of services and work in partnership with parents.

The Audit Commission noted that neither health nor social services were aware of what was needed in their catchment areas, that the existing services' objectives were vague and that the outcomes were unclear. They found a lack of meaningful collaboration and strategic planning. The Commission report outlined some ideas on how different agencies could work jointly. They stated that, for example, family centres could provide a suitable focus for joint work between health, social services, education and voluntary organisations. The whole range of problems and issues could be dealt with at one place with input from different professions. Indeed Pinkerton, Higgins and Devine (2000) found that family centres they investigated provided a forum for group work for mothers or both parents, counselling, parent-training, playgroups for children, advice on housing and social security benefits, and advice on legal matters.

While there are still problems with making family support work in an informed way, progress is being made. Provision of help for children in the community in terms of services and therapeutic intervention is gradually becoming more multi-dimensional and multi-faceted, reflecting the different needs of children according to their developmental stages and presenting problems. There is some positive movement in relation to children and young people with disability (Monteith and Cousins 1999). The comparison of service availability and information regarding this client group prior to the implementation of the Children (NI) Order 1995 and three years after showed considerable change both in their recognition as children in need and in the provision of better co-ordinated resources. However, much remains to be done on the multi-professional level to meet their long-term needs and those of their carers.

Looked-after children

Besides reformulating the bases for addressing the needs of children living in the community, the new legislation reinforced positive parenting in substitute care provided by the local authorities. It became the duty of local authorities to provide improved standards for children in their care, preferably approximating to that expected of reasonable parents. The Children Act 1989 requires not only the provision of care to protect children from further harm, but also the opening of opportunities to prepare them for life. Local authorities, therefore, should act towards children in their care as any well-meaning natural parents would towards their own offspring. This means provision of a home; of a good quality of physical and emotional care; of a sense of security and continuity; of a feeling of being wanted, respected and treated fairly; of access to education and all-round health care; and of good models of how to behave and communicate, how to deal with stressful events and how to approach problem-solving. Additionally, in order to become well adjusted and prepared for life and independent living, children must be helped to acquire the necessary information about the environment in which they live, the culture to which they belong and the prevailing moral code that shapes behaviour and attitudes. While most carers and residential workers try to meet children's developmental needs (and at times do so under adverse circumstances), some children looked after by local authorities in residential and foster care cannot always claim that good quality care was provided. The changes in service provision were long overdue and require rigorous attention.

To promote the welfare both of children in need living in the community and of those looked after away from home, Children's Services Plans have become mandatory. These are meant to be based on careful assessment by local authorities of the types and levels of need in their areas and of the services available or required to meet those needs. In order to have coherent and comprehensive child care plans, and thereby make sure that children's needs are satisfactorily met, all agencies providing services for children have been requested to make plans together. As the Act requires co-operation between different departments and the voluntary sector in looking at all aspects of children's needs, such as health, education and social welfare, the implementation of Children's Services Plans is being welcomed by all those who care about child welfare. It is important, however, to assess how far ideals of co-operation and partnership are being put into effect.

As new policies and practice developed following the implementation of the Children Act some difficult issues have begun to emerge, particularly in the areas of child protection and parental rights and responsibilities. The thrust to shift resources from formal child protection to family support has created decision-making and ideological problems for managers and practitioners. In the midst of organisational and policy changes, children in residential and foster care have often been forgotten. Research findings from the inspection of 27 social service departments in England and Wales, the Warner (1992) and Sir William Utting reports (1997), and other research projects identified several worrying problems which demanded considerable revision of policies, practice and ideology associated with children in care. They found a high level of placement breakdowns; the average child was moved to approximately five different homes. The Who Cares? Trust, in their research paper *Remember My Messages* (Shaw 1998), found that 9 per cent of 11-year- old and younger children moved more than ten times. Of those who had been in care for five or more years, nearly a quarter (24%) had been in 11 or more different placements. For many of those children, who have drifted from one home to another with little or no possibility of ever being able to return home, adoption clearly could have been the best option to provide permanence, security, identity, and development of lifelong attachment to a family.

Choice of placement was found to be poor: children were often placed on the basis of vacancy (not suitability), and seldom were their wishes heard as to where they preferred to be placed. There was also a serious shortage of placements, preventing appropriate and suitable matching. Many research reports consistently pointed out serious inadequacies in the way placements were dealt with and the negative effect this had on children's well-being and behaviour (Berridge and Brodie 1996; Utting 1997; Triseliotis 1999). The 1990s have seen the documentation of the distinctive experiences and associated needs of black and minority ethnic children who are looked after in public care. These include discrimination in daily life, insensitive referral processes and neglect of family strengths. More positively, examples of good practice have been recorded. Although black children are still over-represented in the care system (especially those of mixed parentage), far more than formerly are now placed in families with a similar background (Barn, Sinclair and Ferdinand 1997; Ince 1998; Moosa-Mitha 1999).

Berridge and Brodie (1996) drew attention to the plight of children in residential care, pointing to the fundamental lack of interest, commitment and resources to make residential child care effective and successful. Residential care suffered, of course, from a collapse of confidence because of abuse of children by residential child care workers and malpractices in behaviour management. There were also ideological reasons why residential child care has been undermined (and subsequently neglected) in the preference for foster care. Institutional placements were regarded as inappropriate for preparing youngsters for life and meeting their developmental needs. Consequently children were not given a choice or even asked where they would like to live. Yet the evidence is that residential units and schools can have a positive impact on many of the residents. Among the vital ingredients appear to be clear leadership, careful planning, staff consensus and involvement of family members (Triseliotis *et al.* 1995; Sinclair and Gibbs 1998).

Children old enough and capable of making decisions should be allowed a choice: many, though by no means all, older children prefer residential care, as they often feel that they already have a family. A few are so grossly disturbed that no single family could cope with their behaviour: they are simply unfosterable. Attempts to do so only leads to placement breakdown and consequently to more problems for everybody concerned. Yet we also know that some children want to belong to a family and to be a part of a normal family unit. For some, to live in an institution, regardless of how good it might be, is degrading and stigmatising. Young children are better off in foster care as well. The fact is that both are needed if informed decisions are to be made about the best choices for children. Much can be learned, and better policies and practice put in place, if children and young people are listened to and their messages based on their experiences while in care taken on board. Children need stability, security and a sense of belonging in order to develop secure attachments to the people with whom they live. Attachment affects every aspect of a child's life, as it is at the core of emotional well-being: its development requires consistency of care and the opportunity to develop trusting relationships with carers, the basis on which the child can build future relationships (Howe 1995).

Education of children in care required urgent attention and collaborative efforts between social services and education departments, and more tolerance and flexibility from the schools (Jackson 1994). This has been recognised as a major shortcoming of current services, especially as successful attainment at school would more often than not determine self-advancement and opportunities for job satisfaction. More than 33 per cent of children in care were not receiving education, and one in four of those aged 14–16 did not regularly attend school. Many had been excluded from school, and had no regular educational placement. At the point of leaving care three out of four children had no qualification and eight out of ten had no job to go to (Utting 1997).

The Who Cares? Trust (Shaw 1998) found that only 57 per cent of children had care plans, in spite of their being a legal requirement for all children looked after by local authorities. Thirty per cent of children were unsure about whether they had one, and 13 per cent did not have one. Furthermore, only two-thirds of young people know how to make an official complaint about the way they were looked after in care.

Many researchers found that the plight of children leaving care was serious (Stein 1990; Pinkerton and Stein 1995). They felt abandoned, lost and totally helpless, drifting from one bad situation into another. The Who Cares? Trust (Shaw 1998) reported that one out of four young girls leaving care was pregnant, 22 per cent of them ended up in prison, and about 33 per cent were sleeping on the streets.

Quality Protects

In response to these disturbing research findings on the way children in state care were looked after, the Government issued a White Paper entitled *Quality Protects* (Department of Health 1998), which highlighted eight specific objectives for children's services:

1. To ensure that children are securely attached to carers capable of providing safe and effective care for the duration of childhood. The main aim here is to reduce the number of placement changes to promote stable, secure attachment to significant carers.

2. To ensure that children are protected from emotional, physical, and sexual abuse and neglect. A key issue concerns how significant harm is to be defined and assessed. It is necessary to redevelop reliable operational threshold criteria based on child development and risk factors.

3. To ensure that children in need gain maximum life-chance benefits from educational opportunities, health care and social care. This implies provision of services which meet the needs of all children and counteract the disadvantage of families in need of support.

4. To ensure that children 'looked after' gain maximum life-chance benefits from educational opportunities, health care and social care. Poor educational attainment by children looked after has been identified as a major shortcoming of current services. The aim here is to bring those children closer into line with the experiences and achievements of other local children.

5. To ensure that those young people leaving care are not isolated as they enter adulthood and participate socially and economically as citizens. Local authorities should have an 'open door' policy for

these young people until they are 19 years of age, or 21 if they are in education.

6.   To ensure that children with specific social needs arising out of disability or a health condition are living in families or other appropriate settings in the community where their assessment needs are adequately met and reviewed. Disabled children and their families are often neglected and services that they require are fragmented and poorly co-ordinated. Multi-disciplinary service plans are needed and should be well co-ordinated.

7.   To ensure that referral and assessment processes discriminate effectively between different types and levels of need and produce a timely service response. Service provision must be based on competent assessment and acted upon promptly.

8.   To ensure that resources are planned and provided at levels which represent best value for money and allow for choice and different responses for different needs and circumstances. Services and accommodation for children must take account of the children's wishes and provide options for both service users and professionals. Whenever possible provision should be based on evidence about effectiveness in relation to costs.

Outline of the book

This book aims to provide readers with information and findings arising from current research, addressing many of the issues described above. It covers the core areas of social work practice and service provision with children and families, ranging from child protection through family support to substitute care. The book is divided into three parts according to the three major themes:

- *Part I* discusses research findings and policy and practice developments for children and families living in the community.

- *Part II* deals with some issues arising from *Quality Protects*, the Government White Paper on 'looked after children'.

- *Part III* looks at some important research findings in the child protection field and discusses their implications for policy and practice.

Chapter 2, written by Chief Social Services Inspectors from Scotland and Northern Ireland, stands on its own and is not linked to any part of the book.

This chapter presents current issues and policies relating to the functions of personal social services (PSS) in both countries. Recent developments in research and development (R & D) strategies are briefly discussed.

Part I: Services for children in the community

In Chapter 3 Kay Tisdall, Bernadette Monaghan, and Malcolm Hill review the ways in which the development of Children's Services Plans in Scotland has reflected and been influenced by the evolving relationships between voluntary organisations and local authorities. Examples of positive co-operation are described in the context of a framework for considering inter-agency collaboration.

Chapter 4 deals with operationalisation of the definition of 'children in need' as contained in Article 17 of the Children (NI) Order 1995. Patrick McCrystal discusses three themes in this chapter: the definition of children in need; the operational indicators of need; and inter-agency co-operation.

In Chapter 5 Andrew Percy examines the principles underpinning needs-based planning and applies these to family and child care services in Northern Ireland. Clear definitions and systematic procedures for needs-based planning are described, with attention given to the roles of commissioners and providers. Recommendations for further developments in this area are provided.

In Chapter 6 Kathryn Higgins presents findings about the range of services which constitute family support. She also draws readers' attention to the methodological complexities involved in evaluating the diverse array of approaches used in very different family support settings.

Chapter 7 explores the experiences of young people with disabilities leaving school and their transition to adulthood. Marina Monteith discusses her findings of how appropriate transition planning can effect smooth and positive progress to adulthood.

Part II: Looked-after children

In Chapter 8 Suzanne Wheelaghan and Malcolm Hill share the findings and conclusions of the pilot evaluation study of the use of the Looking After Children (LAC) documentation records in six Scottish local authorities. The authors provide an overview of the system and identify its perceived advantages and disadvantages. Suggestions are made concerning the ways in which the materials are used.

In Chapter 9 Moira Borland reports key findings from our extensive review of research into policy and practice in relation to the education and educational attainments of children looked after by the local authorities.

Details are provided of initiatives designed to overcome long-standing difficulties in achieving effective co-operation.

In Chapter 10 Satnam Singh, Vijay Patel and Patricia Falconer report on the provision of services to meet the needs of black and minority ethnic children as required by the Children (Scotland) Act 1995. They examine to what extent the Children Services Plans have addressed and incorporated the needs of ethnic minority children.

Part III: Child protection

In Chapter 11 Dorota Iwaniec writes about the outcomes of her 20-year longitudinal study on children who fail to thrive. She discusses psychosocial factors affecting the progress of former non-organic failure-to-thrive subjects and the effectiveness of social work intervention as perceived by service users, e.g. parents or carers. She puts forward several recommendations on prevention of significant harm and improvement of practice.

Chapter 12 discusses the importance of effective communication with children, based on visual signals in child-to-child and adult-to-child interactions. Gwyneth Doherty-Sneddon, Sandra McAuley and Ozlem Carrera share results from their experimental research on communicating with children and discuss how good communication strategies can improve the use of the live link with child witnesses in court work.

In Chapter 13 Malcolm Hill and Dorota Iwaniec draw together the messages emerging from the previous chapters and discuss how these findings should influence policy and practice in a wide range of child and family welfare work.

The Legal and Policy Context for Children's Services in Scotland and Northern Ireland

Angus Skinner and Kevin McCoy

Scottish legislation and practice

The Children (Scotland) Act 1995 has been implemented for some time now and its new provisions and terminology have become commonplace. Before discussing some of its key principles, I would like to consider briefly the relationship between the new legislation and Scottish social work practice. I wish to argue that the law provides a springboard for professional decision-making and imaginative practice, not a narrow straightjacket.

Local authorities and practitioners often cite legislation as placing clear boundaries on what they may and may not do. The law is nevertheless open to considerable interpretation – hence the calls for guidance from the Scottish Executive. But is there a question to be posed? Does children's legislation only limit the scope for agencies' action and therefore reinforce agencies' need for instruction and prescription from politicians and policy-makers on how they may use their resources and how they may intervene in family life? After all, Scottish children's legislation was developed after extensive consultation and is based on a wide consensus. It is only one of the tools alongside local resources and services and professional skills and judgement which local authorities and voluntary organisations use to improve the quality of life and experience of children in their areas. Perhaps practitioners and agencies could and should use the law creatively to achieve the outcomes they seek, as could parents and families, with far less oversight by the Scottish Executive than has happened hitherto.

Similarly, using legislation and carrying out statutory work does not necessarily mean frequent recourse to the courts. Indeed the Children

(Scotland) Act 1995 includes a number of sections that support the use of minimum necessary intervention, consistent with promoting the welfare of the child. The Act also supports 'partnership' between agencies and with families. For instance, the Act requires corporate planning and places a duty on other agencies to assist the local authority in discharging its duty to safeguard and promote children's welfare [section 21]. Local authorities should be engaging in a dialogue with families and others about how to fulfil their responsibilities towards children, both on an individual basis and through Children's Services Plans.

In developing the guidance on the Children (Scotland) Act we tried to strike a balance between clarity about the intention of the law and flexibility to enable agencies to act independently and imaginatively. And as the guidance approaches its third reprint we began to feel we might have got the balance not too far wrong! However, we think that there is still too much paper emanating from the Scottish Executive and are doing our best to reduce this. It is interesting that Scotland provided three volumes of guidance to its Act, whereas Northern Ireland has six volumes of guidance on the Children (NI) Order and England and Wales nine volumes on the Children Act 1989.

Core principles in the Children (Scotland) Act 1995

Some of the key themes in the Children (Scotland) Act 1995 are as follows:

- making explicit parents' and public agencies' responsibilities towards children
- improving families' access to supportive and responsive welfare services
- making public agencies more accountable in their work with families
- listening to the concerns of children and their families.

Parental rights and responsibilities and the corresponding responsibilities of public agencies towards children

The Children (Scotland) Act is a unified piece of children's legislation bringing together aspects of private and public law governing the relationships between children, their parents and the state. Scots law now makes explicit what is meant by parental responsibilities and rights towards their children. These are to:

- safeguard and promote their child's health, development and welfare

- provide appropriate direction and guidance

- maintain personal relations and direct contact with the child

- act as the child's legal representative.

There is now some interest in England and Wales in specifying the nature of parental responsibilities in law as this may make it easier to clarify, for example, the extent to which parents can be held responsible for the actions of offending children. For instance, if parents are required to provide direction and guidance, have they done so and how? This begs questions about what appropriate 'direction and guidance' consists of and the courts may make judgements about this when determining the extent to which parents can be held accountable for the actions of their children.

This kind of question about what society might expect of parents and children abounds in legislation, and such expectations will change over time as social mores alter. The English Children Act 1989 bases the making of care and supervision orders on the likelihood of harm to the child as a result of 'the care given to the child not being what it would be reasonable to expect a parent to give to him.' Department of Health Guidance for England and Wales states that:

> The Court must compare the care being given to the child in question with what it would be reasonable to expect a reasonable parent to give him, having regard to the child's needs.

This introduces the hypothetical 'reasonable parent' as the gold standard to which social workers should refer, although maintaining a focus on the needs of the child in question. Social workers have to ask themselves daily 'how would a reasonable parent treat this particular child (taking into account the child's excellent social skills, or visual impairment, or talent for music, or propensity for car theft), how does this compare with how their actual parent treats them, and how far does the actual parent's care fall short of an acceptable standard (which in itself may vary according to the area or age in which the family find themselves)?'

Though we must remember that we are dealing here with very different legal systems, based on different principles, nonetheless it is useful to compare. Across the UK social workers have always made judgements about acceptable and unacceptable risk, and in general made them well, on the basis of research evidence, professional training and experience, and public policy. Most importantly they make them on the basis of the unique circumstances and potentialities of each individual child and family. The Scottish Executive has been asked to define in guidance the concept of 'significant harm' to assist agencies to decide when to apply for an emergency child protection order. Given the huge range of circumstances and families local authorities work with, would that be desirable, even if it were feasible? In my view, guidance would be unlikely to assist staff in making a decision; it might assist them to defend the decision on the basis that they had 'followed guidance'. But that humiliates the professionals and, much more importantly, de-humanises the children and their families.

The proliferation of guidance and procedures over the last decade has too often rigidified professional and agency responses to families in difficulty. Social work has suffered from the public and often painful scrutiny of its mistakes. But there is no hiding place in a risk-aversive reliance on procedures.

Here research evidence – the theme of this book – can have an important part to play. The priority is not for research that assesses whether or not agencies are following the legislation or procedures or regulations. Rather we want research that will point the way ahead: that will surprise us in some ways. While both academic and practitioner researcher can provide valuable information about how current interventions are working, just as important is to identify changing social circumstances and needs and to indicate innovative approaches.

Commissioning and reading research can be just as demanding a discipline as conducting it. Just as we all tend to be more receptive to research findings that confirm our presumptions or aspirations, so we may tend to commission research that is likely to prove, as it were, the wisdom of our policies and approaches. It takes thought to minimise such tendencies. It also takes quite an imaginative effort to envisage what it is we will want to know in four, five or six years time when the research is complete, and to commission research which will address the questions that we are then likely to be asking. Some of the questions will likely be the same, but many will not.

The active promotion of children's welfare

In Scotland, an extensive Child Care Law Review took place in the late 1980s. This had a considerable influence on the subsequent 1995 Act, alongside other developments such as the Clyde Report on the Orkney Inquiry and experience in England and Wales of the Children Act 1989. The Child Care Law Review proposed updating the existing welfare provisions relating to children. The general duty of local authorities to promote social welfare in their areas is retained and remains in the bedrock of Scottish social

work services [section 12 Social Work (Scotland) Act 1968]. The Children (Scotland) Act imposes a duty upon local authorities to provide welfare services to children in need. This gives greater emphasis to the 'positive promotion of children's welfare', rather than, as previously, the prevention of children being taken into care or referred to a Children's Hearing. (For details of the Scottish Children's Hearings system, see Lockyer and Stone 1998.) Help for families should be geared towards supporting the care of the child in their own family and community. Children's Services Plans should set out how local authorities expend their resources to achieve this and, in consultation with communities and other agencies, their priorities for future development.

The Scottish Executive examined the first set of Children's Services Plans produced in Scotland in 1998 to see what pointers they provided for the future. Many aspects of the plans are very good, but authorities generally found it difficult to spell out clear targets and specify how these could be achieved. This was frankly disappointing. There is not a lot of point to plans that are not based solidly on analysis of the current position and realistic, worked-through decisions on how key goals will be achieved. There seems to be a strange arrangement in some authorities to separate 'strategic planning' from financial and operational planning, with its annual round of budgets and real decisions. This is unlikely to enhance the value of the planning effort. Other aspects of Children's Services Plans are considered in the next chapter.

Local authority accountability and the courts

Any intervention in the life of a child or family should be on formally stated grounds, properly justified in close consultation with all the relevant parties. In Scotland the removal of children from their families where there are fears for their safety must be authorised by a Sheriff. Families have rights of appeal against court orders concerning their children. Courts and Children's Hearings may not make an order or supervision requirement unless this is clearly better for the child than not doing so. This is often termed the 'no order principle' and is often linked with the principle of 'minimum intervention' by the local authority.

However, minimum intervention has become a misused term. Some interpret this concept to mean that the local authority should not become involved with a family *unless* there is sufficient evidence to warrant exercise of statutory powers. As a result the local authority's initial contacts are often designed to investigate the extent to which a family is failing. This has been associated with a disproportionate focus on child protection investigations in social work services for children and families. That distorts the intentions behind the minimum intervention principle, which should refer to taking the least intrusive action required to support the family in successfully caring for their child, or in helping them make other appropriate arrangements. The least intrusive action should entail the minimum interference with families' responsibility for and rights in respect of their children and power to make decisions about their lives. For some families, though, that may mean extensive support, not minimal or no assistance. Minimum intervention is entirely consistent with very extensive involvement by the local authority at an early stage in family difficulties – i.e. early intervention.

Where a local authority has persistent concerns about a child's welfare or safety, then these should be set before the Children's Hearing or the court so that families have an opportunity to represent their views and be heard in a proper judicial forum. One of the things we need to look at more in Scotland is the nature of families' representation in Children's Hearings. This connects with the wider issue of participation by children, young people and their families in decision-making.

Children's and parents' views

The Act requires local authorities, courts and Children's Hearings to find out and take into account the views and wishes of children, their parents and other significant people in their lives when making any important decisions. This is not the same as agencies being required to do only what children want, or abrogating responsibility for intervening when parents' views may compromise a child's safety.

Some commentators suggest that provisions in the Children (Scotland) Act 1995 relating to children's views conflict with earlier legislation such as the Education Act 1980, which places emphasis on parents' wishes for their children's education. Children's needs are inextricably linked with their parents; the Children (Scotland) Act does not replace parents' views with children's views but adds an important dimension to agencies' consider-ations. Where there is disagreement and difficulty within families the task of professionals – and particularly social workers – is to work directly with people, listen and seek to understand the different perspectives, and apply their skills to help families resolve their problems. Unitary local authorities have a responsibility to help families achieve solutions which work for them, and not simply apply legislation rigidly. Thus education departments should not look only to the Education Acts, nor should social work services simply follow the Children (Scotland) Act: they should seek to act co-operatively, bearing in mind the principles of both (*see also* chapter 9). The Children

(Scotland) Act places duties on the local authority as a whole (rather than specific services) to act in a corporate fashion in the interests of children. This requirement can be used imaginatively and creatively to promote children's welfare through collaborative planning and co-operation in practice.

The legal and policy context in Northern Ireland

The Children (NI) Order of 1995 came into effect in November 1996. Unlike the Children (Scotland) Act 1995, the contents of the Children (Northern Ireland) Order 1995 mirror almost exactly those of the Children Act 1989. However, the local context for implementing this legislation is very different from that in England and Wales. As Kelly and Pinkerton (1996) observed:

> The fact that the Children (NI) Order 1995 is being introduced as the peace process gathers momentum is coincidental but fortuitous. It adds to the sense that perhaps this is the opportunity for fundamental change, The Order sets an agenda for realigning child care away from being a monitoring and policing service and towards empowerment through partnership. (p.53)

Before the 1995 Order Northern Ireland, in contrast to England, Wales and Scotland, had not had any significant children's legislation since 1968. The Order has four major public policy goals:

- the establishment of children as citizens in their own right
- a contemporary definition of parental responsibility
- a redefinition of the role of the state to support parents
- an emphasis on partnership with parents and other organisations.

Among the related major changes brought in by the new Order were the following:

- harmonising of public and private law
- the introduction of a unified family court system
- new duties to promote the welfare of children 'in need'
- the promotion of partnership with parents
- a range of court orders intended to match more closely children's needs for care and protection, in the context of continuing parental responsibility.

Whereas in Great Britain local authorities provide statutory social work services, in Northern Ireland the responsibility lies with joint health and social services boards and trusts. The Order has been amended to place a duty on health and social services boards to produce Children's Services Plans with an emphasis on the special needs of their populations and the shaping of services to meet these needs.

In addition to this legislation, consideration has also been given to the need to restructure the pattern of residential care for children to ensure an adequate level of differentiated provision with appropriate regimes and staffing levels. The final development in Children's Services worth noting is the establishment of the Guardian ad Litem Agency and the likely impact that this will have on decision-making in the courts and on social work practice.

The implementation of the 1995 Order has taken place alongside a number of other key policy developments, which both affect children and family services and give an important place to research.

The research context

The specific local context in Northern Ireland has encouraged the creation of new arrangements for research and development to shape the child care research agenda in the short to medium term, as the Order is implemented and its impact evaluated. A number of major changes have taken place or are planned. A single funding stream has been created for research with respect to health and personal social services (HPSS). This brings together research expenditure by the Department of Health and Social Services, health and social services boards, health and social services trusts, and special agencies. A linked development is the creation of a Research Strategy Group with representatives from a wide range of agencies. The integrated approach is also to be promoted by the Establishment of Commissioning and Grants Committees for Biomedical Sciences, Health Care and Social Care and ad hoc committees for research training and dissemination of research.

Regional Strategy 1997–2000

The distinctly close links between social welfare and health policies and organisations in Northern Ireland is illustrated by the Regional Strategy document for the years 1997–2000 (Department of Health and Social Services 1996b). This document set out four main aims. These were to encourage public policy which promotes health and social well-being, to support Community Development, to enhance the role of Primary Care and to place increased emphasis on effectiveness and measuring outcomes. This last accords a key role for evaluative research in monitoring and developing policies and services.

The Department of Health and Social Services wishes to see decisions about services and interventions throughout the health and personal social services being based on firm evidence of effectiveness in order to gain the greatest health and social gain from the resources available. The importance of achieving better outcomes is emphasised throughout the strategy. There are some interventions whose effectiveness lies beyond dispute, but many are subject to varying degrees of uncertainty and debate. It is recognised that professionals within the health and personal social services must be committed to evaluation of their work and dissemination of evaluation results.

As well as the four principles, the strategy sets out four interconnected strategic themes. These are:

- Promoting Health and Social Well-Being
- Targeting Health and Social Need (THSN) which relates to inequalities
- Improving Care in the Community
- Improving Acute Care.

The strategy identifies eight key areas where improvement is required and targets have been set within each of these key areas. For children there are targets in relation to stillbirths and infant mortality, children in need, child care services and child abuse. The strategy recognises that both qualitative and quantitative research is vital. The Northern Ireland Survey of Health and Social Well-being will be a major source of information for monitoring the strategy and for future planning. More attention needs to be given to the collation and use of data from many sources and to the identification of information needed to inform purchasing for effectiveness. Alongside outcome evaluation, process evaluation is equally important, as this can provide an assessment of how programmes should be implemented, what kinds of interventions work in what conditions and what level of effort and resources is required. Methods in process evaluation have been less well-defined and require development and investment.

'Well Into 2000'

The policies of the new Government to tackle social exclusion and inequalities in health and well-being are set out the document 'Well Into 2000' (Department of Health and Social Services 1997). This policy statement includes a number of goals for the health and personal social services. Provision should be based on systematic and vigorous assessment of the health and social care needs of the population. The appropriate methods for doing this are reviewed in chapter 5. Those needs are to be met efficiently and effectively through appropriate responses and well-targeted services that are underpinned by research and evaluations. Services are expected to give priority to tackling inequalities in health and social well-being.

In this document the Government calls for improvements in the administration of services. Some of these have a particular health focus, such as the elimination of wasteful and inappropriate prescribing of medicines. Others also have medical implications, but could readily be applied to child and family social work, e.g. the reduction of unproven interventions and the elimination of unnecessary investigations. The elimination of duplication and bureaucracy has implications for any welfare organisation. The importance of research is again stressed. The paper calls for careful and critical appraisal of existing patterns of care, the full evaluation of new techniques and treatments before their introduction and, more generally, increased use of evidence-based decision-making. The Department and commissioners and providers of service are responsible for ensuring high-quality services and positive outcomes, taking account of evidence about effectiveness. In this they will be supported by the new Research and Development Office described above, which has been charged with ensuring that research findings are widely shared, and that a knowledge-based culture is promoted throughout the health and social services.

Fit for the Future

The Government issued a consultative paper inviting views on the way in which the health and personal social services can be reformed and modernised to meet the challenge facing them in the next millennium. This document sets out the seven principles upon which the new health and personal social services will be based. These are:

- equity
- promoting health and well-being, including reducing inequalities
- quality
- a local focus
- partnership
- efficiency
- openness and accountability.

The document also acknowledges that the main changes needed include better use of research findings.

Conclusions

A number of common developments are apparent in both Scotland and Northern Ireland, as in England and Wales, although the expression and relevance differs according to the context in each jurisdiction. The children's legislation of 1995 aimed to create more positive relationships between public social services, families and children, with a stress on key principles such as partnership, participation and shared responsibility. The minimum intervention principle in Scotland is intended to promote optimum family support in the least intrusive manner consistent with the child's welfare. It is not meant to restrict access to services only to circumstances where a need for formal child protection intervention has been established.

An emphasis is also placed on collaboration among statutory services. In Northern Ireland, especially, government objectives for children's services are integrated within more general policy documents embodying goals for the health and well-being of the population. These all stress the importance of decision-making based on systematic relevant evidence.

There is a great emphasis on needs assessment at both the population and individual level. Children's Services Plans are a vital vehicle for collating needs information and matching this with a strategic overview of service provision. The initial plans in Scotland, however, lacked specificity over future provision and funding.

New public policy goals have been established for professionals and organisations. How successfully these will be achieved needs to be addressed. Social work practice will be under considerable scrutiny through working in partnerships with parents and other organisations. The paternalistic approach adopted by some social workers in the past will be severely challenged by the demands of users to be more involved in the planning and delivery of services. New organisational arrangements will force us to consider how we deliver services to individuals, populations and localities in the future. Both quantitative and qualitative research evidence must form part of the constant reassessment of the appropriateness of services.

PART I

Services for Children in the Community

CHAPTER 3

Communication, Co-operation or Collaboration? The Involvement of Voluntary Organisations in the First Scottish Children's Services Plans

Kay Tisdall, Bernadette Monaghan and Malcolm Hill

Introduction

During the 1990s, inter-agency co-operation was very much emphasised in such fields as community care and child protection. Most attention focused on public agencies working together, but the role of voluntary organisations has also been promoted in the context of the 'mixed economy of welfare' (Johnson 1990). This chapter examines the relationship between voluntary organisations and local authorities within the context of other kinds of inter-agency and inter-departmental relations in Scotland.

For children's services, the requirement for inter-agency co-operation was set out by the Government in the 1993 White Paper *Scotland's Children*:

> Children have the right to expect that professionals, from social work, health, education and other services will collaborate in a child-centred way by fulfilling their own role while understanding and respecting the contributions of others. It is most important to ensure that all the efforts of all those working for children benefit children. (Scottish Office 1993, para 2.17)

Inter-agency collaboration is a key principle of the resulting Children (Scotland) Act 1995, to be applied both to provision for individual children and planning of services. The Act deliberately contains provisions to promote such collaboration. Local authorities can ask other agencies, such as health services, for help in providing services under the Act. They must publish information on 'relevant' services, which may include information on voluntary and private sector services. The Government underlined the 'corporate' definition of local authority within the Act, so responsibilities towards children lie not only with social work departments or their equivalents but also with all other local authority services, ranging from housing through education to leisure and recreation.

Central to inter-agency collaboration is the new requirement for local authorities to produce Children's Services Plans (CSPs). Section 19 identifies a range of 'relevant' services that must be covered in CSPs, including references to education, disability and criminal legislation as well as social work. Furthermore, Section 19 identifies particular organisations that local authorities must consult on their CSPs: health boards and trusts, parties within the Children's Hearings System, housing agencies and voluntary organisations. Specifically, voluntary organisations must be consulted when they appear to represent the interests of likely or actual service users, or provide 'relevant' services. Secondary legislation requires local authorities to indicate within their plans the volume of services and expenditure planned, including services by voluntary organisations and the private sector, and states that the first plans should be published by 1 April 1998.

Thus, inter-agency collaboration for children's services is explicitly intended to go beyond collaboration between statutory services to include collaboration between statutory and voluntary organisations. This recognises the voluntary sector's traditional and considerable contribution to children's services, both in creating innovative services and in advocating for vulnerable groups (Hill, Murray and Rankin 1991; Murray and Hill 1991). It also recognises the policy promotion in the 1980s and 1990s of the 'mixed economy of welfare' and the 'enabling authority' (Scottish Office 1994a). Voluntary organisations have the opportunity – the necessity, if they wish to gain funding – to contract with local authorities for services as well as to receive more loosely specified grant-funding.

In the 1990s, children's services faced an additional challenge to that provided by increasing pressure to 'contract-out' new legislation and planning requirements. In 1996, local government was reorganised in Scotland. Twenty-nine unitary councils were created from the previous nine regional councils and 53 district councils, with the three unitary island councils continuing as before. Most of the new mainland councils were considerably smaller than their regional predecessors: for example, twelve of the new authorities had populations of less than 100,000. Social work and education services, previously delivered by regional councils, became the responsibility of very much smaller units. These changes dramatically affected virtually all voluntary organisations. National organisations previously working with nine regional councils now had to negotiate with

29. Voluntary organisations established originally within regional boundaries sometimes found their services straddling several local authorities. The smaller local authorities had less potential for economies of scale than their larger predecessors and some no longer wanted or could afford to support specialist services provided by voluntary organisations. New authorities, with new political make-ups, had new priorities, leading to insecurity and sometimes ended funding for voluntary organisations. Local government reform came at a time of considerable financial constraints for local authorities; in turn, this affected funding for voluntary organisations who received grants and/or contracts from local authorities. (For further description and analysis, see Kendrick, Simpson and Mapstone 1996; Craig *et al.* 2000.)

Local government reform also provided opportunities for some voluntary organisations to develop or expand services, as smaller local authorities realised their needs for particular services or deliberately sought to promote a 'mixed economy' (Craig *et al.* 2000). Pressure from voluntary organisations at the time resulted in Scottish Office guidance to local authorities on funding during local government reform and eventually *The Scottish Compact* (Scottish Office 1998a). This compact considers national government's relationships with the voluntary sector, but the process of its creation and the final product may in turn affect relationships between local authorities and the voluntary sector as well.

The research described in this chapter began in 1996 to examine how, and to what extent, the voluntary sector had contributed to Scottish children's services planning. Scotland was the first UK jurisdiction to have a legal requirement for CSPs, although English and Welsh guidance had promoted plans (1992 and 1994 respectively) and 1996 legislation made CSPs mandatory. The Baring Foundation supported the two-year study, which had two stages. First, a national survey was undertaken of the processes, structures and issues surrounding voluntary organisations' contributions to children's services planning. The survey was undertaken in 1997–98, as the plans were being produced. It involved semi-structured interviews with representatives from all 32 Scottish local authorities and most of the large voluntary organisations involved with children's services. A sample of smaller voluntary organisations was also interviewed and draft plans were considered. Second, four case studies were selected representing diversity in practice, in order to look more closely at the CSP process (including implementation plans and reviews) and to consult a range of smaller organisations. (For more details of the research design, see Monaghan, Hill and Tisdall 1998.) In this chapter, the findings from the research's first-stage interviews were used to examine inter-agency collaboration for local authorities' first CSPs.

Producing the Children's Services Plans

In order to underline that local authorities were to improve inter-agency collaboration by taking a corporate approach to children's services, the Scottish Office guidance wrote of the 'considerable advantage' (1997, p.10) of local authorities' Chief Executives assuming overall responsibility for plan preparation. In practice, some local authorities did give primary respons-ibility to officers within Chief Executives' departments but social work or combined housing and social work departments were far more likely to take the lead co-ordinating role. A few authorities designated a particular staff member full- or nearly full-time to the plans. More often, senior managers co-ordinated the plan amongst many other existing responsibilities, in-cluding overall implementation of the 1995 Act.

Three main mechanisms were used to prepare the CSPs, which involved other departments and agencies in varying degrees and ways:

Committees and groups

While the names of groups and committees varied greatly, the most typical local authority pattern was to have three tiers:

1. The top tier was a *policy* or *decision-making* committee, often chaired by someone from the Chief Executive's department. Membership at this level was usually confined to the senior staff of the authority. In six authorities, however, such committees were jointly composed of councillors and officials.

2. The middle tier was usually an *inter-agency steering or co-ordinating group* of senior statutory officials charged with overall planning and co-ordination.

3. The lower tier was composed of *working groups*. These groups were most commonly organised around types of services (e.g. early years, family support) and client groups (e.g. 'looked-after' children), while some centred around issues (e.g. children's rights) or a combination (e.g. children and education).

Consultation sessions

Virtually all local authorities held seminars, conferences or consultation sessions, by selective or open invitation. Such consultation might happen before or after the production of the draft plan. Four authorities used

consultation events to obtain the views of service users. Voluntary organisations usually played a major role in such events, particularly when young
people were invited.

Consultation by mail

Draft sections or a draft of the plan itself were sent out by local authorities to
a list of voluntary organisations. Several local authorities identified key
questions that consultees might address, as plans were often lengthy.

These three mechanisms roughly map onto three layers of co-operation,
in which the degree of decision-making power usually corresponded to the
membership.

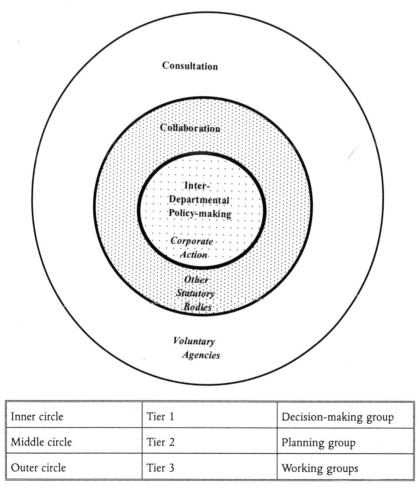

Inner circle	Tier 1	Decision-making group
Middle circle	Tier 2	Planning group
Outer circle	Tier 3	Working groups

Figure 3.1 Local authority co-operation in children's services planning

Distinctions are deliberately made in Figure 3.1 between 'consultation' and 'collaboration', drawing on the typology produced by the Social Services Inspectorate (SSI) (1996). In their analysis of Children's Services Plans, SSI lays out a range of co-operative models (see Figure 3.2).

Communication of agency position: Uppermost planning relationship is confined to one agency telling another what it intends to do.

Consultation on agency plan: Involves activities where an agency asks another for opinion, information or advice before finalising a plan.

Collaboration: Involves a degree of joint working on plans, mutual adjustment and agreement on the extent and limits of each others' activities, but operationally the agencies provide services independently.

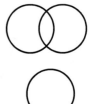

Bilateral planning: Implies an overlap in service provision, so that although each agency will retain its own plan there will be operational interaction arising out of common planning.

Joint planning: Implies planning with a view to different agencies working operationally on the same plan.

Figure 3.2 Social Services Inspectorate's typology of co-operation
Source: Social Services Inspectorate 1996, pp.24–25

The SSI report recognises that this diagram represents bilateral relationships, whereas practice more generally relies on multilateral relationships: hence the use of concentric circles in Figure 3.1. The typology, however represented, suggests that the panacea of 'inter-agency collaboration' is often used for a variety of relationships, which have different levels of closeness and power. These differing relationships will be further considered below.

Communication, co-operation and collaboration

The SSI found that English social services departments producing their plans in 1993/94 were most frequently involved in consultation and considerably less frequently in collaborative or joint-planning relationships. With the Scottish Office's explicit promotion of corporate responsibility, Scottish local authority respondents in 1996 often prioritised the need and opportunity to create and improve inter-departmental collaboration within the local authority. Social work representatives who were leading the planning process on behalf of their authorities were anxious to ensure that their departments alone were not left with the cost of statutory service priorities. This is exemplified by one local authority respondent:

> Politically, we were very concerned that other departments also took responsibility for this Plan, so the Steering Group was set up with that in mind as well.

The key decision-making group, at the core of Figure 3.1, was thus often deliberately composed of officials from a range of local authority departments, and sometimes of elected councillors. Respondents recognised that, despite the rhetoric and even commitment to corporate children's services, competition between departments continued to be a threat. As one local authority respondent described:

> It is useful to acknowledge the competitive element of the Children's Services Plan and that would apply within the local authority as well as outwith. Education and social work, in particular, need to give things up and reach more shared understanding about how to deliver services to some of the types of vulnerable children who cut across traditional boundaries.

Respondents identified at least two reasons for this 'competitive' element. Some referred to the different philosophical approaches of education and social work: education services are primarily concerned with the collective entitlement of young people to education and exam success, as well as with developing individual potential; social work is primarily concerned with the well-being of the individual child. The other reason was financial, as one respondent explained:

> The reality is that, however much the Act stresses the need for us to collaborate, when you are looking at council policy and council budgets, the Directors are in competition with each other. One of the obstacles to co-operation is that we are all strapped for resources.

Inter-departmental collaboration, or 'joint planning' under the SSI typology, was a priority for many of the local authority officers leading on the plans;

even though the research focused on local authority–voluntary organisation relationships, respondents continually returned to discussing inter-local authority relationships instead. The Scottish Office review of the published Children's Services Plans was complimentary regarding their corporate approach, naming it as 'one of the main areas of strength' (1999, p.2). Recent English research (Hearn and Sinclair 1998) noted that local authorities (i.e. education and social services) had to work well internally in order to be able to liaise well with the voluntary sector: 'While the giants banged heads the voluntary sector was invariably left knocking on the door or having to squeeze in through the cracks' (p.42).

Other statutory bodies, such as health services, the police and parties within the Children's Hearings system, seemed to be second on local authority officers' list of priorities, involved in 'collaboration' or occasionally 'bilateral planning' under the SSI typology. Some representatives of statutory bodies, for example, could generally be found in the second tier of groups or second circle in Figure 3.1, which were core planning groups. Voluntary organisations seemed to be a lower priority for most local authority respondents, which resulted in voluntary agencies often being consulted at the third tier of working groups or the outside circle as indicated in Figure 3.1. The same voluntary agency might have different levels of involvement across different local authorities. The agencies did not expect to have a high level of involvement in authorities where they were not delivering services.

While voluntary organisations were usually a lower priority than interdepartmental and inter-statutory co-operation, many local authority respondents expressed their desire, and indeed recognised the local authorities' legal obligation, to consult with such agencies. Working groups were a central means of needs and service analysis and thus almost invariably provided the material content for the plans. Working groups differed, however, from other higher tiers as they were not involved in decision-making. Voluntary organisations that were not represented on the working groups also had opportunities to participate in day events or comment on written documents. In other words, voluntary organisations were most likely to be involved in communication and consultation rather than collaboration or planning.

A small minority of local authorities did not follow this pattern and involved voluntary organisations in the core decision-making and planning groups. For this purpose, they chose either local umbrella groups or one or two large voluntary organisations with strong local connections. Such involvement, which was explored in greater depth in the second research stage, was the exception rather than the rule.

These findings are supported by the results of research undertaken by the Children in Scotland forum (1998) on the 1995 Act. When asked about their involvement in CSPs, 44 per cent of the 132 responding Scottish voluntary organisations reported not having been involved at all. Of the 66 per cent who had been involved, 16 per cent said they had commented on a draft plan and 7 per cent reported having both commented on a draft and attended a consultation. Only 5 per cent of respondents were involved in a working or planning group. Similarly, The Scottish Office review (1999) was critical of published plans' lack of links with the voluntary sector:

> While a few plans outline work with the voluntaries and include them in their objectives and specific targets for service provision, this particular area is another weakness in many of the plans. In the main details about work with the voluntaries is descriptive and rarely quantified in terms of cash, number of children involved and plans for the future. (p.3)

The review noted the failure to provide specific detail on the volume and cost of services to be purchased from the voluntary and independent sectors, which had been one of the specific points of the secondary legislation (p.1).

Whereas the local authority staff usually thought they had fulfilled their duties by offering consultation, this was often experienced as inadequate by voluntary agency staff. Only collaboration or bilateral planning were perceived as full 'partnership' by many voluntary organisation respondents. Service level agreements between voluntary organisations and local authorities were described as forms of partnership, but partnership in the CSP process itself was seen as quite rare. If voluntary organisations were asked solely to comment on a completed draft plan, they felt it was too late for their contribution to be meaningful (*see also* Children in Scotland 1998).

Expectations and realities of children's services planning

The levels of collaboration and communication can be partially explained by the respective sectors' expectations and hopes for children's services planning. Local authority respondents identified a range of desirable outcomes from CSPs:

- To break down barriers and build up mutual trust and respect across departments and with different agencies; to establish clear service priorities; to plan for needs-led rather than service-led resources.

- To make their CSP meaningful, not primarily for heads of services or service managers, but as a reference document for front-line workers so that they could also influence the planning process.

- To establish an ethos of listening to children, in which service user consultation and participation in developing services should be vital.

- To promote the best use of available resources and to facilitate equality of access.

- In the longer term, to change attitudes and ways of thinking within the local authority and externally.

These desired outcomes overlapped with many aspirations expressed by voluntary organisation respondents, providing a common basis for working together. For example, voluntary organisations saw planning as a process allowing children, parents and other service users to have a say in shaping and improving services. They expected CSPs – the finished product – to have clear goals and priorities, against which local authorities could be measured; to be, as one person from a voluntary organisation said, '*a benchmark from which you can approach things in a more ordered way*' . Other outcomes wished for by voluntary organisations had different emphases from those of the local authority. For example, several voluntary organisation respondents thought plans should promote local ownership of services and empower service users, whereas local authority respondents spoke of consultation and participation of service users, but not community ownership.

Many voluntary organisation respondents acknowledged that they had little control over the nature and extent of their participation in planning; control rested primarily with the local authority. One person described the approach taken by her organisation as '*waiting proactively*' to be involved. Voluntary organisations hoped for a high degree of involvement in CSPs at a strategic policy level because of their expertise in and knowledge of both service provision and users' needs and views. Large child care voluntary organisations, for example, expected to be involved at a level at which they could influence policy and practice. They stated that any consultation with them and service users should be meaningful, taking place at an early stage in the process rather than when the CSP was effectively a 'fait accompli'.

As referred to above, local authority respondents were positive about consulting and communicating with the voluntary sector. Respondents frequently referred to the importance of voluntary sector views, particularly in relation to their ability to represent or facilitate service users' views. But local authority respondents did not often feel that voluntary organisations should be invited into discussion about service priorities and policy, due to a conflict of interests as potential service providers. Certain local authority respondents expressed a reluctance to name specific voluntary organisations within CSPs, for fear that plans might become a lever by which voluntaries argued for future funding.

This practical concern is underpinned by the changing perceptions of the voluntary sector held by those working in local authorities. For example, in research on community care, Lewis (1996) reported similar concerns in local authorities:

> It seems increasingly clear that voluntary agencies are regarded as providers, and as purchaser/provider splits become firmer this has important implications. In some authorities voluntary sector represent- atives play a part in the production of the first and second community care plans, as opposed to just being consulted. They did so usually by virtue of being invited onto the joint planning machinery. However, as joint planning becomes joint commissioning, so statutory authorities are raising questions about the membership of the joint commissioning groups/teams. The 1993 Guidance on Joint Commissioning suggests that if voluntary agencies were to continue to participate, then they might need to separate their advocacy and provider roles, just as the social services department has separated its purchaser and provider functions. (p.103)

Such views on community care may have influenced views on planning for children's services, particularly as many lead officers on CSPs had previously been involved in community care planning. As voluntary organisations expand their direct core service provision role, their traditional role of advocacy risks coming into conflict.

Voluntary organisations are not the only agencies with role tensions. As some local authorities move more to 'enabling' and arms-length services, one respondent expressed concern for his own and colleagues' professional role:

> We are in a debate about what public services you actually have. For example, we have a counselling service for children who have been sexually abused. If we keep contracting that sort of thing out, what do social workers, who trained over twenty years ago to be case workers, do within the authority? Do they become brokers, referring to people on to the particular service? There will be people who say that maybe that is what local authorities should be. I don't think we have had that debate properly yet.

This debate was echoed among comments from voluntary organisation respondents, for example:

> There is a still a propensity among some local authorities to regard voluntary organisations as not really partners but as people who will

come in and tinker around the edges: they are not committed, they are unprofessional, they are amateur, they rely on volunteers. None of which is necessarily true at all. Therefore, they are not equipped to taking on central services. Now that varies widely and I can see massive changes. Some of the contracts we have won recently would indicate that local authorities are saying increasingly, 'we want to do business and we want to work in partnership'.

Voluntary agency respondents said they did not consider involvement in planning as primarily a route to promote themselves, guarantee funding or secure additional business. They presented themselves as having a positive altruistic role, primarily in consulting with parents and service users on behalf of local authorities. They felt that they had specialist knowledge and expertise in relation to specific categories of children. Large voluntary child care organisations, according to respondents, could transfer the knowledge and experience they had gathered from one part of the country to another.

One Scottish local authority stood out as having engaged with voluntary organisations in joint-planning, according to the SSI typology. Soon after this authority was created, it established a partnership with two national child care organisations, whereby the organisations would provide services required under the Children (Scotland) Act 1995. These two voluntary organisations were involved in the uppermost tier of committees, which made strategic planning decisions. Following joint agreement on their undertaking major service provision activities, these voluntary agencies' other roles as national experts and representatives of service users' views could be incorporated into such a planning tier.

Further, both organisations had their own charitable funds to contribute to the eventual service provision. Voluntary agency respondents generally felt that they were increasingly expected to 'match-fund': that is, to contribute funding of their own to contracts. This favoured national voluntaries over smaller voluntary organisations, particularly those smaller organisations depending completely on local authority funding. Voluntary organisations felt that their capacity to bring resources 'to the table' should not become the deciding principle for local authorities in terms of quality of service or joint working. While several voluntary organisation respondents expressed this concern about match-funding, no local authority respondent made reference to it.

The significance of financial resources

The funding crisis and the tight timetable for producing the plans were practical constraints on both local authorities and voluntary organisations. Only one authority appointed a lead officer whose sole task was to produce the CSP; hence, most lead officers had limits on the time they could devote to organising consultation. Local authorities might well not wish to raise expectations through extensive consultation if resources were unlikely to be available to meet needs. One local authority respondent described some voluntary organisations as 'unrealistic' in their approach to planning:

> It's difficult to get the budgetary issues just now and there are huge issues about how voluntary organisations will manage to adapt and survive in view of all the cuts. There's not going to be a lot of money around and there doesn't appear to be the same realism among voluntary organisations. Some of the responses to the planning process were about new services and what voluntary organisations could do. I'm not sure that they're getting to grips with the extent of the financial crisis.

Local authorities felt pressurised by the financial crisis and the urgent needs of children, with the related requirement to assess needs and consult on services, whereas voluntary organisations could perceive the constrained agenda as being service-led rather than needs-led and failing to explore all the possibilities before deciding on priorities.

Voluntary organisation respondents were nevertheless acutely aware of the funding crisis. One respondent, for example, sympathised with a local authority's need to focus on 'children in need' to avoid

> ending up in a tremendous soup of confusion and vagueness and a lack of specificity which does not sit easily with times of actual hardship and the need to be disciplined about how you spend your resources.

Respondents from voluntary organisations most often mentioned the funding crisis in relation to their own organisations' survival. Their organisations continually had to reinvent themselves and keep reviewing their services in line with local authority strategies and funding priorities. Annual contracts and grants, compared to three-year service level agreements, were described as too short-term to take proper account of the needs of children. Campaigning and advocacy groups were particularly affected by short-term funding and found themselves tied up negotiating for their survival with local authorities rather than doing what they had originally been funded to do – which might have been representing their interest group in children's services planning.

Service users' interests and views

In preparing their CSPs local authorities must consult with voluntary organisations that represent services users' views. Several local authority respondents expressed a deep commitment to accessing service users' views, but their mechanisms for meaningful consultation were questioned by several voluntary agencies representing young people. Some local authorities had organised conferences and one-day events to enable young people to put their views directly to policy-makers. Voluntary agencies considered such events to be useful as a form of consultation, except when the young people were merely asked about their awareness of existing council services. Furthermore, voluntary organisation respondents felt that young people should not be involved simply as a way of legitimising local authority plans. They said that young people expected to be consulted on their terms and have the opportunity to set their own agendas. The incentive for them to participate, in what was seen as largely a local authority process, was the chance to raise their concerns, give critical feedback and have issues included in the CSPs. They were most interested in influencing the eventual services and not the CSP document itself.

The research team was told of four authorities establishing separate structures for consultation with young people. One authority had a 'consultation group' as one of its working groups for the CSP whereby a voluntary organisation was commissioned to carry out a consultation with children in schools and youth groups. Three local authorities set up a form of youth council specifically aimed to include views from young people who were disaffected or isolated from mainstream service provision. These councils, while addressing broader issues, linked into the local authorities' CSP structures.

Further work is required to ascertain the effectiveness of such desired good practice, particularly from the perspectives of the young people themselves. The Scottish Office review was critical of the lack of evidence of consultation in the plans:

> Authorities have in the vast majority of cases ensured wide consultation during the preparation of the Plans and appropriate consultation with both internal and external interests as the move towards completion. However it would appear that in many instances, there may not have been consultation with children and young people themselves. (1999, p.3)

Who makes up and speaks for the voluntary sector?

Research undertaken by Bemrose and MacKeith (1996) on community care planning found that local authorities were often unclear about which were the relevant voluntary organisations to consult. This was partly because information was scattered among different departments and individuals. One local authority department might be funding the same voluntary organisation for the same service as another department. The expertise of one department in dealing with the voluntary sector was not necessarily shared with other departments. At the same time, the voluntary sector itself was seen as fragmented. One respondent was quoted as saying: 'It's not often that there is a single clear view or spokesperson' (p.25).

Such confusion was also apparent in this research. From the local authority point of view, the voluntary sector is diverse and generally lacks a single point of contact or a consortium, which could collectively represent their interests, though local umbrella groups sometimes partially undertook this role. Voluntary agency respondents too felt that such co-ordination was lacking, though it would allow voluntary agencies to be more effectively involved in consultation and decide who should represent them, rather than local authorities exercising their preferences.

With no consortium or evident local umbrella group, local authority respondents described asking voluntary organisations to participate on the basis of knowledge of existing organisations and people or historical links. The ad hoc nature of this selection was criticised by these two local authority respondents:

> There is an issue about who should be involved. Should it be local organisations who feel that they have a right to be involved because they are local? Is it the people you are already working with? There are a number of prejudices about which voluntaries we work well with. So it's an issue about who you select and why you select them.

> There are personal prejudices about what experiences you've had with certain voluntaries in the past and whether you think that their philosophy will fit in with your own.

The reliance on working groups as the core means of producing the detailed contents of most plans logically required some selection of voluntary organisations – too large a group would be unwieldy and a changing membership unhelpful. One local authority decided to advertise for interested organisations through the local Council of Voluntary Services' newsletter, which thus allowed voluntary organisations to put themselves forward. The local authority still retained the power of selection.

The large child care voluntary organisations, as well as Scottish Women's Aid and Who Cares? Scotland (representing looked-after children), were the ones most often invited to participate in working groups, because of their client groups and local involvement. Smaller and single issue groups, who depended completely on local authorities for grant funding, were more likely to be asked to comment on published draft documents.

Concluding remarks

The involvement of voluntary organisations in the preparation of Scottish Children's Services Plans was highly selective. In only a few authorities were one or two allowed to engage at strategic planning and decision-making levels. All authorities included some voluntaries in lower-tier working groups and consultation events, but these too were only a small proportion of the potentially relevant agencies. Local authority and voluntary organisation representatives often disagreed on who should contribute to the plan, in what way and with what purpose. With a few exceptions voluntary organisations wanted more mutual collaboration, but lesser forms of consultation and communication were on offer.

This pattern links into the debate about the scope and role of the voluntary sector. Numerous typologies have been created, based on such factors as ownership (community, user and donor) and complexity (Taylor, Langan and Hoggett 1995), and covering bodies which range from religious charities to political parties (Marshall 1996). For their CSPs, local authorities need to identify from this complexity which voluntary organisations they are to consult with. Legislation requires two categories – those that provide children's services and those that represent service users – but the spread of voluntary organisation in these categories is still large and diverse, ranging from small local voluntaries to large national ones, from self-support groups to major service providers. Further, most local authority lead officers did not have a comprehensive list of relevant voluntary organisations, in part due to recent local government reform. Even if local authorities had been clear in principle about what type of organisations should be involved, they did not know necessarily know what organisations existed in their area.

Much has also been written about the changing role of voluntary organisations (e.g. Bemrose and MacKeith 1996; Thompson 1997; Rickford 1998). Voluntary organisations are increasingly becoming involved in direct and core service provision and are thus required to become more 'professional' and regulated (Lewis 1996). Numerous commentators have feared that the contractual role will increase competition between voluntary organisations rather than promote networking, and decrease voluntary organisations' ability to innovate and advocate as they become cosy with and/or even subservient to their funders (*see* Downey 1995; Kendrick *et al.* 1996). In this research, respondents from large voluntary organisation felt able to contribute strategically, if invited, to children's services planning. Most local authority respondents, however, felt that in certain organisations there was a fundamental conflict between their roles as actual or future service providers and as advocates; as such, most local authorities included voluntary organisations not in decision-making but instead in information gathering through working groups. Taylor *et al.* (1995) are critical of such a view:

> Some authorities see consultation with potential suppliers as prejudicing planning. To see the voluntary sector in particular solely as a pool of suppliers in a market is to ignore the dual role which many have played in supplying services and drawing on that experience to influence policy. Whether private or voluntary, independent organisations between them have a fund of knowledge on the way in which need has been and can be met in local areas, which can contribute considerably to the development of knowledge in purchasing and planning authorities. (p.64)

Taylor *et al.* do not, however, directly suggest any means by which to resolve the dual role, although statutory services themselves can have both roles as well. However, Taylor *et al.*'s support of umbrella groups and voluntary organisation networks may provide one. Such intermediary bodies can 'act as nurseries for new organisations, provide the infrastructure smaller organisations need and encourage organisations of all sizes to work together' (p.65). They can thus facilitate co-operation rather than competition between voluntary organisations and provide smaller and new organisations with the capacity to participate alongside larger national organisations.

A key descriptor of voluntary organisations is their ability and indeed often remit to represent users or their communities (Taylor *et al.* 1995). Finding the best way to consult meaningfully with children, young people and families is difficult for most organisations, including local authorities. Some Scottish local authorities sought to consult directly with service users whereas others asked voluntary organisations to facilitate or carry out such consultation on their behalf. The effectiveness of these various approaches for different groups of service users has not been evaluated; it is an area being further considered in the second stage of the research. Lack of consultation with service users, and particularly young people, was a weakness noted in recent English research on children's services plans (Hearn and Sinclair 1998) and even more strongly criticised in relation to English family support services by the SSI (1997; 1998).

Both voluntary organisation and local authority respondents had expectations and hopes for the voluntary–statutory relationship in the first Children's Services Plans. The SSI (1996) typology of planning relationships provides a compatible template for the research reported here and its findings are not dissimilar. Most Scottish local authorities were preoccupied with bilateral or even joint planning between internal departments and at least collaboration with other statutory agencies. Just as the SSI reported of English local authorities, consultation or even just communication were more common relationships between local authorities and the voluntary sector. Most voluntary organisation respondents were dissatisfied with this more limited partnership. Arguably, only one local authority saw voluntary organisations as *equal partners* in planning, combining the roles of service providers and experts, and knowledgeable about need in the same way as the local authority. Even then, this strategic partnership was confined to two national organisations (since expanded to three), with smaller agencies having much less influence.

Sutton (1995) points out that the SSI typology does not inherently value one type of relationship over another, for it would be virtually impossible for any local authority to have close relationships such as joint planning with every other possible agency. Instead, the typology provides the potential for clarity on what relationships are and what they might be. What the typology does lead one to assume is that both partners have a common understanding of what the relationship is. This research has raised another critical factor of co-operation, which has been less explored by the major publications on Children's Services Plans from England and Wales: the expectations of the different agencies involved. The mismatch between the expectations of local authority and voluntary organisations resulted in as much frustration and disappointment as the actual degree of co-operation.

Further, the typology suggests that agencies are equal in their relationships. The concentric circles of Figure 3.1 better describe the power relations between local authorities and the voluntary sector: essentially, local authorities largely had the power to determine what their relationships with voluntary organisations would be. Voluntary organisations could refer to local authorities' legal obligation to consult and could proactively suggest to local authorities that they be involved. They could not, however, determine who local authorities asked to participate and how. Local authorities have the statutory responsibility to produce Children's Services Plans and largely retain the decision-making and funding powers.

The call for improved 'inter-agency collaboration' gives little recognition to this differential in power, created by legislation and funding. Like other terms with considerable political currency (such as 'community' and 'partner-ship'), inter-agency collaboration is promoted as being almost inevitably positive. Instead, the relationships covered by such collaboration may not be equally understood and experienced. One 'partner' in the relationship may lack the resources to participate, or the burden of collaboration may be incommensurate with the outcome. As respondents frequently commented within the research, consultation had to be meaningful to be productive – and, ultimately, it has to result in better services for children and their families.

CHAPTER 4

Operationalising the Definition of Children in Need from UK Child Care Legislation

Patrick McCrystal

Introduction

This chapter will report upon the findings from a recent study undertaken by the Centre for Child Care Research, Queens University Belfast, on the operationalisation of the definition of children in need contained in Article 17 of the Children (NI) Order 1995. The definition is repeated verbatim in Section 17 of the Children Act 1989 and is virtually identical to that contained in Section 93 of the Children (Scotland) Act 1995 (Tisdall, Lavery and McCrystal 1998). A review of relevant literature produced following the implementation of this legislation will set the scene for the presentation of the main findings. Three themes in this chapter are the definition of children in need; the operational indicators of need; and inter-agency co-operation.

History and origins of the Children (NI) Order

The Children (NI) Order is the product of a number of influences – local, national and international – over a long period of time. It contains little that originated in Northern Ireland itself. The impetus for change can, however, be traced to the *Report of the Children's and Young Person's Review Group, Legislation and Services for Children and Young People* (The Black Report) (Department of Health and Social Services (Northern Ireland) 1979). This advocated an emphasis on inter-agency co-operation, prevention rather than intervention, the separation of care proceedings from proceedings for children who offend, and the development of a Guardian ad Litem agency.

The sequence of new child care legislation in the UK during the last decade of the twentieth century saw England and Wales receive their children's legislation first, with the Children Act passed in 1989 and implemented in 1991. Northern Ireland and Scotland had to wait several years for their parallel children's legislation, the Children (NI) Order 1995 and the Children (Scotland) Act 1995, to make its way through the Westminster parliament. The three pieces of legislation have similarities. These include shared terminology such as 'children in need' and 'looked-after', although the exact meaning is sometimes different (Tisdall *et al.* 1998).

Children in need: Definitions and research findings from the Children Act 1989

The Children Act laid a duty on local authorities to safeguard and promote the welfare of children in need by means of family support services (Gibbons and Wilding 1995). Colton, Drury and Williams (1995a) noted that this is what 'many see as the heart of the Act' (p.1). They felt this had great potential to pave the way for a wide spectrum of new services for families and children. Section 17(1) of the Children Act reads that a child is in need if:

> a) he is unlikely to achieve or maintain, or to have the opportunity of achieving or maintaining, a reasonable standard of health or development without the provision for him of services by an authority under this Part;
>
> b) his health or development is likely to be significantly impaired, or further impaired, without the provision for him of such services; or
>
> c) he is disabled.

This was incorporated verbatim into Article 17 of the Children (NI) Order. Aldgate *et al.* (1994) believe the definition of children in need as provided in the Children Act represents a fusing of the concepts of prevention and family support. They argue that the definion is wide in order to embrace the proposed changes resulting from the implementation of the Children Act 1989. Packman and Jordan (1991) believe that 'the Act takes a quantum leap from the old restricted notions of "prevention" to a more positive outreaching duty of 'support for children and families' (p.323). It combines in one legal category children who face some level of greater as well as lesser risk to their health or welfare (Section 17(1) of Act). Since the expression 'children in need' is a legal term defined in the Act, social services departments are essentially obliged to follow the definition given Ryan (1994) argues that one of the driving forces behind the concept of children in need and the preventive strategies contained in the Children Act has been the need to provide a clear legislative basis for work with children and their families.

More detailed descriptions of need may be developed by any authority to interpret more fully the legal definition. Aldgate *et al.* (1994) argue in favour of a wide-ranging interpretation in accordance with the spirit of the Act, whereas Ryan (1994) supports a more restrictive approach as a result of the need to conserve scarce resources by targeting particular categories of children. A third alternative is for the authority to avoid the whole dilemma by accepting the definition of need as it stands in the Act and in doing so failing to offer social workers additional interpretation. This raises the question of the value of clear advice and guidance for social workers charged with the task of operationalising the definition. Colton, Drury and Williams (1995b), in their study of how social services departments in England and Wales operate the definition of children in need, reported that policy documents revealed these authorities were offering very little, if any, guidance to social workers on how to interpret the concept in practice. They found that social workers were accordingly using their own interpretations.

Sinclair and Carr-Hill (1995) state that the definition of a child in need contained in the Children Act cannot be regarded as an operational definition, but describe it as 'one which enables local authorities to easily determine which child or group of children should be regarded as "children in need" (p.3). In their survey, 86 local authorities in England and Wales were asked to provide their current criteria for classifying a child as 'in need'. They found great variation, from very precise definitions to broader criteria to be applied in particular circumstances. In fact they claimed that 'most local authorities have devised their own criteria for assessing who is a child in need' (p.3).

Evidence from the early 1990s indicated that the notion of children in need was often being confined to those deemed to be at risk. The Audit Commission (1994) found that social workers regarded children in need as 'a separate group with low priority'; and that there was a need for 'some rebalancing in order to help family support services develop' (Gibbons and Wilding 1995, p.59). The Commission called for a rebalancing of services for children and families from individually-focused investigations towards more broadly-based supportive provision. Similarly, the research reviewed by the Dartington Social Research Unit (1995) suggested that much work under the Children Act was performed under the banner of child protection. This again raised questions about whether the balance between this and the range of supports and interventions available to practitioners is correct.

Despite the obvious difficulty of identifying a population which has not been adequately defined, Colton and his colleagues found that the majority of departments in England and Wales had taken steps to identify overall need and had done so in co-operation with other statutory agencies. They argued that the process of identifying children in need is most effective when it is carried out in conjunction with other agencies. At least half of the departments examined had agreed a joint protocol with education and housing authorities, and three-quarters had agreements with the health authority. Agreements with the police and probation services were less frequent, and least common were agreements with youth agencies and social security departments.

Operationalising the definition of children in need in Northern Ireland

The Children (NI) Order 1995 introduced the concept of children in need to Northern Ireland and requires health and social services (HSS) boards and trusts to assess the needs of vulnerable children and provide appropriate services as outlined specifically in Article 18(1)(3). It has raised expectations of a radical new departure for children and their families in their dealings with the State. Lessons could be learned from the experience of the 1989 Act. Peyton (1996) noted that the 'experience of implementing the Children Act in England and Wales has been variable' (p.24). She concluded that a number of issues had to be addressed to ensure a co-ordinated approach across the province. These are:

- agreement on the specific operational definition of children in need
- mechanisms which ensure that existing and new services are targeted towards children in need and their families
- ensuring a balance between prevention and protection.

Whilst the legislation defines children in need, the legal definition requires operational interpretation as the concept is critical to ensuring that the required support for children and their families will be provided. Much concern has been expressed about the breadth of the definition of children in need and how it will be interpreted across the four HSS boards in Northern Ireland (Wilson 1996). *The Interim Policy and Procedures Handbook on Family Support, Volume One* (Children (NI) Order Implementation Officers Group 1996) notes that the concept of 'need' within the Order is deliberately wide so as to reinforce the emphasis upon preventative support and services to families (5.1). The four HSS Boards were aware of the potential for difficulties with the operationalisation of the definition and undertook preparatory work in advance of the implementation of the Order. This involved a province-wide consultative process undertaken by Social

Information Systems Ltd (SIS), who also engaged in a similar process in England (1994) and Wales (1994).

The resulting work produced a 'position statement with respect to children in need' (SIS 1995). The key aspects considered by the SIS were:

- the development of an operational definition of children in need
- the processes developed for identifying and locating children in need, and the current and projected level of demand for services by such children
- the costs of service options available to HSS boards to meet the needs of children operationally defined as children in need by the boards.

The SIS report notes that the definition contained in the Order encompasses a wide range of groups, and with the exception of children with disabilities, leaves the groups unspecified. The work of SIS, led by Tutt and Giller (1995) originally resulted in considerable clarification as to what is meant by children in need through the development of operational indicators of need. It emphasised the clear distinctions in the Children (NI) Order between

- obligations to children in need (Part IV)
- responsibilities for care and supervision (Part V)
- child protection (Part VI).

Commentators believed that the SIS proposals would ensure close attention to the development of support services and facilitate planning by HSS boards and trusts (Harbison 1996; Peyton 1996).

Operational indicators of children in need

The actual identification of needs for any child will, of course, be dependent on a process of assessment. An important distinction is drawn in the legislation between all children and children in need. This results in certain outline priorities, such as that services must be provided to reduce compulsory intervention; the identification of particularly vulnerable children and their protection from abuse and neglect; and the targeting of resources to children in need (Harbison 1996). However, as Scally and Shabbaz (1995) note, whilst the Children (NI) Order seems to provide a clear and comprehensive agenda for service provision to all children in need the absence of firm criteria and priorities leaves each HSS board and trust in Northern Ireland 'free' to decide its own level and scale of services appropriate to children in need in its area.

The operational indicators of need were developed to assist this process. They initially consisted of eleven categories of need. These were documented in the *Interim Policy and Procedures Handbook* (1996). Subsequently the revised and increased *Policy and Procedures Handbook on Family Support Volume One*, has amended the original eleven indicators of need and increased the number to thirteen. Where children fall into any of these categories, an assessment to determine eligibility for family support is offered.

Other issues for professional practice

Operationalising Article 18 of the Children (NI) Order will have an impact on many aspects of professional practice for social workers. The results will include closer liaison with other agencies in both the statutory and voluntary sector and increasing levels of partnership between social workers and parents.

The Children (NI) Order requires HSS boards to commission services for children in need. A key consideration here is whether existing structures for co-operation and co-ordination between the various statutory bodies are sufficient to facilitate the coherent approach to the needs of children which must develop if the vision of the Order is to be achieved. One potential vehicle for the development of inter-agency joint planning and action is the concept of Children's Services Plans (Harbison 1996). The need for collaboration is further highlighted by the requirement to produce an inter-agency Children's Services Plan for each HSS board area (Peyton 1996). The Department of Health and Social Services *Regulations and Guidance* (1996a) require this plan to be based on a reliable and comprehensive knowledge base; a thorough analysis of need and supply; the views of service users and the local community; consultation with other agencies; and monitoring and feedback.

Within the province there are a number of existing fora that provide good models for inter-agency working. Area Child Protection Committees include senior representatives of all agencies with an interest in protecting children from abuse and neglect. Approaches and service developments which involve two or more agencies and require joint funding are becoming more common. Recently formed Area Early Years Committees have responsibility for implementing the *Policy on Early Years Provision for Northern Ireland* (DHSS and Department of Education (NI) 1994), and agencies are required to work together to co-ordinate and promote the extension of high-quality services for children under 12 years of age, which are targeted to those in greatest need. Different philosophies, policies and criteria of need must inevitably be addressed and working definitions negotiated if scarce resources are to be maximised and duplication kept to a minimum.

Whilst partnership is not mentioned explicitly in the primary legislation it is one of the key principles on which the Children (NI) Order is based:

> Parents with children in need should be helped to bring up their children themselves and such help should be provided in partnership with parents. (DHSS (NI) 1995)

The Children (NI) Order is underpinned by the concept of children's rights as well as other value positions such as defence of the birth family, child rescue and minimal state interference. It is attempting a radical harmonization of divergent opinions and attitudes about child rearing and the role of the State to intervene in family life, which have been prevalent to some degree over the last half-century. By focusing on consensus the Children (NI) Order can appeal to a broad constituency of opinion in which meaningful partnerships can develop (Houston 1996).

A spirit of partnership between parents and staff is probably more widespread in family support services than elsewhere in the child care system (Wilson 1996). There are real opportunities within the legislation to begin honestly to engage and empower parents but this requires all parties involved to 'power share'. This requires professionals to look creatively at how we can enable parents to advocate on their own behalf and when they feel their voice is not being heard, and have access to a complaints procedure that ensures that their concerns are heard and responded to. Partnership with children raises even more challenges. There is no doubt that children and professionals are in an unequal relationship due both to differences in age and experience and the power inherent in the worker's role/organisation. The legislation has the paramountcy of the child as its motivating theme and this is reflected in duties on HSS boards and trusts to ascertain the wishes and feelings of the child. This is a crucial element when weighing up any considerations in relation to a child. However, reference is often made only to carers' wishes without any real attempt to ascertain directly the wishes and feelings of the child in any meaningful way (Wilson 1996).

The study

This research was conducted in the early stages of implementation of the Children (NI) Order 1995, i.e. 12–18 months after implementation. An overview from eleven HSS trusts in Northern Ireland in relation to the requirements of Article 18 was obtained from child care management in each trust. The professionals with responsibility for ensuring operationalisation of policy are those at Senior Social Worker (SSW), Assistant Principal Social Worker (APSW) and Principal Social Worker (PSW) levels. As a group they are in a strong position to reflect current practice and the extent to which it meets the requirements of Article 18 of the Children (NI) Order, as their work involves an interface between operationalisation and practice.

A self-complete questionnaire was developed to assess this group's perception of the operationalisation of the definition of 'in need' contained in the legislation. Each child care manager received a copy of the questionnaire with a stamped addressed envelope for return. One hundred child care managers completed a questionnaire. This represents a 68 per cent response rate. Responses were received from each HSS trust in Northern Ireland. Also, research interviews were held with four child care managers from each HSS trust, two at PSW/APSW level and two at SSW level. These interviews enabled a fuller investigation of the issues addressed in the research. Following this, two focus groups were carried out with a sample of child care managers to discuss further the issues addressed in the research through the shared experience of those participating. As anonymity was assured for all child care managers who participated in the research, individual trusts will be identified by a letter from A to K, with HSS boards numbered 1–4.

To avoid confusion, results tabulated with a possible total of 100 responses (n=100) contain information from the postal questionnaire, whilst results tabulated with a possible response of 44 (n=44) contain information from the interview survey. The views of PSWs and APSWs will be presented together with all SSWs presented as a group. A further column is added to most tables indicating the number of HSS trusts that each response was obtained from.

Definition of children in need

Ninety-nine per cent of child care managers surveyed were familiar with the definition of children in need contained in Article 17. The one exception worked in child/adolescent psychiatry. Over one-third of all child care managers surveyed (40%) felt that the definition contained in the Order was adequate for professional practice; the others did not. One-third (33%) of PSW/APSWs felt this was adequate, rising to 44 per cent of SSWs. Seventy-five per cent of those who felt that the definition was adequate for practice also indicated that their trust provided guidance regarding the definition. Comments made by all those surveyed are presented in Table 4.1. This table also shows whether those making the comment felt the definition was adequate for practice (yes) or not (no). A small number of respondents made more than one comment, others did not comment at all.

Table 4.1 Comments made by child care management on the adequacy of the Children (NI) Order 1995 definition of children in need (n=100)			
Comment	Number	Yes	No
Very wide (could apply to most children)	35	11	24
Open to interpretation	26	4	22
Requires further explanation	16	1	15
Clear and concise	6	6	–
Other	14	8	6
No answer/Missing	5	–	–

Other comments included: the definition does not acknowledge the prioritisation of need (3); it covers health development and disability (3); it is reasonable (3); it should not be used in a prescriptive way (2); it has a clear focus on the child (2); and it is stigmatising (1).

It is interesting that among those child care managers who feel the definition is very wide, open to interpretation and requires further explanation, a significant number felt it was both adequate and inadequate for professional practice. For example, approximately one-third of those who feel the definition is very wide believe that it is adequate for practice, but two-thirds of those who feel this way question its adequacy for practice. Similarly, four of those who believe it is adequate for practice feel that it is open to interpretation, although those who feel it is not adequate are more likely to think this way.

These views are further supported by the comments made by child care managers interviewed for the research. A higher proportion of those interviewed (57% from ten trusts) felt it was adequate for professional practice; 30 per cent from seven trusts felt it was not, with the others from three trusts unsure. One PSW noted that the definition is 'fine for legislation but needs an operational and practical focus'; however, SSW views ranged from 'it's not particularly useful, it's left totally to interpretation' to 'it's all embracing, it can take in everything and doesn't rule out anything'. Others took a more pragmatic view in commenting that 'interpretation can be difficult but you don't want to be too prescriptive'. Among child care managers in the field of disability the position was more positive, with one SSW saying that 'it's a brilliant piece of legislation for children with a disability. The role of children with a disability was not well defined before'. However one disability services manager noted that 'it needs to be operational for disability, which is being done'. Table 4.2 presents the comments received from child care managers interviewed on their views regarding the application of the definition of children in need to practice. Not all those interviewed made a specific comment.

Table 4.2 Comments on the application of the definition of children in need to practice (n=44)

Comment	Number	Trusts
Open to interpretation	14	9
All-embracing	5	5
Could be more specific	4	3
Operational indicators clarified this	4	2
Other	5	3

Other comments included 'it is good for children with a disability' (2), 'not initially' (2), and 'difficult to come to terms with' (1).

Nearly three-quarters (72%) of all child care managers surveyed indicated that their trust provided guidance regarding the interpretation of the definition of children in need. Nearly one-quarter (24%) believed their trust did not, and four respondents did not answer the question. There were contrasting views in a number of HSS trusts. In five trusts all child care managers surveyed were aware of guidance provided by their trust. However, among the other six trusts a number of child care managers did not think such guidance existed. For example, just over half of those surveyed in trusts E, F, G and I, and three-quarters of those in trusts A and H, believed their trust did provide guidance. There was some measure of satisfaction with guidance given by HSS trusts, as just over half of all child care managers who responded felt this was either satisfactory (49%) or very satisfactory (4%). All PSWs were satisfied with interpretation provided by their trust, as were 52 per cent of SSWs, but only 35 per cent of APSWs felt this way, with a further 35 per cent unsure. The most popular source of guidance was the trust's *Interim Policy and Procedures Handbook*, followed by the operational indicators of need, Children (NI) Order training, DHSS regulations and guidance, and a copy of the legislation. A number of respondents said their trust was currently working on guidance.

Assessment of children in need

Schedule 2 of the Children (NI) Order outlines the 'Provision of Services for Families: Specific Powers and Duties', which include that 'every authority shall take reasonable steps to identify the extent to which there are children in need within the authority's area' (Schedule 2(1)). Child care managers were asked if they were aware of their trust taking steps to identify overall need in their area. Only one-third (33%) of child care managers surveyed were aware of this, and nearly half (48%) were unsure. Nineteen per cent reported that their trust was not undertaking this. Forty-one per cent of PSW/APSWs were aware of this, with 37 per cent unsure, but only 29 per cent of SSWs were aware, with 57 per cent unsure. Only two trusts (B and I) registered no awareness of this, although in the remaining nine trusts responses were not unanimous. For example, in trust A three child care managers were aware of this, four did not know, and eleven were unsure; in trust H six child care managers were aware of this but six were not. Child care managers were asked what steps their trust was taking towards identifying overall need in their area. The main source of information was either referrals only, membership of predetermined groups, or a combination of both. However, it is interesting that a number of child care managers from each HSS trust were either unable to answer or chose not to.

Forty-eight per cent of middle management agreed that they had encountered problems in seeking to identify children in need in their area. The most problematic issue regarding the identification of children in need appears to focus on the definition of this group and the lack of a systematic method for this. Interestingly for child care managers, another issue centred around the fact that only families with children referred to social services come to their attention.

Twenty-one per cent of child care managers indicated that there were categories of need which their trust did not feel able to tackle satisfactorily, with 64 per cent indicating that they did not know. There did not appear to be an overriding problem that trusts were unable to tackle. Among the problems highlighted were issues around after-school provision, residential provision, and young offenders.

Social workers are encouraged under the Children (NI) Order to assess need in a comprehensive manner. In view of this, child care managers were presented with the list below and asked which of the following they take into account when assessing the needs of children. Table 4.3 represents their responses.

Table 4.3 Categories taken into account when assessing needs (n=100)		
Categories	Number	Trusts
Emotional and developmental behaviour	95	11
Health	92	11
Education	91	11
Family and peer relationships	90	11
Social presentation	85	11
Age-appropriate self-care and competence	83	11
Identity	75	11
Other	34	11

Other categories taken into account when assessing needs included the needs of the family indices of deprivation (6); disability – effects on the child and family (6); children on the child protection register (5); equal opportunities (4); peer support networks (4); social integration/inclusion (3); availability of resources (2); health/development milestones (1); and expressed needs (1). Two social workers commented that assessment tends to focus on the presented problem.

As Table 4.3 shows, child care managers appear to be generally aware of the need to take a wide variety of different considerations into account when assessing the needs of children. The data would appear to refute assertions that the sole criterion was the risk of abuse and neglect, and show clearly that other factors are taken into account when assessing the needs of children.

Views on operational indicators of need

Child care managers were presented with the operational indicators of need (SIS 1995). The original list of 11 indicators was used in this research due to the timing of the questionnaire survey, which was administered before the implementation of the revised *Policy and Procedures Handbook* in April 1998, which included the new list of 13 indicators (Children (NI) Order Implementation Officers Group 1998). Respondents were asked if each indicator was used by them in practice. The responses are presented in Table 4.4.

At least 61 per cent of all those surveyed indicated that they used all indicators of need. 'Children subject to a child protection assessment' was the most commonly used operational indicator, as indicated by 81 per cent of child care managers surveyed. Over three-quarters of those surveyed also indicated 'Children ceasing to be "looked after" by the Trust'; 'Children at risk of family breakdown'; 'Children experiencing psychiatric, psychological...'; and 'Children whose parents or carers are unable...'. Three-quarters of child care managers also indicated that 'Children with a disability' was used as an indicator of need. These findings perhaps raise the question whether child care managers were using the lists as general indicators of a child in need rather than as specific criteria for assessing children.

Child care managers interviewed were asked about the value placed on the operational indicators. These were seen as giving direction but open to interpretation. For some respondents the operational indicators were seen as fulfilling a statistical role.

Table 4.4. Use of operational indicators of need (n=100)	
Operational indicators of need	Yes
Children who are living in poverty, are socially disadvantaged, and whose health or development is likely to be significantly affected should services not be provided	64
Children subject to child protection assessment	81
Children with a disability who require services	73
Children for whom no one exercises parental responsibility	71
Children whose parents or carers are unable, for whatever reason, to provide reasonable standards for their child	76
Children at risk of family breakdown likely to lead to significant harm	79
Children experiencing psychiatric, psychological, emotional or behavioural difficulties suffering or likely to suffer significant harm	76
Children for whom offending and its consequences are significant features of their lives	63
Children whose welfare is likely to be significantly prejudiced as a result of homelessness	63
Children ceasing to be 'looked after' by the trust	76
Children who are carers	60

There was a general feeling among those interviewed that the operational indicators have an important role in giving direction to practitioners. However, one SSW believed they are 'just seen by social workers as ticking another box on the referral form. I don't think social workers needed the list.' Whilst views were generally favourable towards their use, the precise nature of this use varied between trusts. For example, for some child care managers they were used at the point of referral. One APSW commented that 'They provide a clear and focused set of criteria. They provide a framework within which to operate;' for senior social workers 'they provide a framework within which to operate' and are seen as 'the backbone of the service. They are broad enough to allow for good service development and a preventative approach. We rely on them more in contrast to Article 17.'

However, a number of child care managers viewed them as additional bureaucracy, with one SSW commenting that 'they are just another indicator. They operate as a measuring tape so we can have some idea. They are no more than this. They lead to a fuller assessment and are tailored to those participants' needs. It's tying them (children in need) into little boxes.' Further concerns were raised by one PSW who noted: 'I think they are generally recognised as key areas where we will be responding. But it's very early days and we are not fully into what they mean. There is concern that if someone doesn't fit a category then "no can do" is possible.' Further confusion was raised at a focus group discussion in which it was noted that:

> Social workers are familiar with the operational indicators and they do play a part in one team's practice, but this was a specialist setting and clients have already been referred and assessed for this service. As many operational indicators have already been used for referral, there is no need to categorise as one or other category of need. The operational indicators are not built into the referral forms, only factual information is required. SOSCARE requires this type of coding, codes 8 and 23 were the most common.

However, there appears to be a general agreement that the operational indicators can make a valuable contribution to practice, with one APSW summing up the current situation in stating that: 'they are very useful. I feel they are the first agreed indicator of what the province is using. After the legislation we were left asking "What should we do? What does this mean?" – but they are still very broad.' For some they provide further guidance on the operational definition of children in need, with one SSW suggesting that with their implementation 'they add understanding to the broad definition of children in need.'

The implementation of the operational indicators of children in need has received a varied but generally favourable response. Although the revised list has been available to all HSS trusts from 1 April 1998 its use is at a relatively early stage. To some extent the perceptions of its value for practice appear to be based upon the progress made by individual trusts towards its implementation.

Interagency co-operation

The process of identifying children in need is most effective when it is carried out in conjunction with other agencies. Article 18(5) states that every authority

> (a) shall facilitate the provision by others (including in particular voluntary organisations) of services which the authority has power to provide by virtue of this Article...

> (b) may make any such arrangements as it sees fit for any person to act on its behalf in the provision of any such service.

Child care managers were asked if they were aware of plans/strategies in place with any statutory agencies. Their responses are presented in Table 4.5.

Table 4.5 Strategies or plans for co-operation with other statutory agencies (n=100)	
Agency	**Number aware of a strategy/plan**
Health	61
Education	59
Police	51
Housing	44
Probation	36
Youth	29
Social Security	17
None	18
Other	16

Other agencies mentioned included community/voluntary organisations (8); district councils (2); inter-agency groups (2); Environmental Health (1); Area

Child Protection Agency (1); Training and Employment Agency (1); and the Northern Ireland Office (1).

As Table 4.5 shows, child care managers were most aware of strategies or plans with health and education. Only trusts G and J did not indicate this to be the case, although only in trust D was this unanimous among respondents. A lower proportion of child care managers surveyed were aware of plans/ strategies with police, housing and probation, with again only trust D in unanimous agreement among those surveyed. Plans/strategies with youth and social services were less frequent. Eighteen per cent of child care managers were not aware of any such arrangements, a figure which includes responses from all trusts except trust D. In all other cases, with the exception of co-operation with police and social security, a higher proportion of PSW/APSWs compared with SSWs were aware of co-operation.

When asked specifically if their HSS trust has agreed joint protocols with other statutory agencies, child care managers produced the responses detailed in Table 4.6.

Table 4.6 Has your HSS trust agreed joint protocols for identifying children in need? (n=100)	
Agency	Number of positive responses
Police	26
Health	26
Education	22
Housing	18
Probation	11
None	14
Youth	6
Social Security	5
Not known	47
Other	3

Other protocols were agreed with voluntary agencies (1); through net-working/liaison at Team Leader level (1); and through the referral service (1).

Police, health and education were the agencies most likely to have agreed joint protocols with HSS trusts. Child care managers in trust J did not indicate that joint protocols existed with a statutory body. Such protocols were less likely with housing and probation. Only six child care managers indicated that such an arrangement existed with social security, and only four said that this was the case with youth services. Perhaps significantly, nearly half (47%) of child care managers surveyed indicated that they did not know whether their trusts had agreed joint protocols for identifying children in need. At least one child care manager from each HSS trust felt this was the case, including half those from trusts D, F, G, A and H. Over half of SSWs (52%) indicated that they did not know this, compared with 45 per cent of APSWs and no PSWs.

Table 4.7 Level of communication and co-operation existing between your HSS trust and statutory agencies (n=100)

Agency	No answer	V. high	High	Moderate	Low	V. Low
Education	7	27	39	17	4	6
Health	21	45	21	5	1	7
Police	13	27	30	17	5	8
Probation	2	17	32	27	10	12
Youth	0	10	28	34	13	15
Social Security	1	10	24	32	16	17
Housing	3	21	33	22	12	9

Perhaps not surprisingly, child care managers indicate that health services have the highest level of communication and co-operation with their HSS trusts (Table 4.7). Over two-thirds of respondents felt there was at least moderate communication and co-operation with education (73%), and over half felt communication and co-operation was at least moderate with housing (57%), police (60%) and probation (51%). Communication with social security and youth was more limited.

Over half (53%) of child care managers reported that they have encountered problems in working with the statutory agencies listed above. Forty-six child care managers cited specific problems. The most common problem was a lack of clarity of roles and responsibilities, followed by agencies not fulfilling their responsibilities and pushing their own agendas. Limited resources was a recurring theme.

Clearly, child care managers in a number of HSS trusts will have to overcome significant problems in order to improve inter-agency working. Identification of such issues is an important step towards this.

Child care managers were then asked how they felt these problems might be resolved. Responses are presented in Table 4.8.

Table 4.8 Resolution of problems encountered with statutory agencies (n=100)	
Resolution	Number
Better liaison, networking, joint training	33
Joint strategies	10
Better understanding of each other's role and responsibility	9
Enforcement of statutory obligation	5
Consistent interpretation of categories within trusts	4
Complete rethink of child abuse investigation and support	3
Other	13

Other ways of resolving the problems mentioned include: better funding for these agencies (to fulfil statutory responsibilities) (2); more resources (e.g. increased public housing) (2); more staff (2); service becoming more needs-led (2); earlier identification of needs assessment (2); more adherence to Area Child Protection Committee (1); youth service more focused (1); recognition that refinement of 'in need' definition is essential (1).

Clearly it was felt that there was a case for improving liaison, with joint training as perhaps one way of clarifying issues that are relevant to all agencies involved. One-third (33%) of all child care managers felt that this was an important step towards improving co-operation between HSS trusts and other statutory agencies.

Conclusions

Within each HSS board there was evidence of consistency across the trusts located in that geographical region. This, however, was not the case across the four HSS boards. As some HSS boards are at a more advanced stage than others in implementing the *Policies and Procedures Handbooks*, this may explain the more positive attitudes to the operational definition of children in need in such boards. This provides evidence for the value of this approach to developing the operational requirements of Article 18. It also suggests that lessons can be learnt from the experience of such trusts and the HSS boards in which they are located. The findings also provide support for the argument that there is a need to standardise practice in relation to children in need across all four HSS boards, which was one of the problems highlighted in the literature from England and Wales.

The findings also suggest that the implementation of Article 18 of the Children (NI) Order is creating a transition in practice. Whilst it is clear that child protection will continue to take priority, often at the expense of family support, the ethos of Article 18, with its refocusing of practice from protection to prevention, is beginning to influence practice, at least in the attitudes of practitioners. However, only when the transition currently being experienced is complete will we have a clear picture of the position of family support provision against child protection. There are indications from this research that practice is moving in the direction of the former.

CHAPTER 5

Needs-based Planning for Family and Child Care Services in Northern Ireland: Problems and Possibilities

Andrew Percy

Introduction

The planning and delivery of family and child care services is inextricably linked to the concept of 'need'. From the organisation and management of services at national and regional levels through to the point of local service delivery, the needs of children and families *should* determine the extent and nature of services provided to them.

There is a clear expectation within the 1995 Children (NI) Order that service planners and providers should undertake, in collaboration with other agencies, a thorough analysis of the 'need' and 'demand' for services within their area, and their supply. This needs assessment is expected to influence the strategic planning, organisation and, ultimately, the delivery of family and child care services to children and families in need. With the advent of Children's Services Plans (Children's Services Planning Order 1998) this expectation has been made explicit. Service commissioners and providers now have a statutory requirement to plan and manage services on the basis of local needs.

In light of this requirement, this chapter will attempt to define what the needs-based planing process actually entails, to assess the extent to which needs-based planning, as defined above, can be undertaken by commiss-ioners and providers, and finally to provide some recommendations for the further development of the family and child care service needs-based planning process within Northern Ireland. While the chapter will consider some of the issues surrounding supply and demand, its principal focus will be on 'need' and its assessment at both the population and individual level.

Key terminology

A useful starting point in the discussion of needs-based planning is to clarify what is actually meant by '*need*', '*demand*' and '*supply*'. This is far from simple, as numerous definitions exist for each of these key terms. The various professional groups involved in the planning process, such as social workers, health economists and senior PSS operational managers, may each have their own slightly different understanding of these concepts.

Need

Social work, by and large, has tended to employ an *individualist* view of need, looking at which services are most appropriate for individual children and families in response to their individual sets of needs. Bradshaw (1972) labelled this '*normative need*' – need as determined by 'experts' in relation to personal, cultural and professional norms and values. Here, individual need is constructed through the interplay of:

- professional knowledge, values and ideologies
- personal views and opinions
- appreciation of the legislative imperative
- client expectations and experiences (which Bradshaw termed *felt need*)
- the demands of the job such as caseload management, availability of resources and individual skills and expertise (Ritchie, Christie and Wilson 1996).

Colton, Drury and Williams (1995b) found that social workers tended to construct definitions of need closely aligned with notions of minimum human rights and requirements, such as adequate food, warmth, clothing, education, hygiene and emotional support; appropriate developmental progress; or a childhood free from abuse or neglect. This approach is also embodied in the UN Convention on the Rights of the Child, which specifies the minimum requirements and standards for the treatment of all children. Article 24, for example, specifies the right to the highest standard of medical care, while Article 27 outlines the right to adequate standards of living and housing (see Children's Rights Development Unit (1994) for more details on the UN Convention). The dominance of a welfare/rights model of need within social work is understandable given the historical development of the profession. Jordan (1997) observed how the social work profession has its origins in the 'charitable visitor' aiming to protect or compensate the weakest members of society. Even in more recent times the profession has been dominated, to an extent, by the welfare rights movement, which seeks to alleviate material deprivation and income maintenance problems (Hill 1997).

This individualist perspective on need is somewhat different from that employed by other professional groups such as epidemiologists and health economists. Here, need tends to be defined in terms of a population's 'ability to benefit from health or social care'. Bebbington, Turvey and Janzon (1996) argued that 'need' should not be conceptualised as a set of absolute characteristics or conditions of welfare, as in the social work individualist approach, but rather as an instrumental or subjective assessment of the need for social care. As a result, it must take into account the circumstances of an individual relevant to their need, current assumptions about what services are appropriate to meet that need, the cost of those services, and, finally, the resources available to purchase those services. In Bradshaw's terminology (1972), this perspective can be reformulated in terms of *comparative need* – need statistically determined with reference to the level of resources available to others – and *expressed need/demand* – the number of referrals to social services – as well as *normative* and *felt need* (Ritchie *et al.* 1996).

Sheppard and Woodcock (1999), in a recent review, also draw a similar distinction between these two main conceptualisations of need. They term the first the 'deficit state' approach, where need is seen as 'falling below some expected standard, one which is applied to everyone' (p.69). This is similar to the individualistic view of need outlined above. The alternative to this, as seen by Sheppard and Woodcock, is a 'differentiated concept of need' which consists of three main components, a statement of a problem, a statement of the support or service that would alleviate the problem and a statement about the resources required to provide the service. Although specified on an individual and not a population basis, there are clear parallels between this conceptualisation of need and that employed by health economists. Sheppard and Woodcock argue that if family and child care services are to achieve a 'needs led' operation, there must be a move away from the traditional deficit approach to need, with its single taxonomy of needs areas (for example the NI Operational Indicators of Need (SIS 1995)) towards a differentiated conceptualisation of need, with its three taxonomies: problems, services and resources.

Demand

Within a micro-economic model of health care services, *demand* is traditionally considered to be the health care services people may wish to use within a free system, or may wish to pay for within a market system (Stevens and Raftery 1994). Such demand derives from the individual's desire to be healthy or at least not to be unwell. However, within social services demand is unlikely to be expressed in this direct manner. While some families may know that they are '*unwell*' (i.e. have certain problems that would benefit from the provision of family and child care services), most families in crisis may not be in a position to recognise the signs or to demand help or support. Others may be reluctant to contact family and child care services because of the stigma associated with it. Many may also simply be unaware that support and help is available. It may be worth noting that many of these issues apply not just to social services, but also to certain aspects of health care (e.g. HIV care). As a result of the above, the demand for family and child care services is not expressed by families; rather it is determined by social workers acting for children and families who are often referred to them from a number of different sources including GPs, teachers, police and members of the public.

Supply

Supply can simply be stated as the extent and range of services provided to the general public. At present the supply of family and child care services is unlikely to match the extent of existing need (Higgins, Pinkerton and Switzer 1997). Knapp (1997) identified numerous social and economic factors that have contributed to this increasing needs/service provision gap. Economic pressures, market forces and government cutbacks may reduce the resources that can be allocated to local service provision. In parallel, broad socio-demographic changes may act to drive need upwards. These include increasing numbers of lone parents, widening social and family expectations, and the growing gap between the poor and the 'well off'.

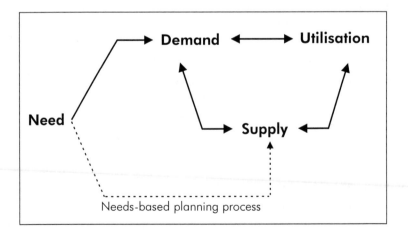

Figure 5.1 Interaction between need, demand and supply

The interaction of need, demand and supply

Need, demand and supply cannot be considered in isolation (*see* Fig. 5.1). The amount of need within a local community is one of the principal determinants of demand for family and child care services, but by no means the only one. The extent to which need actually translates into demand will depend on other factors, including the willingness of families to seek help, the identification and referral of families to social services by local communities, and the referral and assessment procedures employed by local health and personal social services (HPSS) family and child care teams. Demand is also interdependent with supply. The availability of family and child care services (e.g. the number of social workers operating within a particular patch, or the number people willing to foster children) will influence the size and nature of the social work caseload and the service decisions taken by social workers.

As can be seen from the above discussion, social workers sit at the very nexus of need, supply and demand for family and child care services. That position with respect to need, supply and demand is not uncommon. GPs in particular are themselves simultaneously required to assess individual need, moderate demand and designate supply (Stevens and Raftery 1994).

The role of needs assessment in the planning process

Given the health–economic definition of need outlined above, the overall aim of needs-based planning could be formulated as the effective development and use of available resources to achieve the maximum benefit for the local population. By definition this involves taking strategic decisions around the allocation and distribution of available resources in the most effective way across different client groups and areas according to their assessed need.

Guidance issued by the Department of Health (Department of Health/ Price Waterhouse 1993) proposed a dynamic model of needs-based planning involving the integration of both individual (bottom-up) and population (top-down) needs assessment data. Within this model, such data are used to form the basis of an initial strategic plan, which is then refined by front-line experience, review and further needs assessment work, culminating in 'an increasingly full understanding of the population's ability to benefit from care' (p.6). Bebbington *et al.* (1996) described the needs-based planning process as essentially 'a mechanism for assembling and combining evidence and assumptions about states of welfare, prices, resources and service preferences for a group of people.'

Stevens and Raftery (1994), promoting an epidemiological approach to needs assessment, suggested that needs-based planning should be focused on a particular problem rather than a population group or service type, as need results from problems. Within this model consideration should be given to:

- the actual problem
- the sub-categories of the problem
- the prevalence and incidence of the problem
- existing models of welfare/care
- the corresponding services available
- the effectiveness and cost-effectiveness of those services
- the anticipated outcomes of those services.

Population needs assessment

The starting point for any needs-based planning process is the assessment of need within a given population. This can be achieved in a number of different ways, including the analysis of official client records, the use of survey data (both local and national), and the use of proxy indicators of need, each with its own associated advantages and disadvantages. Here, a distinction should be made between 'need', defined as a characteristic or circumstance which could benefit from the provision of a particular service, and 'in need', i.e. the specific population to whom the legislation refers. As a result it is possible to estimate both the extent of 'need' (the frequency of a characteristic within a given population) and the extent of the population 'in need' (the proportion of the population who fall within the legislative criteria). A further consideration is that in some cases individuals can have multiple needs, so the extent of need may be substantially higher than the size of the total population defined as in need.

Official client records

As social services are required to maintain detailed accounts of client contact, such official records provide a readily available data source for the assessment of population need. However, official records have a number of inherent limitations that reduce their usefulness. First, while they contain extensive material on the child and their status within the care system, official records tend to hold little information on the actual specific needs of the child. Therefore, they can be used for prevalence estimation only.

Second, many vulnerable children, some would say the majority of children in need, do not appear on official records. This constitutes *hidden need*. Even when vulnerable children do come to the attention of social services, and thus appear on official records, not all of their needs may be assessed and met (*unmet need*). Therefore, client record systems hold only a sub-sample of children 'in need' which is unlikely to be fully representative of all the children in need within a local area. In addition, numerous biases are likely to be introduced by the identification, referral and assessment procedures used.

Client records are also heavily influenced by past service provision. To an extent, client records may reflect the policies and practices of local social services teams as much as they do the level of actual need within a local community.

Complex statistical procedures such as capture–recapture methods (Higgins 1998) or small area utilisation modelling (Carr-Hill *et al.* 1997) can be used to overcome some of the limitations within official record systems. Capture–recapture methods can be employed to estimate the size of populations hidden/missing from official records. As the name suggests, they require multiple samples or observations of the client population (in this case, of children referred to social services). These observations can be made across different services' utilisation databases or within a single database across time. Through the statistical examination of the overlap between the various samples (i.e. those cases that are observed twice or more) it becomes possible to estimate the number of families or children in need who do not appear in any of the samples (Higgins 1998). However, they do require the use of complex statistical procedures (e.g. Poisson modelling, log-linear modelling or Markov and semi-Markov modelling). While such procedures have been extensively employed in other fields of study, such as drug-use prevalence research (Wickens 1993), they have been under-utilised in child care research.

In contrast, small area utilisation modelling has been applied to child care needs assessment. It was the methodology recently employed in the development of a new resource allocation formula for family and child care services in England and Wales (Carr-Hill *et al.* 1997). It is also currently under consideration as the basis for family and child care service resource allocation within Northern Ireland (Percy *et al.* 1998).

Small area utilisation modelling is a class of approaches that examine variations in service utilisation (and its associated service costs) across small geographical areas (i.e. wards) in relation to the socio-economic characteristics of those areas. In essence, this approach uses current utilisation as a proxy for need so as to identify a range of variables derived from census questions that appear to be correlated with need. These variables can then be used as robust areal indicators of the relative need for family and child care services. While the approach incorporates a proxy for need (current utilisation) rather than a direct measure, specific techniques (the use of dummy variables within the model) can be employed to control for variation in utilisation, which is determined by possible service supply factors and historical service policies and practices. As with capture–recapture, small area utilisation modelling is reliant on complex statistical procedures such as multi-level modelling.

While both these approaches attempt to address some of the core limitations of official records, the quality of any estimates of population need produced in this way is determined by the quality of the record data used. In many cases considerable errors may exist within the client records. A recent audit of the SOSCARE database, the principal HPSS client and activity recording system in Northern Ireland, found considerable problems with the robustness and completeness of the family and child care component (Deloitte and Touche 1997a; 1997b). In particular, fundamental problems were identified within the data collection and input stage. Percy *et al.* (1998) also identified weaknesses in SOSCARE relating to the quality of postcode information, boundary issues regarding children with disabilities, lack of detailed information on specific services utilised, and lack of information on the amount of social work activity per case Before SOSCARE could be employed within any needs assessment exercise, these data limitations would need to be addressed.

Survey approach

General population surveys can provide an alternative data source to agency records. The advantages of using surveys is that they may uncover hidden need that has not come to the attention of PSS. They also provide an independent assessment of need that is not influenced by variations in local policy or practice (*unmet need*). In addition, surveys can be used to collect detailed data at an individual level on both individual characteristics, the extent of individual need, and actual individual service utilisation. Because of the standardised way in which surveys are conducted, they can be used to measure trends in the variation of need across time: for example, the rates at which individuals become needy, take up services or no longer require services.

However, surveys do have a number of weaknesses. First, surveys, like all data sources, are subject to a range of errors, including sampling, non-response, coverage and measurement error (Moser and Kalton 1971; Alwin 1991). For example, coverage error occurs within most large-scale general population surveys, as people living in non-household accommodation (those in hospital or residential homes) tend not to be included within the sampling frame. The accumulation of such errors within national or regional surveys can make results at the small area level (e.g. below local authority/ board level) statistically unreliable. This problem can be overcome, to an extent, either by conducting local surveys of population need, although these tend to be disproportionately expensive when compared to national surveys, or by calculating synthetic estimates of local need from existing national survey data (*see* Bebbington 1996).

The second problem affecting surveys relates to the type of data that can be collected. As surveys are usually based on individual interviews, they cannot collect information which is not related to the characteristics of the respondent. It is generally not possible within a survey to measure neighbourhood characteristics such as the extent of community support or social control, although it is possible to attach some geodemographic information to individual survey case data.

The third problem is related to this general point. Survey assessments of need, because of the limitations of the individual interview, tend to be rather superficial when compared with the broad, detailed information that would be collected via a comprehensive individual social work assessment. As a result they do not easily translate to potential services or resource requirements (Turvey 1995). In some cases surveys do not even attempt to measure the extent of actual individual need but simply assess individual service utilisation. However, it is possible, using a two-stage interview process, to include a full clinical assessment for certain respondents within a population household survey. Finally, surveys are on the whole very expensive and time-consuming.

Surveys of the need for family and child care services are technically feasible, and many of the problems listed above could be overcome by the use of more sophisticated sampling designs – incorporating some form of standardised independent needs assessment – or improved measurement instruments. However, undertaking such work can be both practically and methodologically difficult. The direct interviewing of children about family and child care problems within a household or school survey would pose major ethical problems. This would restrict any survey needs assessment to either asking parents about their relationship with their child(ren) or asking adults about their childhood experiences.

A survey of parents on their need for family and child services may be a more practical option than asking children directly. In fact, surveys of this kind have been conducted in the USA (Hemenway, Solnick and Carter 1994; Ross 1996; Finkelhor *et al.* 1997; Straus *et al.* 1998). However, such surveys are likely to underestimate need, as some parents may be unwilling to disclose very sensitive information within the confines of a survey interview. They also fail to consider the views of the child, which are an important and required component of any family assessment. Notwithstanding these methodological issues, surveys of this kind still produce estimates of need several times higher than other methods (Straus *et al.* 1998).

Surveys of adults on their own childhood experiences are also possible (Baker and Duncan 1985; Ghate and Spencer 1995). However, estimates of need produced in this way would be dated and of little value to the service planner. Also, a survey of adults may under-report childhood incidents of abuse or neglect because of memory problems, embarrassment, a wish to protect parents, or a conscious wish to forget incidents (Widom and Morris 1997; Widom and Shepard 1996).

Surveys have been used for population needs assessment purposes for other forms of HPSS. Buckingham *et al.* (1996) used specific questions from the 1991 General Household Survey (GHS), the 1994 GHS and the 1996 Omnibus Survey to estimate the probability that a person with a given set of characteristics would be a community health service user. The UK Disability Survey was used in a similar way by Bebbington *et al.* (1996) in relation to community care service use.

The use of proxy indicators

When the measurement of actual need within local communities is difficult and costly to undertake, as in family and child care services, the use of proxy indicators of need may be a cheaper and more manageable alternative to conducting full-scale population needs assessment. If population or area characteristics can be identified that predict the extent of local need, and which are observable and readily available, they can be employed as proxies for need. The guidance issued by the Department of Health recognised the legitimacy and benefit of using proxy indicators to ensure an adequate information basis for planning purposes (Department of Health/Price Waterhouse 1993).

However, few studies have directly examined the relationship between population characteristics and the need for family and childcare services. Those that have been completed have been almost exclusively restricted to child physical or sexual abuse, which is only one aspect of need, albeit an important one, relating to only one area of service provision, that of child protection.

In general many of these studies have also have been weakened by a number of methodological limitations in the research designs employed, including over-reliance on clinical populations and retrospective data, failure to take account of variations in the severity and chronicity of the child maltreatment, and poor operational definitions (Dingwall 1989; Aspinall 1996). It is only in recent years that emotional abuse and neglect have been fully recognised as forms of child maltreatment requiring service provision (*see* O'Hagan 1993; Iwaniec 1995).

In a major review, Belsky (1993) concluded that the abuse and neglect of children 'is multiply determined by factors operating at multiple levels of analysis (developmental, immediate-situational, demographic, cultural-historical, evolutionary' (p.427). As well as a range of psychological and personality factors, child maltreatment was associated with a lack of community and social support, poverty, low parental educational attainment, unemployment, unplanned pregnancies, larger families, short space between births, and stepfamilies. In addition to these, Aspinall (1996) cited age of the mother, bonding failure (breast feeding may be a proxy for this), type of family, spousal violence, alcohol and drug use, and previous history of abuse as potential causes of child maltreatment.

Research undertaken by Browne and Stevenson (1983), identified nine indicators which retrospectively differentiated between abusing and non-abusing families, including parental indifference to the child, history of family violence, socio-economic problems, low birth weight, parental history of abuse, step-parent or cohabitee present, single parent, mother under 21 at time of birth, history of mental illness, problem drinking or drug use, and post-delivery mother–child separation exceeding 24 hours. Spacing between births was not found to be a significant predictor of child maltreatment. However, in a follow-up prospective study, the psychosocial indicators listed above were poor at identifying those families that were subject to a case conference within the next two years (Browne and Saqi 1988). The authors concluded that the failure to take account of the parent–child relationship within the list of indicators weakened their predictive power.

In a study of admissions into care in England, Bebbington and Miles (1989) found that children from certain kinds of families were at considerably higher risk than other children of being admitted into care. These were families with only one adult in the home; where the head of household was on benefits; living in crowded conditions; or living in rented accommodation. Children with mothers under the age of 21 or of mixed-race parentage were also more vulnerable than others to reception into care.

The overall conclusion from the above research is that there are a range of factors associated with the need for family and child care services in general. A number of these factors operate, or can be measured, at an aggregate community or area level, and may therefore form the basis of potential proxies for need. However, there are a number of practical problems that would have to be overcome. The main source of data on local areas is the census. However, this becomes dated, as a full census only occurs every ten years. The last census was in 1991. As a result it is unlikely to accurately reflect the current geodemographics of a small area. Diamond *et.al.* (1997) compared the 1981 census-based ward and parish population estimates for 1991 with the actual 1991 census counts. Inaccuracies of between 2–4 per cent for the total population, and 10–30 per cent for five-year age groups were found. Non-adjusted 1981 census counts differed between 15 per cent to over 40 per cent from the 1991 counts across the five-year age groups.

There are also a range of statistical and methodological problems which must be taken account of when using local base and small area census statistics (Cole undated). These include:

- *data suppression* – areas have to contain a certain minimum population size (Local Base Statistics (LBS) thresholds – 1000 residents, 320 households)

- *data modification* – census data is blurred to prevent inadvertent disclosure of information about identifiable households (Barnardisation)

- *small number problems* – this occurs when small random fluctuations in numerators and/or denominators result in large fluctuations in percentages.

Finally, one potential needs proxy – income – is not collected within the census. However, many of the census indicators of material and social deprivation are either the causes or consequences of low income (Davies, Joshi and Clarke 1997). Yet, as Davies demonstrated, such deprivation indicators do misclassify a sizeable proportion of the poorest households and also those households on higher incomes who choose not to spend on cars or home ownership.

Census-based geodemographic classification systems provide a commonly used alternative to individual census variables. One such system – ACORN (A Classification Of Residential Neighbourhoods) – classifies local neighbourhoods (enumeration districts) into one of 7 categories, 17 groups or 60 types, according to the census characteristics of the households living there. The dimensionality of the census data is conveniently reduced, as is the multicollinearity of the census variables (many of the potential census needs indicators are highly correlated, which causes problems in modelling the data). However, many of the range of census variables used to construct different geodemographic profiles will in fact be distal indicators of the need for family and child care services. Their automatic incorporation within any area profile will reduce its efficiency as an accurate proxy for need. Cole (undated) lists a range of other limitations, including subjectivity of classification, scale transference problems (i.e. ecological fallacy), misclassification due to the quality of census data at the ED level, and the spatial misallocation of postcoded data.

Similar problems arise with the use of deprivation indices such as the Robson Index (Robson, Bradford and Deas 1994). Theoretically, the need for family and child care services is unlikely to be related to general deprivation per se, but rather to specific aspects of it.

Given the limitations of each of the principal methods of assessing population need outlined above, it is unlikely that any single approach will provide a comprehensive and reliable measure of a population's need for family and child care services. A more promising strategy may be to employ a range of different population assessment methodologies within any one exercise. Here, national/regional survey estimates of population need could be considered alongside survey-based synthetic estimates of local need. The findings from this national/local comparison could then be considered in the light of local indicators of need and service utilisation patterns.

Individual needs assessment

As mentioned previously, the Department of Health guidance on needs-based planning recommends the integration of both population and individual needs assessment data. Individual needs assessment and care planning data provide the linkage between population-assessed needs and required service provision. By examining individual case histories it is possible to gain an insight into how social services have responded to assessed need.

Individual client assessment has always been a core component of social work practice, although the process has taken numerous forms and guises over the years (Lloyd and Taylor 1995). Even though it is now over ten years old, the 'Orange Book' on child protection (Department of Health 1988) is still the most comprehensive statutory guidance on individual needs assessment relating to child abuse. Key components of the Orange Book assessment procedure include in-depth examination of:

- the nature and extent possible of child maltreatment
- the child
- family composition
- carer profile

- parental relationships and family interactions
- family networks
- family finance
- physical conditions and the home environment.

Within Northern Ireland, subsequent guidance has recently been issued by the four health and personal social services boards (Children (NI) Order Implementation Officers Group 1998). Even though the Orange Book has been criticised for being more about assessing risk or screening for legal intervention than for assessing need for services, it still forms the core of the HPSS guidance on assessment processes for both child protection and family support services. However, greater emphasis is placed on a multi-disciplinary/multi-agency approach to comprehensive assessment. It is suggested that where appropriate, other professionals such as health visitors and clinical and educational psychologists should assist in the assessment of child and family need.

In addition to understanding of how services currently respond to actual presented need, information is also required on the quality of those services provided, and in particular on the comparative effectiveness and efficiency of alternative intervention modalities. In theory, such information, together with an assessment of need from both an individual and a population perspective, can be combined to form what Bebbington et al. (1996) referred to as the 'welfare technology – what is likely to be required in order to achieve a particular improvement in the state of welfare for a person in a certain initial state' (p.9). At its core is the concept of 'client/intervention matching' – the provision of the most appropriate intervention required to meet the specific needs of the client. Without such information the quality of planning decisions around the allocation of specific services within any location in accordance with its need profile will be compromised.

At present a considerable debate exists on what the most appropriate methods are for the evaluation of personal social services. On the one side, some argue for the application of experimental methods, and randomised control trials (RCTs) in particular, as the gold standard approach to the evaluation of human services. The main point that they make is that the random allocation of clients, the hallmark of RCTs, maintains high internal validity within the study, which then allows the researcher to make strong inferences about whether the intervention under study had or did not have an impact on the children and families who received it. However, RCTs have a number of other methodological conditions that must be met. The client population participating in the study must be homogenous; the interventions being evaluated must be standardised across all clients; and the study population must not have multiple needs, as they may have a confounding effect on the intervention. It is these conditions that are attacked by proponents of a more naturalistic approach to evaluation. They argue that social workers never deal with homogenous populations, and do not provide standardised interventions but rather interventions that are open-ended, self-correcting and tailored to the individual needs of the client. As a result such critics suggest that RCTs do not and cannot evaluate interventions with families and children as they are actually delivered in practice (for a full discussion of these issues *see* Hill 1999a; Shaw and Lishman 1999).

Needs-based planning for family and child care services in Northern Ireland

The discussion above provides a brief outline of both population and individual needs assessment, two essential components of the needs-based planning process. Such methods attempt to provide answers to questions that lie at the core of the planning process:

- What is the extent of need within a given population?
- How do social services respond to that identified need?
- How should they respond?
- What are the expected outcomes and benefits of those responses?

At present within Northern Ireland there is limited evidence that current service planning is undertaken along such lines. This is unsurprising given the paucity of detailed information available to those involved in the planning process. No comprehensive national or regional survey of the need for family and child care services has been conducted; nor has a capture–recapture type study been undertaken. Much of the population needs assessment work that has been undertaken has fallen within the proxy indicator approach. Bearing in mind the lack of evidence about the relationship between population and areal characteristics and the need for family support services, such community profiling on its own provides little by way of accurate or detailed information about the actual extent of local need beyond the general statement that the 'demand' for family and child care services greatly exceeds current 'supply'.

There are a number of probable reasons for this lack of population needs assessment. First, population needs assessment research is expensive and time-consuming. As family and child care services account for only about 5 per cent of the overall HPSS budget within Northern Ireland there may be a reluctance to undertake such research. Research effort may be concentrated on more costly programmes of care such as that for the elderly. Second, needs assessment in relation to family and child care services is technically and methodologically difficult. While standardised measures of child abuse and neglect may exist there is little agreement on the conceptualisation and operationalisation of the wider concepts of 'the need for family and child care services' and 'children in need'. Finally, there is a lack of published guidance or examples of needs-based planning in relation to family and child care services. To date such work has been restricted almost exclusively to hospital inpatient services and community care. As a result, the general needs-based planning methodology is less advanced in the area of family and child care services.

Problems also exist in relation to individual needs assessments, in particular the extent to which a coherent 'welfare technology' could actually be established for family and child care services. Effective matching presupposes the availability of a wide range of alternative family and child care services/ interventions to which clients with differing needs can be matched, and that clients are able to access those services. However, recent research conducted within Northern Ireland has highlighted variations in the provision, availability and access to family and child care services (Higgins *et al.* 1997; Monteith and Sneddon 1999; Pinkerton and McCrea 1999). The extent to which current service provision actually resembles the welfare pluralism necessary for appropriate intervention matching is debatable.

As well as the appropriate service options being available to facilitate matching, practitioners must have information on the comparative effectiveness and efficiency of the service/intervention options available. However, within family and child care services there is a distinct lack of high-quality intervention evaluation studies (MacDonald and Roberts 1995). To take the example of family support – the major focus of the post-Children Order restructuring – few randomised control trials have been conducted within the UK. There are a number of reasons for this including the diversity of work that falls within the banner of family support; the diversity of clients that receive family support-type services; the open-ended corrective nature of the therapeutic work undertaken; and the organisational pressures of managing risk and preventing harm to children.

Defining what is meant by family support has also proved a major theoretical challenge. Relevant services range from universal primary prevention projects aimed at alleviating or reducing poverty, stress or poor housing amongst families through to intensive crisis intervention attempting to keep children out of care. In many cases, services defined as family support differ little from other services defined as child protection, up to and including the temporary removal of children from their family (respite care) (Higgins, Pinkerton and Devine 1998b).

In addition to the lack of quality evaluations of family and child care services, few of those that have been conducted have included an analysis of the cost benefits/cost effectiveness of services provided (Knapp and Lowin 1998). As a result, little information is currently available to the service planner on the comparative effectiveness and comparative costs of different family and child care service/intervention modalities. To a large extent, questions as to what are the most effective family and child care interventions, and as to who benefits most from what, remain unexplored and unanswered.

The way forward

This paper has argued that, while there is a statutory requirement on Northern Ireland HPSS boards and trusts (and on local authorities in England, Wales and Scotland) to deliver needs-led services, the existence of major planning information gaps, specifically in relation to both population and individual needs assessment, have restricted the extent to which this has actually been achieved in practice. These planning information gaps have been recognised within the Children's Service Plans recently published by NI HPSS boards. For example, the Western Board plan identified the need for the *construction, through sharing of information, of a common database to enable effective needs assessment to occur* as part of a new planning infrastructure, the need to undertake *interagency needs assessment exercises* and the need *to begin the process of identifying services* (family support) *for piloting and evaluation* (Western Area Children and Young People's Committee 1999, pp.15, 30, 38). Similarly, the Eastern Board plan set a number of key objectives including the identification of *vulnerable children, families and communities*, the introduction of *research and dissemination strategies which will gather evidence and disseminate findings on what works in supporting children in need*, and the development of *evidence based interventions with individuals/groups vulnerable to abuse and neglect on a cross-agency basis* (Eastern Area Children and Young People's Committee 1999, pp.12, 15, 18).

Northern Ireland is not unique in this respect. Little work of this nature has been undertaken in the rest of the UK. There, the community care legislation, which excludes family and child care services, has been the principal driving force behind methodological and data developments in needs-based planning (*see* Department of Health/Price Waterhouse 1993;

Turvey 1995; Bebbington 1996). As a result little of this expertise has been directed towards family and child care services.

If the requirements of the Children's Services Planning Order are to be met these planning information gaps must be addressed. To this end three principal research priorities can be identified:

- *Epidemiological research* – research towards estimating the extent and nature of the population of children and their families who would benefit from the provision of personal social services.

- *Risk factor research* – research to identify those environmental, social and individual characteristics or experiences associated with the need for family and child care services. A risk factor is an experience, characteristic or condition that increases the likelihood of a child or family being in need. By contrast, *protective factors* refer to those experiences, characteristics or conditions that reduce the likelihood of a family being in need.

- *Evaluative research* – research to assess the efficiency and effectiveness of family and child care interventions provided by social services.

Consideration should be given to the establishment of a regular regional general population (probability) survey of families in Northern Ireland assessing need in relation to family and child care provision. While such a study would be unable to cover the full range of family needs, its ability to assess both 'hidden' and 'unmet' need and its ability, assuming consistency of method, to track trends over time, reinforce its central position within the needs-based planning process. Such a regional survey could be built upon by small, localised prevalence studies, using proxy needs indicators or capture–recapture approaches.

As well as basic prevalence and incidence data, cross-sectional surveys can also collect data on those cognitive, behavioural and social factors that may be associated with increased family and child care needs. These factors are not included within the census. Such information may have major implications for the design and delivery of prevention services aimed at reducing the need for social work interventions in family life.

While it is recognised that a survey of this nature would pose considerable practical and methodological challenges, particularly around defining and measuring need, these should not prove insurmountable. National cross-sectional surveys of other sensitive issues have all been successfully undertaken within Great Britain, including illicit drug use (Ramsay and Percy 1996; 1997); rape, indecent assault and sexual harassment (Percy and Mayhew

1997); and sexual behaviours including homosexual experiences (Wellings *et al.* 1994).

There is a strong argument for not only a core regular survey of population need but also a fundamental overhaul of the family and child care administrative and client record systems. As mentioned previously, the recent audit of SOSCARE – the principal family and child care utilisation database (Deloitte and Touche 1997a; 1997b) – revealed major data quality problems. These limit the extent to which it could be exploited for population or individual needs assessment purposes. Before this could occur, major improvements in the data collection procedures, quality control systems, and the range of information collected would have to be made. There is also considerable scope for the further integration of the administrative data sources that exist across social services, health services and education. Work of a similar nature has been undertaken in the USA (*see* Goerge, Van Voorhis and Lee 1994; Goerge *et al.* 1995).

Cross-sectional prevalence and incidence data, whether from surveys or administrative records, provide only a partial picture of need. While they answer questions on the distribution of need across a population, they provide little by way of information on the onset, development and course of specific family and child care needs. Here, a longitudinal cohort study tracking sample families over time would be of more value. Questions such as how specific needs arise within families, whether such needs vary over time and what the acute and chronic impact of specific needs on family life is could be addressed in this type of study. In addition, cohort studies permit the investigation of risk and protective factors. Identification of risk and protective factors may have major implications for the design and delivery of preventative services such as family support. Protective factors, in particular, are important in the study of resilience – why some families manage to cope with extreme adversity while others fail to.

It can be argued that prevention will never be effective unless it is delivered in a comprehensive and co-ordinated manner, via a number of different channels, each either attempting to mitigate a specific risk factor or range of risk factors, or promoting the development of a protective factor or series of protective factors (*see* Coie *et al.* 1993 for more details). In relation to service planning, risk factor research provides an accessible conceptual framework for the provision of universal and targeted interventions aimed at reducing the occurrence of family and child care needs within a local population.

The final piece in this proposed research agenda is evaluative research. To date little is known about the effectiveness or efficiency (or cost-effectiveness) of family and child care services. Both experimental outcome studies comparing various intervention modalities, and more naturalistically-orient-ated investigations examining how interventions are provided by social workers on the ground, are required. Such studies would move social work towards 'evidence-based practice'.

CHAPTER 6

Understanding and Developing Family Support in Northern Ireland: The Challenge to Policy, Practice and Research

Kathryn Higgins

Introduction

This chapter presents the contribution made by a three-year study to the understanding and development of family support in Northern Ireland. It begins by placing the research within the general context of the Children (NI) Order 1995 and its allied new policy direction. The overall aims, objectives and parts of the project are described, and conclusions from Part One are summarised. However, this chapter is concerned mainly with Part Two, which focuses on the evaluation of family support services in Northern Ireland. As well as presenting the main findings, the chapter highlights the methodological challenges presented by the evaluations and the means by which researchers sought to address them. It is hoped that attention to methodological issues will provide an appreciation of the complexities involved in devising an approach suitable for evaluating very different family support settings.

The picture of family support as captured by the project at the level of policy and practice provides a launching pad for suggestions of a future family support agenda. In line with the perspective of the chapter, it is the agenda for research that will be explored in more detail. Such an agenda is mindful of the prevailing 'Zeitgeist' of evidence-based practice and the necessity for those involved in social care to demonstrate that their processes and interventions are effective and open to systematic evaluation. Accordingly, the chapter's final conclusion is an assertion of the need for future research on family support that addresses effectiveness.

Background and policy context

The Children (NI) Order 1995 has been described as:

> The most comprehensive piece of legislation ever enacted in Northern Ireland in relation to children … [which] will have a profound effect not only on children and families but also on a wide range of organisations and disciplines in the social services, voluntary organisations, the courts, the education system, the health service and on individuals providing child minding, day care and other services for children. (DHSS (NI) 1995, p.1).

Expectations of the Order were heightened by the fact that, in contrast to the situation in England and Wales, there have only been three major pieces of child care legislation in Northern Ireland since 1945 (Kelly and Pinkerton 1996). As with the Children Act 1989, which it closely follows, the Order has two main aims: first, to simplify the law and make it more accessible; and second, to create a new balance in the relationship between parents, the state and children. Achieving the new balance is seen to require attention to the twin principles of the paramountcy of the welfare of the child and the promotion of parental responsibility. The Order reasserts the pivotal position of prevention, reframed as 'family support', in the balance between the state, parents and children. This new policy direction is endorsed by the Department of Health and Social Services (DHSS) Regional Strategy for Health and Social Welfare 1997–2002 (DHSS 1996b; 1997), and is also a policy direction for which there is considerable professional support. It expresses not only a UK-wide but also a growing international consensus on how best to meet the needs of children and their carers (Children's Rights Development Unit 1994).

The family support research project

At the heart of this project lies a concern to assess the practical application of the laudable principles outlined above. The overall aim is to provide empirical data and informed comment as a contribution to the planning, monitoring and evaluation of the initial impact of the Children Order on family support services. The project has three objectives:

- to provide an overview of family support services in Northern Ireland with relevance to child care policy prior to the Children (NI) Order

- to select, describe and evaluate a range of family support settings

- to identify and analyse changes in family support provision during the initial 12 months after implementation of the Children (NI) Order and to assess the early impact of the Order.

The project was designed in three parts so that each objective could be addressed in turn whilst building on what went before. For the purposes of this chapter only parts One and Two will be discussed.

1. Family support prior to implementation of the Children (NI) Order

Part One of the study (Higgins, Pinkerton and Switzer 1997) focused on the situation concerning family support before implementation of the Children (NI) Order. It considered the historical development and legislative intent of, and the social policy choices and constraints posed in relation to family support. It also reviewed the English and Welsh experience of prevention and family support, and the existing information on needs and services within Northern Ireland.

Three main perspectives were identified on the meaning of family support:

- *A legal perspective.* Articles 17 and 18 of the Children (NI) Order 1995 do not use the term 'family support' as such, but set out duties of statutory service provision with respect to children in need. Further detail is given in Schedule 2 of the Order and supporting Regulations and Guidance Volume 2.

- *An empirical research perspective.* This drew largely on features of successful preventive and early years provision suggested by existing research primarily undertaken in England and Wales (Holman 1988; Cannan 1992; Gibbons 1990, Gibbons and Wilding 1995; Statham 1994; Smith 1996).

- *A theoretical perspective* – a model of preventative child care developed by researchers at the University of Leicester (Hardiker, Exton and Barker 1991).

The main components of these three are outlined below.

Legal perspective – Part IV of the Children (NI) Order

Article 18 sets out a general statutory duty

- to safeguard and promote the welfare of children who are 'in need'

- to promote the upbringing of children in need by their families, as long as this is consistent with the children's welfare

- to provide a range and level of personal social services appropriate to the children's needs.

Article 17 sets out criteria for determining which children are deemed to be 'in need':

- the child is unlikely to achieve or maintain, or to have the opportunity of achieving or maintaining, a reasonable standard of health or development without the provision of services by a trust
- the child's health or development is likely to be significantly impaired, or further impaired, without the provision of such services
- the child is disabled.

Empirical research perspective

Seven features of successful prevention are:

- partnership with service users
- locality-based services
- sensitivity to cultural traditions
- inter-agency and interdisciplinary co-operation
- creative and responsive resourcing
- outreach and engagement
- clarity about the relationship to child protection.

Theoretical perspective
1. TYPES OF WELFARE STATE

Developmental	The state accepts responsibility for meeting social need through increasing individuals' control over their lives and access to resources
Institutional	A mixed economy of welfare provides for a range of social needs
Residual	Informal, voluntary and private sources provide for individuals' social needs, with the state providing a last resort/safety net service

2. LEVELS OF PREVENTION

Level One	Universally available services that can be expected to strengthen family functioning

Level Two	Support services targeted on families in early difficulties where the risk of breakdown is low
Level Three	Work with families who are suffering severe and established difficulties
Level Four	Work with children in the care system to minimise the ill-effects resulting from their separation from their home and/or their involvement in the care system

A number of conclusions arose from this analysis of existing literature and information. Considerable confusion and various possible interpretations were apparent regarding what family support meant in policy and practice. However it was defined, family support was a broad concept covering a huge amount of potential need. Readiness to respond to the new requirements for family support was highly variable among policy-makers and practitioners, across both the statutory and voluntary sectors. Consequently no dramatic shift towards family support within the child welfare system was to be expected in the first twelve months of the Children (NI) Order.

2. Perspectives from practice

The aim of the second phase of the study was to explore the realities of family support. This was done by undertaking process evaluations of six settings engaged in delivering family support. The intention was not to assess the outcomes of the individual services, but to examine how they illuminated the application of family support principles in practice.

Developing an appropriate design to cover six very different settings posed a number of methodological challenges. It is useful to explore these, not only to enhance understanding of research processes, but also because the issues in many ways mirrored the practical struggles the social care world at large was having with the concept of family support. In a similar vein Tunstill *et al.* (1996), discussing the assessment of family support in England and Wales, asserted that the methodological challenges 'of this apparently simple task were considerable and in many ways this illustrated the complexities of section 17 implementation for Local Authorities' (p. 45).

Selection of the research settings

It was desirable to include in the study settings that were in some way representative of the range of family support services. Deciding which settings to select and how to select them presented the first challenge. In the first place, given the lack of any consensus about what exactly was meant by

family support, it was hard to establish where the boundaries of relevant
services lay. Identification of suitable settings was also hampered by the
absence of sufficiently detailed information on the types and numbers of
family support services. Without a sampling frame which would allow
representative settings to be identified the solution posed was the selection of
settings on the basis of theoretical sampling – in which 'one samples for
information in a focused manner, based on a priori theory that is being
evaluated and/or modelled', (Kuzel 1992. p.39). In particular, sampling was
based on including different 'levels of prevention', using the framework
described by Hardiker *et al.* (1991). In addition, legislative and empirical
sources suggested subsidiary criteria for the choice of services to be studied
(*see* Table 6.1). This ensured that the study included statutory and voluntary
provision for children at different ages, in both rural and urban areas.

Table 6.1 Selected settings by level of prevention and other criteria					
Setting	Level of prevention	Age group	Urban/ rural	Provision for disabilities	Statutory/ voluntary
Family Resource Centre (pilot)	Tertiary	Young children	Both		Voluntary
Playgroup	Primary	Young children	Rural		Voluntary
Day Centre	Secondary	All ages of children	Urban	[Yes]	Statutory
Child Care Team	Tertiary	All ages of children	Both		Statutory
Leaving Care Service	Quaternary	Older teenagers/ young adults	Urban	[Yes]	Statutory
Children's Centre	All	All ages of children	Both		Voluntary/ statutory

The *Family Resource Centre* was used for piloting the research and was not
included in the subsequent analysis. The *Playgroup* offered a service based on
the High/Scope approach to pre-school children living around the small
Nationalist village in which it was located. The number of sessions operated

was determined by the number of children wishing to attend. The *Day Centre*, run by a health and social services trust, was a well-equipped, purpose-built facility set within a large Nationalist housing estate. It offered three types of service: child protection, prevention from admission to care and compensatory therapeutic support. The specific services provided fell under four headings: respite, family work, group work, and individual counselling. The Day Centre also provided a specialist respite service for children with a disability. The *Child Care Team* was a front-line statutory service. The methods used were typical of any child care team and included investigation, support and therapeutic intervention.

The *Leaving Care Service* was a statutory scheme providing negotiated responsive support for young people leaving residential or foster care. Services fell into seven categories ranging from a preparation for leaving care programme to an accommodation referral service and support in relation to risk management. The *Children's Centre* was a project jointly run by the local trust and a voluntary agency set within a large Loyalist housing estate. It offered three types of service: support, child protection and recovery work. Under the child protection heading, services included comprehensive assessment, risk assessment and support for children entering or leaving care. Within the family support category, services ranged from summer and holiday schemes to facilities for baby weighing clinics and parenting skills groups. There was also a community development strategy which underpinned much of the work.

Managing the research process and areas of investigation

Managing the research process for such a range of settings presented the second major challenge for the researchers. In order to give negotiation of access and data collection a systematic approach, the research team devised standardised protocols to deal with the establishment of relationships with the settings from initial contact through to site visits through to the signing of formal research contracts. Standardised procedures were also put in place to deal with the engagement of all contributors to the research process, as well as to data collection.

Challenge number three came in the form of the potentially huge amount of material which could be obtained in this evaluation of family support. Order was imposed by identifying four substantive areas for which data were required. These were as follows: expressed purpose of the project/programme; organisation; needs; and services (including the process of delivery).

Data collection

Faced by a wide variety of settings, each with different purposes and types of service, it was necessary to devise a means of collecting data in a consistent and standardised fashion with sufficient flexibility to deal with the differences. Accordingly, a kit was developed, comprising a range of tools including standardised[1] and non-standardised[2] measures utilised in previous research and also research instruments specifically designed for this study. Appropriate instruments were chosen from the kit to fit the nature of each setting (*see* Table 6.2).

		Table 6.2 Techniques used in each setting (with numbers of respondents)					
		1	2	3	4	5	6
Level	Setting	Staff question-naires	User question-naires	Staff interview schedule	'External' interviews schedule*	Community survey	Documentary analysis framework
P	Play-group	**	19***	1**	2	n/a	✓
S	Day Centre	25	20	3	2	n/a	✓
T	Child Care Team	37	19	3	0	n/a	✓
Q	Leaving Care Service	26	12	1	2	n/a	✓
All	Child-ren's Centre	14	11	3	2	155	✓
	Total	102	81	11	8	155	

* External interviews refer to those completed with agencies who referred families to the settings or who worked closely with the setting although from an outside agency.

** No staff questionnaires were used in Playgroup, but one semi-structured interview was completed with staff to gain an overview of all children attending.

*** Self-completion.

1   The Malaise Inventory (see Rutter, Tizard and Whitmore 1970)
2   The Family Problem Questionnaire (see Gibbons (with Thorpe and Wilkinson) 1990)

Evaluation criteria

The most difficult challenge was presented by the need to draw the assembled material together to make a useful contribution to the knowledge base on the evaluation of family support. Having acknowledged the utility of using modelling as a way of clarifying alternative types of family support (Higgins *et al.* 1997; Higgins, Devine and Pinkerton 1998c; Higgins *et al.* 1998d), a further development was attempted. This involved devising criteria that corresponded with the ideals for family support identified in the legal, empirical and theoretical material previously reviewed. The criteria were tested on the pilot Family Resource Centre and then applied across the other settings. In all, 23 criteria were developed (*see* Table 6.3), grouped into five clusters:

- Expressed Purpose
- Organisation
- Need
- Services (further divided into style, process and means)
- Outcome.

Table 6.3 Criteria for family support

EXPRESSED PURPOSE

Criterion 1: the setting is based on explicit assumptions about the type of welfare it is promoting ('residual', 'institutional', 'developmental').

Criterion 2: the setting has clearly stated aims and objectives, which are couched in the terms used in Article 17 and 18 ('safeguard and promote welfare', 'promote upbringing of children in families', 'children in need', 'reasonable standard of health or development', 'achieve and maintain', 'impair').

Criterion 3: the setting is explicitly targeted at one or more of the four levels of prevention.

Criterion 4: the setting has an expressed commitment to providing one or more of the types of services set out in Schedule 2.

Table 6.3 Criteria for family support (continued)

ORGANISATION

Criterion 5:   the organisation of the setting includes its service users (adults and or children) in its management.

Criterion 6:   the organisation of the setting encourages effective and flexible working across disciplines, agencies and sectors.

Criterion 7:   the organisation of the setting encourages a close and co-operative relationship with representatives of the neighbourhood(s) in which the children in receipt of its services live.

Criterion 8:   the organisation of the setting ensures the capacity to deliver a wide range of services.

Criterion 9:   the organisation of the setting ensures attention to staff needs and creates an effective and integrated staff team.

NEED

Criterion 10:   The programme delivers services to children in one or more of the Inter-Departmental Group (IDG) 'in need' categories.

SERVICES

Criterion 11:   services are delivered in a manner that is responsive to the opinions, wishes and feelings of both children and parents/carers who use them (style).

Criterion 12:   services are delivered in a manner that enhances existing strengths and skills of the children and parents/carers who use them (style).

Criterion 13:   services are delivered in a manner that expresses understanding and respect for issues of race and culture in the lives of the children and parents/carers who use them (style).

Criterion 14:   services are delivered through a clearly planned and managed but flexible process (process).

Criterion 15:   services are delivered using an explicit set of methods, techniques and skills which promote engagement and creativity (means).

Table 6.3 Criteria for family support (continued)

Criterion 16: services are delivered in a manner that draws effectively on the expertise of other service providers (means).

Criterion 17: services are delivered in a manner that draws effectively on the contribution of relatives, friends and neighbours (means).

Criterion 18: services are delivered in a manner that incorporates concern for child protection (style).

Criterion 19: services are delivered in a manner that minimises the effect of children's disabilities (style).

OUTCOMES

Criterion 20: the setting contributes to children achieving or maintaining a reasonable standard of health or development.

Criterion 21: the setting contributes to the prevention of significant impairment of children's health or development.

Criterion 22: the setting contributes to minimising for children the effects of being disabled.

Criterion 23: the setting promotes the upbringing of children.

Data contributing to criteria 1–5 were derived from the documentary analysis; 5–9 from documentary analysis, interviews with staff and external referrers and service users; 10 from staff questionnaires; and 11–19 from analyses of documentation, staff questionnaires, staff interviews and service user interviews. Criteria 20–23 covered the area of outcomes, which were derived directly from legislation and are what family support should be achieving.

When all assembled data were analysed the researchers made a judgement on whether the setting addressed the particular criterion or not. The results are shown in Table 6.4.

Table 6.4 Criteria by settings

	Expressed purpose			Organisation					Need		Services									Outcomes			
	1	2	3	4	5	6	7	8	9	10	11	12	13	14	15	16	17	18	19	20	21	22	23
Level 1: Playgroup				✓	✓	✓	✓		✓	✓	✓	✓	✓	✓	✓	✓	✓	✓	✓	✓		✓	
Level 2: Day Centre				✓	✓	✓	✓	✓	✓	✓	✓	✓		✓	✓	✓	✓	✓	✓	✓	✓	✓	✓
Level 3: Family and Child Care Team				✓				✓	✓	✓	✓	✓		✓	✓			✓			✓		✓
Level 4: Leaving Care Service				✓		✓		✓	✓	✓	✓	✓		✓	✓	✓	✓	✓		✓	✓		
Levels 1–4: Children's Centre				✓	✓	✓	✓	✓	✓	✓	✓	✓		✓	✓	✓	✓	✓		✓	✓		✓

Criteria 1–23

Detailed accounts of how specific settings addressed criteria can be found in the individual setting reports (Devine, Higgins and Pinkerton 1998; Higgins *et al.* 1998c, 1998d, Pinkerton, Higgins and Devine 1998a, 1998b), but here a summary of the overall pattern is provided.

Expressed purpose

Although all the settings had written policy documents that covered the purpose of their work, none met the first three criteria. In other words, they did not make explicit their underlying assumptions about welfare delivery or levels of prevention, nor link their purposes to the legislation on children in need. This separation of aims from the broader policy agenda was likely to hinder the complex public policy shift involved in the Children (NI) Order. Strategic decision-making might also be unclear if there was uncertainty about the levels of prevention at which a setting was operating. For example, the general position of the Day Centre seemed to be shifting from Level 2 to Level 1, and it also continued to have services appropriate to Level 3.

Although all the services had clear aims that were in line with the spirit of the Children (NI) Order, these aims did not use the language of the Order (Criterion 2). As a result they missed opportunities to reinforce the importance of their services as providing for children 'in need', clarify their relevance to children at risk of 'significant harm', and identify the relationship between prevention and family support.

All settings had a written commitment to at least one service that fitted the categories covered by Schedule 2 of the Children (NI) Order (Criterion 4), but none of the settings made that link explicit. From the evaluations it was clear that, at this point in their development, all the settings needed to work on expressing their purpose in a way that was directly linked to the Children (NI) Order and to an agreed vocabulary for expressing basic assumptions about welfare and levels of prevention.

Organisation

All the settings except the Family and Child Care Team scored well on co-operation with the local neighbourhood, but apart from the Playgroup none included service users formally in the management of the setting. Most of the settings provided a range of services, although the Playgroup carried out very focused work. One criterion which produced a unanimously positive score was that regarding the attention to staff needs (Criterion 9).

Need

It was noted earlier that the development of family support services is inseparably linked to the identification of appropriate need. Finding a manageable and meaningful means of assessment has proved very challenging. The needs being presented to the five settings were identified using a range of indicators, primarily related to parental difficulties. The work of Robson *et al.* (1994) on deprivation across Northern Ireland, based on data from the 1991 Census of Population, was used to provide information on the localities in which the five evaluated settings were operating. Robson's work encompasses three aspects of deprivation: degree, intensity and extent. Three of the district councils in which settings were located had figures indicating that at least one-quarter of their population lived within the worst 15 per cent of wards in Northern Ireland. One setting was situated in an area with the second-worst figures for degree and extent, and the worst for intensity of deprivation.

It is also the case that certain families experience levels of deprivation out of keeping with the areas in which they live. Accordingly, 11 variables from the range identified by Robson and his colleagues were selected as appropriate to the families using the settings, and data were collected on these. The first row of Table 6.5 identifies the number of respondents within each setting who experienced more than half the indicators. Information on income and household running costs was also collected. A further consideration was the number of respondents whose income was solely made up from benefits. Financial difficulties were also identified in the Family Problem Questionnaire (Gibbons *et al.* 1990).

It was recognised that socio-economic deprivation is not the sole indicator of need appropriate to family support, and so information on other areas of health and social well-being was also collected. The Malaise Inventory (Rutter *et al.* 1970) has been used in a number of studies to assess the degree of depression and emotional distress experienced by parents. The presence or absence of 24 physical and emotional symptoms is recorded, and scores of seven or more are considered to mark a cut-off between the normal range of reactions and those that might be considered as evidence of clinical disturbance. Further information based on the Gibbons Family Problem Questionnaire was classified into one of four categories: parent/child problems (eight items), partner problems (four items); social contact (four items); health problems (three items).

As Table 6.5 indicates, financial and health/well-being problems were the most common across the sample as a whole. The Day Centre, Child Care

Centre and Leaving Care Services had the highest proportions of parents with difficulties.

Table 6.5 Indicators of need by setting					
	Setting				
	Playgroup	**Day Centre**	**Family and Child Care Team**	**Leaving Care Service**	**Children Centre**
Indicator	n=19	n=20	n=19	n=12	n=11
Socio-economic: 6 or more *Robson indicators*	0	6	3	0	3
Income less/same as running costs	1*	11	6	3	7
Income from benefits only	2**	12	9	8	5
Financial *Gibbons questionnaire*	0	3	5	2	5
Health/well-being *Malaise Inventory*	6	15	8	9	6
Health *Gibbons Questionnaire*	0	5	1	0	1
Parent/child *Gibbons questionnaire*	6	5	4	0	3
Partner *Gibbons questionnaire*	0	2****	0	0	2***
Social *Gibbons questionnaire*	1	8	4	3	7

* missing data for 3 respondents   *** not applicable for 4 respondents
** missing data for 1 respondent   **** not applicable for 5 respondents

Table 6.6 Experience of IDG categories by setting*					
	Play-group* n=37	Day Centre n=25	Family and Child Care Team n=37	Leaving Care Service n=26	Children Centre n=14
Children who are living in poverty and are socially disadvantaged and whose health or development would likely be significantly affected were services not to be provided	18	8	8	7	8
Children subject to a child protection assessment	1	4	19	2	3
Children with a disability who require services	24	9	1	0	2
Children over whom no one is exercising parental responsibility	0	0	1	12	0
Children whose parents or carers are unable, for whatever reason, to provide reasonable standards of care for their child	0	4	12	2	3
Children at risk of family breakdown likely to lead to significant harm	1	7	9	1	6
Children experiencing psychiatric, psychological, emotional or behavioural difficulties suffering or likely to suffer significant harm	3	6	9	13	4
Children for whom offending and its consequences are a significant feature of their lives and those judged to be at serious risk of offending	0	1	3	3	0
Children whose welfare is or is likely to be significantly prejudiced as a result of homelessness	0	0	1	24	0
Children ceasing to be 'looked after' by the trust	1	0	2	14	1
Children who are carers	0	0	0	0	0
Children who have been excluded from school	0	0	0	0	1

*   Categories are not mutually exclusive.
** Information is derived from questionnaires completed by staff for each service user, except for the Playgroup, where staff completed one questionnaire covering all service users.

An alternative approach was provided by the 12 operational indicators for identifying children 'in need' developed by a civil service Child Care Research Inter-Departmental Group (IDG) consisting of the DHSS, the Department of Education (NI) and the Northern Ireland Office. These were based on the work of the four health and social service boards with the consultants Social Information Systems (SIS 1996). Table 6.6 sets out information provided by staff within the settings about the numbers of service users to whom the categories applied. The shaded squares represent settings where the Inter-Departmental Group category applied to at least half the service users.

It is clear from Table 6.6 that the five settings were collectively engaged with all the Inter-Departmental Group categories of need, apart from children who are young carers. The playgroup and Day Centre were most likely to service children with disabilities, while the Leaving Care Service dealt with large numbers of young people for whom there were concerns about significant harm and a high risk of homelessness.

Services offered

In order to explore the question of whether or not the services being provided by the five settings could be appropriately regarded as family support, it was necessary to go beyond the types of services being offered and consider the manner in which they are delivered.

All five settings delivered their services through a clearly planned and managed process that gave attention to referral, engagement, assessment, planning, implementation, review and disengagement. In each case this process reflected the particular purpose and distinctive features of the setting. For example, the Playgroup's overall process was timetabled to reflect the school year. In looking at the means adopted by the settings for delivering their services in an engaging and creative fashion, it is useful to distinguish between methods, techniques and skills. To varying degrees all five settings used the basic skills of questioning and confronting, information-giving and explanation, and listening and empathy. For techniques and methods, there is a much more varied picture, as can be seen from Table 6.7.

On the whole the settings were using means of working similar to those that have been traditional within social care.

Most settings co-operated with other service providers. Once again, this occurred to varying degrees and took different forms as appropriate to the particular setting. For example, Day Centre staff were able to draw on other disciplines within their Trust throughout the various stages of their work, from referral through assessment and planning to intervention, evaluation and disengagement. They also had a thriving relationship with agencies in the voluntary and community sectors.

Table 6.7 Extensive use of methods, skills and techniques

	Playgroup	Day Centre	Family and Child Care Team	Leaving Care Service	Children's Centre
	n=37	n=25	n=37	n=26	n=14
Methods					
Individual counselling	28	14	25	12	8
Couple counselling	0	0	4	0	1
Group counselling	0	1	3	0	4
Individual therapy	0	6	9	0	1
Marital therapy	0	0	0	0	0
Family therapy	0	0	1	0	0
Play therapy	28	18	3	0	5
Group therapy	0	21	2	0	0
Community action/development	28	3	1	0	6
Techniques					
Build on existing family strengths	28	9	20	14	2
Agree criteria for judging results	0	5	21	6	8
Take calculated risks	0	2	6	14	1
Skills					
Questioning and confronting	14	4	19	16	6
Information-giving and explanation	28	16	22	19	7
Listening and empathy	28	17	25	20	11

A rather more mixed picture emerged from consideration of the extent to which the settings drew on the contributions of relatives, friends and neighbours. For example, the explicit community-orientation of the Play-group, Day Centre and Children's Centre led to them having strong links in the local areas, though these tended to be more about enabling and providing resources for community development than being directly case- related links to informal networks. By contrast, it was the needs of particular young people leaving care that required the Leaving Care Service to understand the possibilities and the restrictions within their family circle, peer group, local service networks and locality.

Partnership with service users, both children and their adult carers, is central to the style of work appropriate to family support. Such partnership requires that services are delivered in a manner that is responsive to user opinions, wishes and feelings and enhances their existing strengths and skills (Criteria 11 and 12). All the settings were committed to partnership and attempted to be responsive to service users. There was recognition that this should directly include children. Settings were making efforts to be child-centred environments and develop appropriate means for direct communication with children and young people. This was particularly apparent in the settings with their own buildings. All the settings saw themselves as fairly successful in this, and that view was generally endorsed by the opinions of the adult service users.

The relationship between family support and child protection is increasingly recognised as being not about alternatives but rather degree of focus. This was clearly the case for the five settings, all of which included child protection as an aspect of their work. A third important aspect of the style of work appropriate to family support is that it expresses understanding and respect for issues of race and culture in the lives of service users. All the settings recognised the importance of this and attempted to operationalise the written policy commitment they all had to it, but there was little evidence of any particular success. In part this was because neither staff nor service users generally saw the direct relevance of cultural sensitivity and anti-discriminatory practice to their immediate concerns. Where it did present as an issue it was dealt with: for example, the Playgroup was conscious of the need to counter sexist stereotyping in play, and the Leaving Care Service gave support around issues of sexuality, such as young gay people 'coming out'. Another block seemed to be the particularly difficult, and potentially physically dangerous, challenge of sectarianism.

A further core feature of all aspects of family support is an inclusive approach to children with disabilities that minimises as far as possible the effect of the disability. All the settings included work with children who were physically disabled or had learning difficulties, and all showed evidence of being receptive to their needs, but only for the Playgroup and the Day Centre was this as a major feature of their work.

Outcomes

Family support is about achieving particular outcomes for children and their parents/carers. These were assessed by drawing on Article 17 of the Children (NI) Order. All five settings were committed to ensuring that the children who used their services achieved and maintained standards of health and development on a par with their peers. Assessment of children's functioning was a part of all the settings' work. Nevertheless, none of the five had a detailed statement of indicators by which this could be measured for the setting as a whole.

Similarly, although four of the settings were heavily involved in child protection, none of them had a detailed statement of indicators or a monitoring system to show that they were effective in achieving this outcome. Three settings which were actively and expressly concerned with promoting the bringing up of children by their own families, also had no way of demonstrating the achievements of, for example, their parenting pro-grammes. Only two settings had a major commitment to the outcome of minimising the effects of disabilities through their services, and again they had no indicators with which to judge their success or otherwise.

The picture of family support provided by the evaluations reinforced much of the view expressed in the Part One literature review. It showed that there were important strengths that could be built upon, but that much remained to be done to achieve the aspirations for family support embodied in legislation, guidance and the literature. The settings may or may not have been representative of existing family support but they were illustrative of what was already possible. Drawing on the experiences of the five settings it was possible to construct the following agenda for further development for family support in the areas of policy, organisation, practice and research.

Developing family support

In relation to policy, the study of family support services highlighted the need to advance a regionally agreed conceptual framework and vocabulary to underpin and extend into practice the work already done on defining children 'in need' and the services set out in Schedule 2 of the Children (NI) Order. Additionally, it suggested that it was necessary to develop regionally agreed criteria for evaluating family support settings, which could take as a starting point the 23 criteria developed for this research. It also stressed the necessity of engaging community representatives and service users as active partners in policy formation, and, finally, that clear strategic directions are needed that fit with the specific circumstances of each setting.

The survey suggested the need to structure organisations to be compatible with the principles and style of working appropriate to family support. Additionally, it stated that it was necessary to find appropriate ways to effectively involve community representatives and service users in the management of settings. Organisations should give priority to ensuring that staff receive support, supervision and training individually and in teams. Finally, it highlighted the requirement to further develop integrated structures for promoting interdisciplinary, inter-agency and, particularly, inter-sectoral working.

In terms of practice, future developments should maintain a focus on the strategic goals of family support as articulated by the organisation. In addition, service providers should help develop and use an agreed conceptual framework and vocabulary of family support. Increased attention needs to be given to finding more inclusive methods of needs assessment. The import-ance of critically evaluating practice using clearly defined outcome criteria was also stated. Finally, the need to explore new methods of working, especially those which suggest more effective ways of drawing on the contributions of relatives, friends and neighbours, was also noted (e.g. Gilligan 1999).

Conclusion

This chapter has presented the contribution to the understanding and development of family support that has emerged from a three-year research study. The basis for the study was derived from the legal framework and research and theoretical perspectives. Some methodological challenges have been discussed, and it was suggested that they reflected the difficulties the social care world at large was having with the concept of family support. The settings examined in the study provided a range of services that were in many ways consistent with family support principles, but policies and practice were not linked to strategic thinking or the wider policy context, while attention to the potential contributions of informal networks was undeveloped.

The chapter will be brought to a close with a consideration of the link between the future agendas for practice and research. Underpinning this is the overarching theme of the need for a more research-minded approach to both policy and practice (Davies *et al.* 1994). This need for a 'research-mindedness' regarding policy is reflected in the future family support agenda outlined previously. The chapter highlighted that many of the challenges encountered by researchers were reflective of difficulties at the level of practice. Such shared difficulty adds weight to the suggestion of a necessarily symbiotic relationship between practice and research.

There is a need for more external research, such as locality cluster studies to explore the combined impact of different settings on need within a geographical area; in-depth, qualitative case studies based on the experiences of service users, both adults and children; and studies using a social care economics approach. However, just as important is to recognise that practitioners as well as researchers need to attend to the growing emphasis on evidence-based practice. For practitioners this may mean reconsidering the nature and relevance of their practice and its knowledge base. Careful stock-taking may involve the necessary culling of practices if their outcomes do not hold up under evaluation. It will also require structuring of the rationale, planning and delivery of interventions in a way that facilitates ongoing and systematic evaluation reiterating the need for a research-minded approach. Both researchers and practitioners need to place more stress on measuring outcomes. More outcome-focused research will involve meticulous analysis of research technique. Effective research design is essential for gaining confidence that a particular set of outcomes is attributable to actions or interventions.

As discussed by Hill (1999b), the 'levels of evidence' approach is favoured by many in the social care field who, whilst accepting the value of the robustness offered by experimental design, also recognise the real-life difficulties of researching children and families. However, others suggest that a systematically controlled approach to the evaluation of interventions provides agencies and policy-makers with the best data for providing effective services (McDonald and McDonald 1995). Exploring these perspectives will be an interesting task, not least because of the inherent difficulties and attendant controversies that come with research of this kind. As Trinder (1996) succinctly summarises, research is highly political. Methodologies are not neutral sets of techniques to be picked out of textbooks!

CHAPTER 7

Making Progress? The Transition to Adulthood for Disabled Young People in Northern Ireland

Marina Monteith

Introduction

This chapter explores the transition to adulthood for young people with disabilities and describes the findings of a two-year study carried out in Northern Ireland by the Centre for Child Care Research (Monteith and Sneddon 1999). It also examines how transition planning can effectively assist successful progress to adulthood.

The transition to adulthood for young people covers a period of life from the early teens through to the mid-twenties, and even beyond that. Adulthood is defined legally in terms of a range of rights obtained between the ages of 14 and 21 years, such as being able to vote at 18, being able to leave school at 16 and obtain full-time work alongside adults (in theory at least), or being able to apply for a driving licence. It is also determined socially through access to adult clubs or groups and to pubs and other licensed premises. The transition to adulthood, therefore, is complicated by the blurred boundaries between childhood and adulthood.

As young people leave school and enter further education, employment training or employment, social groups break up and reform, leading to further uncertainty and change in young people's lives. Young people will have aspirations for the future and part of the transition involves dealing with reality in an adult world and how this impacts on these aspirations. Young people with disabilities may have additional difficulties to deal with in order to achieve adult status. Many social groups (e.g. structured groups such as youth clubs and leisure organisations) do not actively promote inclusion and young people with disabilities may find it difficult to join or be accepted. In addition, the dependent care relationships built up with adults throughout childhood may make it more difficult for disabled young people to develop autonomy and independence.

Developing a conceptual framework

McGinty and Fish (1992) viewed the transition to adulthood as both 'a phase in time and a process of personal growth and development'. Young people with disabilities should have the same opportunities and choices available to them as other young people, in terms of education, training, employment and independent living. The conceptual framework for their transition should be the same as for all young people, and should not be based on a model of existing services and resources. In this way, young people's needs can be identified and assessed, and appropriate resources targeted to service delivery at this time of transition.

McGinty and Fish (1992) identified three main stages of transition, and pointed out that these may occur at different times for different individuals. The three stages were:

1. the final years of school

2. further education and job training

3. the early years of employment and independent living.

A number of conceptual frameworks have been identified in the literature in relation to the transition to adulthood. These usually consist of a number of key transitional goals or adult attributes, which are in some way inter-connected or linked to holistically represent adult life. Theorists of the transition to adulthood suggest that these individual elements do not necessarily occur at the same time, and that there is a degree of disunity between elements. Yet the elements are interconnected, and one element or attribute can impact on the progress of others. Some of the frameworks from the literature are briefly outlined below.

The Organization for Economic Co-operation and Development (OECD)/ Centre for Education Research and Innovation (CERI) study (OECD 1986) provides a useful framework of transitional goals, each representing aspects of adult life. These are:

1. employment or other valued activity

2. independent living and personal autonomy

3. social interaction and community participation, including leisure and recreation

4. adult roles within the family, including marriage and parenthood.

The transition to adulthood can be viewed as a number of interconnected elements based on normative expectations, involving leaving school and entering work or higher education, leaving the parental home to set up a new home, becoming sexually adult, including eventually cohabiting or marrying, becoming a parent, and becoming a full adult consumer (Jones and Wallace 1992; Barnardos 1996; Morrow and Richards 1996).

The nature and timing of transitions have altered significantly in recent years. Based on their extensive literature review, Morrow and Richards (1996) concluded that young people were often economically dependent on their families until at least their mid-twenties due to economic and social policy changes over the last two decades, and that this in turn restricted consumer behaviour. Young people were also delaying parenthood until their late twenties or early thirties, although research suggested that they were sexually active at earlier ages than formerly. Morrow and Richards described the transition to adulthood as a 'disjunction', with a number of interconnected adult attributes occurring at different times in the young person's life. These attributes were political or legal adulthood; financial or economic adulthood; social or sexual adulthood; and parenthood, which together formed an 'ideal' adult status.

These various models of youth transitions include broadly similar components which combine to represent adult status. McGinty and Fish (1992) argued that, although the transitional goals represent different aspects of adult life, in practice they should be tackled through one 'coherent individual transition plan'. This requires the many different agencies involved in working with young people with disabilities to collaborate and to co-ordinate their activities.

The progress towards adulthood and the experiences of a young person can be further understood by consideration of a career route proposed by Bullock, Little and Millham (1998). They present the idea of two dimensions to an individual's development, a life route and a process. The life route involves those decisions made by the young person (and his or her family) that have an impact on life chances. It includes all areas of a person's life from birth and incorporates individual personality. The young person's life route interacts with the second dimension, process, which involves the decisions made by professionals and/or courts which also affect life chances. Process includes health, social services, education, child guidance and the legal

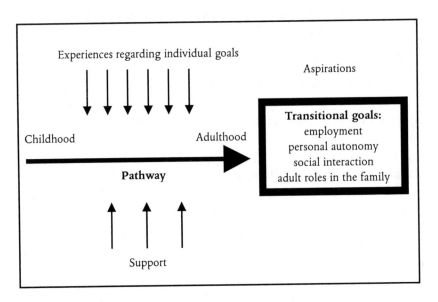

Figure 7.1 Conceptual model of transition to adulthood

system. Perhaps a third dimension would be environment, including social and physical barriers, combining with Bullock *et al.*'s life route and process to make a pathway to adulthood.

A combination of the framework of transitional goals (OECD 1986; McGinty and Fish 1992; Hirst and Baldwin 1994) and the idea of a pathway to adulthood provided a conceptual model for this research (Monteith and Sneddon 1999). This study examined the views and experiences of disabled young people and/or their parents. Their experiences were mapped in terms of these transitional goals, the choices made, progress towards achieving adulthood, and the formal support received, including transition planning and social work services. Professionals working with disabled young people need to adopt a broad conceptual framework that enables them to locate their own services and those of others within a holistic view of the young person's life and his/her needs. A very narrow concept of transition can result in important needs being ignored, not assessed and unmet by service provision. For example, a focus on future employment and job-related skills by those advising young people about leaving school can leave other important needs unaddressed. Before presenting the findings, this chapter briefly reviews relevant legislation and previous studies.

Legal framework in Northern Ireland

A range of key social welfare legislation exists regarding provision for young people with disabilities. Within Northern Ireland, this currently includes the Children (NI) Order 1995, the Disabled Persons (NI) Act 1989, the Chronically Sick and Disabled Persons (NI) Act 1978, the Disability Discrimination Act 1995, and the Health and Personal Social Services (NI) Orders 1991 and 1994. Other legislation pertinent to the transition to adulthood for young people with disabilities include the Education and Libraries (NI) Order 1986 and the Education (NI) Order 1996. Table 7.1 indicates the equivalent legislation in Scotland, England and Wales.

Table 7.1 Comparison of legal framework within the United Kingdom		
Northern Ireland	**Scotland**	**England and Wales**
Children (NI) Order 1995	Children (Scotland) Act 1995	Children Act 1989
Disabled Persons (NI) Act 1989	Disabled Persons (Scotland) Act 1986	Disabled Persons (Services, Consultation and Representation) Act 1986
Chronically Sick and Disabled Persons (NI) Act 1978	Chronically Sick and Disabled Persons (Scotland) Act 1972	Chronically Sick and Disabled Persons Act 1970
Education and Libraries (NI) Orders 1986 and 1987	Education (Scotland) Act 1981	Education Act 1981
Education (NI) Order 1996	Education (Scotland) Act 1996	Education Act 1993
Disability Discrimination Act 1995	Disability Discrimination Act 1995	Disability Discrimination Act 1995
Health and Personal Social Services (NI) Orders 1991 and 1994	National Health Service and Community Care Act 1990	National Health Service and Community Care Act 1990

It is evident that a whole range of legislation can be relevant to young people with disabilities, and this can be confusing for young people and their carers as well as for the professionals involved in the delivery of social care services. For example, while young people with disabilities could have their social care needs assessed as 'children in need' and be provided with appropriate family support services under the Children (NI) Order, they could also be assessed under the Disabled Persons (NI) Act 1989 for a range of personal social services, or have a statement of special education needs made under the Education (NI) Order 1996. The Children (NI) Order did not replace assessments for disabled people under other legislation (e.g. Chronically Sick and Disabled Persons (NI) Act 1978, Disabled Persons (NI) Act 1989, Education (NI) Order 1996). Instead the Children (NI) Order empowers health and social services trusts to combine assessments under the Order with those under other legislation, and facilitates inter-agency working to this end. The confusion created by the range of legislation of relevance to disabled young people is mirrored by the fragmentation of service delivery for them, with many agencies involved in providing a whole range of services. All of these organisations have their own priorities, cultures, definitions and assessment procedures, which can lead to a piecemeal approach to the provision of services for these young people and their parents or carers. The sections below outline briefly legislation in Northern Ireland relevant to the provision of services to young disabled people at this stage in their life. Social welfare legislation is outlined first, followed by key education statutes and other legislation relevant to the delivery of social care services.

Children (NI) Order 1995

The Children (NI) Order 1995 provides a legal framework for the provision of services for disabled children and their families. Young people with disabilities up to the age of 18 (or 21 in some circumstances) are included in the Order's definition of 'children in need' (Article 17). Health and social services trusts have a responsibility to provide a range of services for them and their families where this would safeguard the welfare of the child or young person (Article 18). The Order requires that different organisations, both statutory and voluntary, work together in the provision of family support services. Health and social services trusts must publish information about services provided by voluntary organisations. They must ensure that this information is made available to those who could benefit from these services.

The *Guidance and Regulations* (DHSS 1996c) state that careful assessment and ongoing planning is vital to post-school service provision that takes account of wider personal, social, health, occupational and educational abilities, and the needs of the young person. Such planning should include the views of young people and their parents. The *Guidance and Regulations* state that trusts should have in place 'precise arrangements for working with the relevant agencies in order to ensure that joint planning is followed by joint service arrangements' for young people with disabilities.

Disabled Persons (NI) Act 1989

The Chronically Sick and Disabled Persons (NI) Act 1978 was amended by the Disabled Persons (NI) Act 1989. The 1989 Act, developing further the provisions in the 1978 Act, requires health and social services trusts to assess young people with disabilities, at the time they leave school, for a range of welfare services as outlined in the Chronically Sick and Disabled Persons (NI) Act 1978. The trusts are also expected to give appropriate advice about matters such as employment and further education.

Section 5 of the Disabled Persons (NI) Act 1989 requires Education and Library Boards to notify the relevant trust at the time of the first annual review of a statement following the child's 14th birthday, or at the time of a reassessment after that birthday, whichever is earlier. This notification is required in order for trusts to be able to consider the young person's needs for social services after they have left school. Education and Library Boards are also required to notify the trust between twelve and eight months before the actual date of ceasing full-time education. The Disabled Persons (NI) Act 1989 also gives disabled people rights to representation, to assessment of their needs, and to information and counselling. The statutory provisions relating to representation are provided in Sections 1 and 2 of the 1989 Act, and were intended to give disabled people in Northern Ireland the same rights given in Great Britain by the Disabled Persons (Services, Consultation and Representation) Act 1986. These two sections, ten years on, have not yet been implemented. Carers of disabled people, including those caring for disabled young people, have the right to have their ability to care taken into account (Section 8) and the right to ask for an assessment of the needs of the disabled person (Section 4).

Chronically Sick and Disabled Persons (NI) Act 1978

This Act requires boards or trusts to identify the numbers of disabled people in their area (Section 1) and to publish information about social services provided under Section 2 of the Act. Section 2 requires boards or trusts to make arrangements for social services to meet the needs of disabled people, including practical assistance in the home, transport arrangements to and from home, home adaptations, holidays and help obtaining a telephone.

Education and Libraries (NI) Orders 1986 and 1987

The Education and Libraries (NI) Order 1986 was amended in 1987. Under these two Orders, Education and Library Boards have a duty to identify and assess children in their area who have special education needs and children who they think have or will have special education needs. If the assessment finds that a child has special education needs, the Education and Library Board must issue a statement explaining these needs, which must also detail the special arrangements being made by the Education and Library Board to meet those needs.

Education (NI) Order 1996

This Order provides a legal framework for the assessment and development of special education provision for children with special education needs. It is accompanied by a Code of Practice on the Identification and Assessment of Special Education Needs (Department of Education for Northern Ireland (DENI) 1997), based on its equivalent developed in England and Wales (Department for Education and Employment (DfEE) 1994). This code provides detailed guidance on five stages of assessment, and sets out the procedures and arrangements for

- the identification of children with special education needs
- the assessment of those needs
- the making of provision to meet those needs
- the introduction of an Independent Appeals Tribunal for the determination of parental appeals.

The Code states that the first annual review after the young person's 14th birthday should involve all the agencies who will play a major role during the post-school years. The transfer of relevant information should ensure that young people receive any necessary help or support during their continuing education and training after leaving school. The Code stipulates that specific targets should be set as part of the annual review, so as to ensure that independence training, social skills, and other aspects of the wider curriculum are fully addressed during the young person's last years at school. The first annual review after the young person's 14th birthday (and any subsequent reviews) should include completion of a Transition Plan that draws together information from a range of individuals from both within and beyond the school, so as to enable agencies to plan coherently for the young person's transition to adult life (DENI 1997).

THE TRANSITION TO ADULTHOOD FOR DISABLED YOUNG PEOPLE

Health and Personal Social Services (NI) Orders 1991 and 1994

Under the Health and Personal Social Services (NI) Orders 1991 and 1994, health and social services boards are responsible for assessing the health and social welfare needs of their resident population (including disabled young people) and for commissioning services to meet these needs. Health and social services boards' relationships with trusts, which provide services, are governed by contracts. These Orders brought about the purchaser/provider split in the organisation of health and personal social services, with health and social services boards 'purchasing' services for their resident population and trusts' 'providing' services which were agreed through contracts with health and social services boards.

Disability Discrimination Act (1995)

This Act aims to ensure that disabled people have equal opportunities in terms of access to employment, buildings, and goods and services. It also requires schools, colleges and universities to provide information for people with disabilities.

Disabled young people and the transition to adulthood

Empirical studies in the 1980s suggested that disabled young people often experience significant transition difficulties. These include a high degree of social isolation, which tends to worsen after leaving school, a higher incidence of psychological problems compared to non-disabled peers, a lack of self-confidence, low self-esteem and difficulty finding or keeping a job (Anderson and Clarke 1982; Walker 1982; Brimblecombe 1987). Clarke and Hirst (1989), in a follow-up study ten years after Anderson and Clarke's original data collection, found that few of the young people had made the transition to a more independent adult life. These disabled young people were less likely to have had a paid job, to have set up a household on their own, to have married or to have become a parent than other young people in the general population. They seemed to have experienced either a lengthened or limited transition to adulthood.

Walker (1982) found that young disabled people were less likely to have experienced paid employment, and were more likely to experience unemployment than other young people. In addition, disabled school leavers had very low aspirations for employment compared with their non-disabled peers. Those disabled young people who had found employment were less likely to be in skilled or professional jobs than other young people. A number of researchers have indicated that there is a need for changes in attitudes to enable ordinary life experiences, independent living and employment (Hirst 1984; Parker 1984).

These studies were, however, confined to particular localities, to particular disabilities or to particular services that young people used. In light of this, Hirst and Baldwin (1994) developed a major study that aimed to provide a more coherent overall perspective on the transition to adulthood for disabled young people. This involved interviews with a large sample of the young people themselves, covering all the teenage years and including all types and degrees of disability. The study also included a comparison sample of non-disabled peers. Hirst and Baldwin's study provides a comprehensive picture of disabled young people's experiences of this crucial phase in their lives.

Contrary to the earlier findings, Hirst and Baldwin stated that, substantial numbers of disabled young people were moving towards adulthood without major disruption, anxiety or unhappiness. They showed that many had achieved some degree of independence and enjoyed social activities appropriate to their age. Many had a positive image of themselves and had some feeling of control over their own lives. Hirst and Baldwin concluded that the lives and circumstances of disabled young people can fall within the same range as other young people. Nevertheless, they did report some significant differences between the experiences of these young people and their non-disabled peers. Disabled young people were less likely to be in paid work, and were also often less prepared for, and less likely to be, living independently of their parents. Although most disabled young people had positive views about themselves, a higher proportion than among other young people had low self-esteem and a limited sense of control over their lives. Feelings of low self-esteem and helplessness were particularly common among disabled young people who had attended segregated (special) schools. Disabled young people were more dependent on their parents for their social life or leisure pursuits than other young people, although most disabled young people were satisfied with their social or friendship networks. Non-disabled peers were more likely to have close friendships, more frequent contacts and a wider circle of friends than disabled young people, who were less socially active.

Hirst and Baldwin found that those young people with severe and multiple disabilities experienced most difficulty in the transition to adulthood. These young people had limited social lives and friendships, less of a sense of control over their lives and lower self-esteem, and only a few had obtained employment training or paid work. Hirst and Baldwin found that severely disabled young people were more likely to experience inequalities in both support and opportunities.

The circumstances, experiences and aspirations of disabled young people in Northern Ireland

This section presents some of the findings from a two-year study carried out by the Centre for Child Care Research on the circumstances, experiences and aspirations of disabled young people in Northern Ireland (Monteith and Sneddon 1999). The study included 76 young people with a range of disabilities (physical, sensory and/or learning) and aged between 16 and 21 years. A multi-stage sampling method was used. First, one health and social services trust was selected from each board area, ensuring a mix of urban/rural, religious and geographical representation. Second, young disabled people aged between 16 and 21 years were identified in each trust area. As no obvious sampling frame existed, a combination of snowball and purposive sampling was used. Key individuals in a range of statutory, voluntary and community organisations were selected for their good contacts with disabled young people. They identified young people with disabilities known to them and approached them regarding possible participation in the study. In this way a list was compiled of young people who were willing to participate in the project. The profile of the 76 young people involved in the study indicated an even mix of both genders, a good spread across the age group targeted, and a wide range of types of disabilities.

Semi-structured interviews were conducted using interview schedules that included components adapted from the work of Hirst and Baldwin (1994) and Flynn and Hirst (1992). Interviews were completed with young people themselves where possible. To this end, a degree of flexibility was built into the interview schedule so that, although by appearance it seemed somewhat structured in approach, interviewers were briefed on how to adapt the interview in relation to the young person's needs. Questions were kept short and straightforward in an attempt to involve, as much as possible, young people with learning disabilities in the research. A shorter version of the questionnaire was designed, which the interviewer could use for young people with more severe learning disabilities. Of the 76 young people in this study, 69 were able to participate to some extent (49 completed a full interview and 18 completed a shorter version) while a further 9 young people (with severe learning and communication difficulties) were included by proxy through interviews with their parents. Further details of the methodology are provided in a Centre for Child Care Research report (Monteith 1999).

Gaining employment

Obtaining work provides economic independence and, as such, is a key goal in making the transition to adulthood. Jobskills Training Programmes, work placements, National Vocational Qualifications (NVQs), vocational training, and further/higher education may all play a part in providing young people with adequate skills for future employment.

The study found that disabled young people participated in a range of daytime occupations. In total, 43 young people attended some form of educational institution, on either a full-time (18) or part-time basis (25). Similar numbers attended school (18) and further education colleges (19), while a few students attended residential schools (3) or further education residential colleges (2). Many young people (21) were undertaking a youth training programme (JobSkills), and this usually combined work placements with part-time study for vocational qualifications at a local college. Of the 76 young people, 45 were currently studying for a qualification, with 23 studying for NVQs. Six respondents were studying for A levels and a further six for GCSEs. Small numbers of young people were reported to be studying for other qualifications such as certificates from day centres, or other vocational qualifications from technical colleges (GNVQs or BTEC Higher Certificates/Diplomas).

Although only one person stated that they had no formal activity during weekdays and many young people were occupied with vocational training and/or work placements, only two young people had actually obtained a job which did not involve a work placement. One of these young people was employed on an Action for Computer Employment (ACE) scheme and earned below the minimum wage level for this age group (£3 per hour), which was being implemented in April 1999. The number of young people aged between 19 and 21 years who had moved from the vocational training system to actual employment is low. As might have been expected, many young people aged between 16 and 18 years participated in vocational training and work placement schemes, but it might have been hoped that higher numbers would have progressed to employment. Achievement of adult status in terms of employment has yet to be realised for the majority of young people in the Northern Ireland study. By contrast, Hirst and Baldwin (1994) found that 15 per cent of disabled young people aged 16–22 years in Great Britain were in employment, with this increasing to 33 per cent for those aged 19 or 20 years.

In addition, while many young people in this study were occupied with school or a combination of job placements and college, some had very limited or no weekday occupations. One young person reported no formal activity while a further four had no current activity but were going to commence job training or a job placement soon. One young person attended a day centre full-time, while part-time attendance at a day centre was the sole weekday occupation for six young people. Five others combined attendance at a day centre with participation in vocational education, job training or work placements.

Independent living and personal autonomy

Developing independent living skills and gaining personal autonomy is another transitional goal. As young people grow up they begin to develop some degree of independence. To gain some insight into this area, researchers examined the sources of income of disabled young people and explored the extent to which they managed their own money and made their own purchases, whether they had a house key, and whether they saw their GP or social worker alone.

It was evident from the findings that most of the disabled young people were reliant on benefits and training allowances as their main source of income. Some young people also received income from either their parents (12) or other relatives (6). Only seven people reported an income received through a regular job, five of these were spare-time jobs with small amounts of money involved.

Table 7.2 Source of Income	
Source of Income	**Number**
Disability Living Allowance	51
Severe Disability Allowance	29
Income Support	28
Training Scheme/Placement	22
Parents	12
Regular job (including spare-time jobs)	7
Other relatives	6
Invalidity Benefit	2
Student Grant	1

Note: some young people had more than one source of income.

The majority of young people (65) in the sample said that they had some money to spend each week. Parents and benefits were the main sources of income for many young people. A few had money from earnings or from a training allowance. Money was mainly spent on clothes, food, sweets, going out, magazines/books or CDs. Almost two-thirds of the young people said that they bought their own clothes, while parents (mostly the mother) purchased clothes for the remaining one-third. One young person said his grandparents bought his clothes. Of those who said they bought their own clothes, 38 said they had help to do so. This help came mainly from parents (27), siblings (5), friends (8) and other relatives (2).

Forty-nine young people were asked if any of their money went towards rent, housekeeping, food and other bills. Twenty-nine young people did contribute to household bills, although 13 did not specify an amount. Twelve said they paid amounts ranging from £10–25 per week, while one person said s/he paid for telephone calls.

Three-quarters of the sample of disabled young people put some of their money in a savings account. Twenty-two deposited the money in their account themselves, while parents made the deposits for 32 others. Young people were, however, more likely to get their money out by themselves (35), with only 10 saying that their parents took the money out for them. It would seem that many young people did have access to money of their own, and some were able to make purchases and manage their money by themselves.

Eighteen out of the total sample of 76 young people said that they went to see their GP alone. Of the 18 young people who had seen a social worker in the last year, 8 had done so on their own. Nine were accompanied by their parents, while one young person saw the social worker sometimes by herself and sometimes with a parent. Half of the young people said that they made appointments themselves.

Forty-four of the 76 young people had their own house key, while a further 13 had access to a key (e.g. it was left with a neighbour or hidden in an outhouse/garage), making a total of 75 per cent of young people either having access to a key or having their own key to their home. A slightly higher proportion of young people in rural areas had their own key or access to a key (82%) compared to those living in urban areas (72%). Larger urban areas differed from smaller ones, with young people living in cities (76%) more likely to have access to a key or have their own key than young people living in towns (67%).

Young people with multiple disabilities (54%) were much less likely to have access to or have their own house key than other young people. All young people with physical disabilities only, and 85 per cent of those with sensory disabilities only, had a house key or access to one, compared with two-thirds (68%) of those with learning disabilities only. Thirteen young people who did not have their own house key said that they would like one. Over half (7) of these were young people with multiple disabilities.

Social life and community involvement

This aspect of the transition to adulthood often brings many changes for young people, with friendship groups breaking up and reforming as they leave school and move on to further or higher education, job training or placements, or other options. The research examined the friendships of young people with disabilities and their participation in social and/or leisure activities.

Table 7.3 Number of young people taking part in leisure/social activities at home			
Activity	Young people's responses (n= 67)	Responses by proxy through parent (n=9)	Total number of young people (%) (n=76)
Taking part in outdoor games (at home)	59	8	67 (88%)
Watching TV or video	55	7	62 (82%)
Listening to records, tapes or CDs	29	3	32 (42%)
Using home computer/video games	22	1	23 (30%)
Listening to the radio	16	4	20 (26%)
Reading books	13	2	15 (20%)
Taking part in indoor games	11	2	13 (17%)
Doing a hobby/creative art/craft	10	2	12 (16%)
Looking after pets/animals	5	0	5 (7%)
Gardening	1	2	3 (4%)
Other	15	4	19 (25%)

Note: some young people had several activities.

The sample of young people seemed to have a wide range of leisure and social activities. Table 7.3 indicates the range of activities that young people said they undertook at home, the most popular involving taking part in outdoor games, watching TV or videos, and listening to records, tapes or CDs. Sports, visiting friends and going shopping were the most frequently mentioned activities outside the home (Table 7.4). Almost half (37) the young people belonged to a club, group or society. Some of these were groups for disabled young people such as Gateway clubs and Sportsability, but many were mainstream organised activities, including youth clubs, church clubs, sports clubs, Girl Guides/Boys' Brigade, or the Phab clubs aimed at facilitating interaction between young disabled and non-disabled people.

Table 7.4 Number of young people taking part in leisure/social activities outside the home

Activity	Young people's responses (n= 67)	Responses by proxy through parent (n=9)	Total number of young people (%) (n=76)
Taking part in sports activities	37	1	38 (50%)
Visiting friends/relatives	29	4	33 (43%)
Going shopping	21	5	26 (34%)
Going to pub/café/restaurant	17	3	20 (26%)
Going to cinema/theatre	19	1	20 (26%)
Going to disco/party/dance	17	2	19 (25%)
Going to social/youth club	10	3	13 (17%)
Going for walks	5	3	8 (10%)
Watching sport/games/racing (live – not TV)	6	1	7 (9%)
Going for a drive	6	0	6 (8%)
Going to church/chapel	2	0	2 (3%)
Going to concert/folk club/bands	1	0	1 (1%)
Playing slot machines	1	0	1 (1%)

Note: some young people had several activities.

Nine out of ten young people said that they had friends their own age, and all young people reported having at least one friend. Friends were made through school/college, work or job placement, or through clubs/societies. Some young people also had friends at a day centre. Three-quarters of young people said that they saw their friends in their spare time, outside of college, work or day centre hours. Friends were equally likely to visit the young person's home, or to be visited by the young person. In addition to friends, one-quarter of the sample said that they had a boyfriend/girlfriend. It would seem that many young people had an active social life and took part in several social and leisure activities.

Adult roles in the family

McGinty and Fish (1992) argued strongly that any conceptual framework adopted for transition should 'embrace family roles…as legitimate objectives for young people with disabilities' (p.16). Young people with disabilities have the right to the same aspirations as other young people, including getting married and/or having children. This study examined young people's roles within their household, including developing household skills and carrying out routine household tasks, and aspirations for the future, including living arrangements and views on marriage.

Table 7.5 Number of young people who help with housework at home			
Household task	Young people's responses	Responses by proxy through parent	Total number of young people (%)
	(n= 67)	(n=9)	(n=76)
Washing up	54	3	57 (75%)
Making own bed	51	4	55 (72%)
Washing/ironing own clothes	28	1	29 (38%)
Getting meals ready	31	1	32 (42%)
Cleaning own room	56	2	58 (76%)
Shopping	41	4	45 (59%)

Sixty-seven young people were asked if they helped around the home with a variety of tasks. In addition, a further nine responses were obtained from parents of young people with learning disabilities with whom interviewers had difficulty communicating.

Young people seemed more likely to complete certain tasks such as washing up, making their bed, cleaning their room and doing the shopping, than getting meals ready or washing or ironing their own clothes (Table 7.5). Many young people, however, were involved in the whole range of tasks. Most of those helping reported that they did so all of the time or sometimes. Only a few said that they did not help very often. In this way many young people were developing responsible roles within their household.

Young people were asked whether they would like to leave home in the future (nearly all the young people still lived at home). Forty-three thought that at some stage they would like to leave home. However, the stage in their life that they said they would like to leave home varied greatly. Twenty-nine young people stated an age when they might do so, which ranged from 18 to 50 years. (Some young people were not asked this question as they had difficulties understanding time periods.) Similarly, questions were asked about getting married at some time in the future, and 38 thought that they would like to; of these, 24 thought that they actually would get married at some time. Table 7.6 indicates the age at which the young people would like to either leave home or get married. It would seem that most expected to leave home some time before getting married.

Table 7.6 Age when young person thought they might like to leave the parental home/get married		
Age (years)	Leave parental home (no.)	Get married (no.)
Under 20	8	1
Early 20s	15	2
25	-	8
Late 20s	3	11
30	1	5
30-something	-	1
50	1	-
When I get a job	-	1
As soon as possible	1	-

Fifteen young people said that they would need some help in order to live on their own. Half the young people said they would ask their parents for help. Other sources of aid included carers, friends, other relatives and social workers. Access to accommodation was a major issue for several young people, who felt that adaptations would be necessary for them to be able to live somewhere else.

The findings suggest that the aspirations of young people with disabilities are similarly wide-ranging to those of any young people. Their wishes ranged from the idealistic, such as winning the lottery (how many of us don't wish occasionally for that?), to the more practical, such as to have a good job or a nice house. The most frequently occurring wishes among the young people were to get a job (23), to have their own home (20), to get married (14), to have a boyfriend/girlfriend (6), to be happy (12) and to have children (10). About one-quarter of the sample had a dream of winning the lottery or being rich and/or famous. Some of the young people's wishes are listed in their own words below.

> *I want a boyfriend…and a house key.*
>
> *I'd love to have a job that I love to do with a reasonable salary, and probably get married…if I wasn't deaf, if I could hear — maybe if there was a new device that came out and I can hear.*
>
> *That I'd have a good job, that I'd have children hopefully and settle down.*
>
> *I'll be here all day — come back in half an hour…to be a popular famous singer…get rid of my gambling problem — to arrest it — write that down, to arrest it…to meet the right person and to settle down and get married and have children…to find a pot of gold at the end of the rainbow (laughing).*
>
> *Three wishes…get married…to represent Northern Ireland in the Bowling World Cup and…to have kids of my own.*
>
> *Stay single — what else — get better at snooker — what else — have no more operations.*
>
> *To have a full-time job with good money…to live in my own house with a partner and…maybe have children when I'm older maybe.*
>
> *Loads of money…to have children. I want children. And get married as well. To have a nice boyfriend or be married.*
>
> *Get rid of the epilepsy…be able to drive a car…pass all my NVQs…the main one is I just want rid of my epilepsy.*
>
> *To meet friends…go and sometimes play football.*

Several other researchers (Armstrong and Davies 1995; Shepperdson 1995) have noted considerable change over the last decade in the aspirations of

disabled school leavers regarding access to further education and occupational choices. Many more young people with disabilities are now seeking
further education places and have clear ideas about future occupations.
Obtaining viable employment plays an important role if a young person is to
develop some degree of independence and make a successful transition to
adult life. The research to date shows that although disabled young people
no longer have low aspirations, they are less likely than their non-disabled
peers to have access to employment and the associated financial independence.

The role of formal social support, and in particular transition planning,
plays a crucial part in the extent to which many disabled young people will
successfully achieve adult status. Transition planning and assessments for
support should address the barriers that young people have to face, as well
individual needs for social care. The findings of this study suggested a lack of
cohesion and integration in transition planning. The research found little
evidence of collaboration between education establishments and social
services. While over half (40) of the young people had talked to someone in
school (usually a teacher or careers adviser) about preparing to leave school,
and 28 out of the 76 young people had had an assessment of their needs
carried out by a social worker, very few had actually had a transition plan
drawn up. A number of young people complained that there was too much
emphasis on information about careers, colleges, courses and qualifications,
not enough advice on independent living and day-to-day issues, and not
enough specialised advice relating to their disability.

From the young person's viewpoint, a cohesive, collaborative arrangement for transition planning, as intended by Children (NI) Order 1995, was
not evident. It would seem from these young people's experiences that
transition planning is piecemeal, with different agencies having some input,
but lacking overall co-ordination and direction. In addition, interviews with
the young people (or their parents) seemed to indicate that the social work
resource available to them was limited, and that there was a lack of clarity
about the role of the social worker. Most young people, however, did find
their social worker easy to talk to, approachable and helpful.

Conclusions

The Northern Ireland study supported previous research findings that
disabled young people have the same range of aspirations and expectations
for their future as other young people. However, while some disabled young
people deal successfully with this important phase of their lives, other young
people experience some degree of difficulty, particularly in terms of gaining

employment. Financial independence is difficult for young people to achieve if they are dependent solely on benefits and training allowances as their source of income; this in turn has an impact on other aspects of the transition to adulthood, including living independently.

A range of legislation is relevant to the provision of services for disabled young people, and this is often mirrored by the fragmentation of service delivery and a piecemeal approach to transition planning. In order to overcome these problems, the range of professionals and agencies involved in meeting statutory obligations and providing services to young people with disabilities need to work together. A framework or structure for transition planning needs to be developed which facilitates collaboration between agencies, enables shared assessment arrangements, allows the exchange of information between agencies and professionals, and recognises the young person's own views and right to make choices. Transition planning needs to include regular assessment, review and planning, including educational, vocational and personal preparation for adult life. Different agencies and professionals need to come together to co-ordinate their contributions to the transition plans of disabled young people. The mechanism developed to facilitate such collaboration needs to address issues of the availability and sharing of information between professionals and agencies and across the phases of transition. These mechanisms also need to involve young people and their parents or carers.

The transition planning process under the Education (NI) Order 1996 identifies a framework which could be adopted to enable collaborative and inter-agency working. Disabled young people who do not have a statement, however, need also to be included in the process of transition planning to assist their progress towards adulthood and identify potential problems and possible solutions or options. Transition planning should take place at a strategic level as well, so as to ensure that these mechanisms are properly in place and that appropriate funding and budgets are allocated to this important area of work. Children's Services Plans can play a vital role here in planning appropriate services for disabled young people and identifying key partners for this collaborative work. Transition planning will only be effective through the commitment of everyone involved. A particular difficulty lies in the resources available for inter-agency collaboration, as this in itself requires some financing to sustain. In addition, a successful transition plan requires key individuals within agencies to be identified as responsible for the delivery of key services. As different agencies have their own priorities and service objectives this can be difficult to co-ordinate.

If agencies are effectively to assist disabled young people in their progression to adulthood a collaborative framework of transition needs to be put in place, supported by joint working agreements between agencies that also address the issue of access to necessary budgets for service delivery. Such inter-agency collaboration will involve developing shared values, agreeing upon a structure for working together, understanding each other's roles in the transition process, committing resources, developing joint planning arrangements, and sharing good practice and information. Joint working arrangements exist to some extent already, but these are piecemeal resulting in fragmented services. There is a clear need for a key person, perhaps nominated by an inter-agency working group, to take a lead role in liaising with the various agencies and professionals and working closely with the young person and his/her parents. Initiatives elsewhere, such as the Kurator system in Denmark, may provide important models of good practice for such a development.

PART II

Looked-after Children

CHAPTER 8

The Looking After Children Records System: An Evaluation of the Scottish Pilot

Suzanne Wheelaghan and Malcolm Hill

Introduction

The 1990s witnessed a most unusual development in child welfare. A standardised system of records, produced by academics and supported by the Department of Health in London, was introduced and spread rapidly across first England and Wales and then a number of other countries. Previous record and planning systems had been very diverse and adapted to local circumstances and administrative requirements. It appears that this new set of records, now commonly known as the Looking After Children or LAC system, was sufficiently attractive and adaptable for policy-makers and managers in many different places to decide that now was the time to change and to adopt a more common system.

This chapter reviews research findings on the importing of the LAC system into Scotland, but first we provide a brief overview of the system, its perceived advantages and critiques that have been made.

The Looking After Children materials

In brief, the Looking After Children materials comprise a set of records intended to act as a comprehensive and coherent store of information about children and to assist assessment, communication, planning and reviews. They were designed primarily for children looked after in foster and residential care.

The origins of the Looking After Children programme lie in the work of a group of child care academics set up in England in the late 1980s to examine how to assess better the outcomes for children who experienced public care (Parker *et al.* 1991). The initial concern was that too often the needs of children in care had not been met and that certain aspects of their lives (such as health and education) tended to be neglected (Jackson 1989; Department of Health 1991; Hill and Aldgate 1996).

As a result it was decided to develop a set of questions and prompts for social workers and others to help them assess children's needs across seven broad areas of development. The aims were not confined to assessment, however. The originators of the system also stressed the vital importance of encouraging definite and specific action plans to be formulated and carried out to address unmet needs. The seven core dimensions were:

- health
- education
- family and social relationships
- emotional and behavioural development
- identity
- self-presentation
- self-care skills.

These form the basis of what became known as the Assessment and Action Records (AAR) (Ward 1995; 1996; 1998). Age-related versions were created for children aged

- 0–1 year
- 1–2 years
- 3–4 years
- 5–9 years
- 10–14 years
- 15+ years.

It became apparent that it would be helpful to integrate the AAR with other basic records held by local authorities for children looked after away from home. Information is needed at different stages, from pre-admission through to review of a care plan, so six additional forms were devised. Hence, a package of materials was developed which included two Essential Inform-ation Records (1 and 2), Placement Agreement forms (parts 1 and 2), a care plan and a review form[1]. Although devised later, most of these precede the AAR in a child's care career, at least when first used.

Used together, these materials have a number of purposes with respect to individual children:

- to provide an accurate record of key information and events

- to ensure at least minimal standards of care and encourage optimal care

- to facilitate assessment, monitoring and reviews of the child's progress

- to assist communication among the key parties, including the child

- to help ensure that actions are taken by appropriate people in response to identified needs

- to assess outcomes of care careers.

Potentially, the information from the records can also be collated, analysed and aggregated to give local authorities data on service provision, children's progress and outcomes for their populations of children in residential and foster care. This would serve as a basis for performance monitoring and strategic planning.

It will be seen later that a number of complications arose because of tensions among these varied functions and associated principles when linked to a single record. For example, the desire to have comprehensive information may not fit with young people's and parents' readiness to give or share it. Details required for monitoring progress or future reference might distract attention from current needs and plans. An emphasis on sharing information and partnership among the various key people involved can conflict with confidentiality. Such dilemmas are not specific to this type of record, but the aim of using a standard integrated system sharpens awareness of them.

Moreover, written forms alone could not fulfil the ambitious and diverse purposes of the LAC materials. They could only work well if used by skilled workers and within the context of satisfactory case management and information systems. Successful usage would depend as much on the quality of staff and planning systems as on the forms themselves and associated practicalities.

---

1   Partly as a result of the research, these forms were later amended and re-organised into five: the Essential Core Record and Placement Agreement; Essential Background Record; Care Plan; Day-to-day Placement Arrangements form; and Review of Care Plan.

Despite some improvements over the years, agencies and researchers have often recognised that their previous case records had a number of deficiencies, so that even if LAC did not fulfil all its aims, it might still be better than what went before. Although the records require much time to complete, so did the various forms that preceded them.

The LAC system in practice

The development of the LAC materials has been an extended process, which has involved careful monitoring and adaptation to feedback from participants (Ward 1995). No systematic evaluation of their impact has yet taken place, but indications of their application are available from a small number of reviews, audits and critical appraisals, mainly carried out in England. Policy-makers and managers in a range of other countries have welcomed the LAC materials and introduced them. They have been translated into other languages, e.g. French. (Jones *et al.* 1998, p.220).

The materials are now being used in over 90 per cent of local authorities in England and Wales. An audit carried out in 1996 found great variation across and within authorities in the extent to which records were being completed as intended. The majority had most of the required information, but in many cases there were significant gaps (Moyers 1997). The AARs were less likely to be fully answered than the other forms. One-third had had more than one-quarter of the questions unanswered. A subsequent audit revealed some improvement in completion rates, though linkages between the AAR and the care plans and reviews were often not good (Scott 1999).

Little progress has been made in the use of the LAC materials at a strategic level, and not only because the information on individual cases is incomplete. Poorly developed information systems, diverse databases and the absence of a computer culture in many offices are additional major problems (Kerslake 1998).

As a result, the main impact has been evident at the individual case level. Some social workers have stated that the schedules helped them to discuss difficult issues with older children, foster carers or parents (Parker 1998, p.196). On the other hand, the time taken up by recording can detract from direct work with children, families or carers (Bell 1999). Managers in one London Borough acknowledged that initially they had neglected to involve foster carers fully in the implementation process. Once this was rectified, feedback about the records was largely positive (Phillips and Worlock 1996).

Critiques

The LAC materials have been widely promoted by central government, local government senior managers and a number of child care academics, but they have also drawn criticism on theoretical and practical grounds with respect to both the overall approach and the contents (Knight and Caveney 1998; Bell 1999; Garrett 1999). The arguments against LAC may be grouped as follows:

- The *'checklist' format* that characterises many parts of the records detracts from professional autonomy and oversimplifies complex issues such as identity.

- The LAC materials represent *top-down standardisation and control,* as witnessed previously with respect to child protection, criminal justice and social work education.

- The materials embody an *individualised vision of child development,* with little attention given to the poverty that affects most of the families of looked-after children or the influence of ethnicity, gender and other social factors.

- The records encourage a *structured data-gathering approach to communication* with children, young people and their families, which runs counter to certain principles of direct work such as careful timing and sensitive responsiveness to client-led agendas. 'Children's subjective experiences and right to identify relevant issues for themselves are marginalised' (Garrett 1999, p.36).

- LAC is based on *largely middle-class norms* about parenting and family life, which are presented as universal.

- A *bio-medical rather than a social model of behaviour, health and disability* is espoused, with dangers of imposing value judgements and forcing children to fit into conventional expectations.

Jackson (1998) defended the LAC materials against some of these charges. She said that the influence of deprivation and oppression is well known; the aim of the LAC forms is to try to ensure that disadvantage is not repeated or reinforced when local authorities look after children. Jackson also reasserted that the dimensions have been shown to fit with the views of 'ordinary' parents, but Garrett provided some evidence that the community study that tested this was not fully representative. Jackson said that the records are intended to encourage participation and that a number of social workers have reported that the records helped dialogue and sharing. Moreover, 'good practice requires that they should be used flexibly' (p.52).

At the heart of the debate about the LAC system lie some fundamental divisions regarding the nature of childhood and family life (*see* e.g. Hill and Tisdall 1997; James, Jenks and Prout 1998) and the role and functions of statutory social work. LAC was developed in part because existing practice was perceived to have failed many children (Department of Health 1991; Parker *et al.* 1991). It was concluded that specific guidance and procedures would promote better practice. Critics, on the other hand, fear that the materials may be serving governance and bureaucratic purposes to the detriment of empowerment- based work that gives a central place to the voices of service users.

The present study

The research discussed in this chapter was not designed to provide inform-ation that would resolve arguments about LAC, nor was it on a sufficient scale to do so. It did canvas from varied sources a wide range of feedback that is relevant to assessment of the claims and counter-claims. The study was commissioned by the Scottish office to assess the short-term usefulness and impact of the LAC system as it was introduced in six Scottish local authorities (Wheelaghan *et al.* 1999). The English and Welsh forms had been adapted to take account of the different legislation and organisational context of social work in Scotland (Fabb and Guthrie 1997). The Scottish Office intended the evaluation to inform further modifications before the system was promoted more widely.

The Scottish Office organised a conference in May 1997 in which presentations by people who had developed and used the forms in England and Wales were given. Packs were made available to all local authorities and they were invited to take part in a pilot programme to assess their practical effectiveness and contribute to their revision before full implementation (planned to start in 1999). Eleven of the 32 Scottish local authorities agreed to take part in the piloting of the materials, and of these six agreed to participate in the evaluation by the University of Glasgow.

The study was planned to be primarily qualitative, obtaining perspectives from samples of each of the key participants and stakeholders. The timescale for the research did not allow for the collection of large or representative samples, but care was taken to include respondents at different levels and in different locations across the six participating authorities. Multiple methods were used in the study:

1. Semi-structured qualitative *individual interviews* with:
   - Members of staff with prime responsibility for LAC (26)
   - Social workers and seniors in local teams (19)
   - Foster carers (10)
   - Young people (4)
   - Residential staff (3)

2. Attendance at *implementation group meetings* (15)

3. *Group interviews*

4. *Self-completion questionnaires* (evaluation sheets) completed in relation to 130 records with respect to 53 children

5. *Detailed scrutiny* of 94 individual records for 24 children

6. Brief information obtained by *telephone and letter* from Reporters and panel chairpersons representing the Scottish Children's Hearings (for details of the Hearings system, see Lockyer and Stone 1998).

The study lasted eight months, from November 1997 to July 1998. Its conclusions were therefore inevitably provisional and related to the introductory phase that might well not be typical of longer-term experiences, when motivations, familiarity and other factors would be different. In some ways the climate was favourable to innovation. Local government reorganisation had recently taken place and many councils were open to experimentation or needed to develop procedures of their own (Craig *et al.* 2000). The recent implementation of the Children (Scotland) Act 1995 laid great emphasis on planning and partnership, and some saw LAC as an opportunity to strengthen these. On the other hand, financial stringency, adjustments to organisational change and the new demands of 1995 Act beset many staff in local authorities.

The next section of this chapter presents the main findings of the study, beginning with the processes by which the new records system was introduced. Next, the views of staff, carers and young people are considered. The results of the record scrutiny are then presented, and finally conclusions and implications are drawn out.

Introduction of the LAC system

In view of their willingness to take part in both the piloting of the LAC system and the external evaluation, it was evident that the six participant authorities were especially committed to LAC. This was further demonstrated by the fact that they all decided not only to use the records during the pilot period in 1997–8, but also to introduce them on a long-term basis. Despite the emphasis on corporate approaches to children's services in the legislation and associated guidance, the initiative was taken by social work services, acting largely alone in the first instance, though with some attempts to inform and involve other departments and agencies as the scheme was introduced.

Five of the authorities expected staff to apply all of the LAC records. The sixth authority concentrated mainly on introducing the Assessment and Action Records, since it had only recently set up a new system for routine recording and reviews.

Initially, authorities intended to introduce the forms *prospectively*. In other words, appropriate information, placement and care plan forms would be used for new admissions to residential and foster care. Review forms and AAR were to be completed for children already looked after, as their next review became due. However, before long the majority of agencies began to require workers to complete records *retrospectively*. This entailed filling in information, placement and planning forms on children already accommo- dated. The main reason for this was that senior or review staff saw the value of having uniform and comprehensive details available. Yet this process meant workers and perhaps carers putting together information that was already on existing records. This was to have a significant effect on people's experiences of the LAC forms.

Each authority set up an Implementation Group, although in one council this was an informal arrangement mainly involving just three staff. The groups were composed of a range of staff at different levels (*see* Table 8.1) They all included a service manager at Principal Officer level and an Administrative or IT Officer, although in two instances the latter was only added once the group had started. The involvement of other kinds of personnel was variable. Most groups included a staff member with respons- ibility in residential care and a foster carer. None of the Implementation Groups included officers from other departments such as education or health.

The Implementation Group was managed by a person with designated responsibility for LAC. In four councils this was a Senior Service Manager, in one an Area Team Manager and in one a Senior Social Worker. The less senior organisational position of the project leader in the latter two authorities affected their status and authority, so they were in a somewhat weaker position than elsewhere to insist on particular arrangements.

The tasks undertaken by the Implementation Groups were as follows:

- to decide how and when the forms would be used
- to organise training for LAC
- to promote LAC across the department (project leaders sometimes referred to themselves as 'cheerleaders' or 'champions' of the LAC system)
- to monitor the use of the records
- to handle queries and issues as they arose.

Table 8.1 Membership of Implementation Groups	
Position/role	**Number of authorities**
Senior Service Manager	6
Admin/IT/Research Officer	6 (4 from the start)
Residential Manager/Worker	5
Senior Social Worker	5
Foster carer	4
Training Officer	4
Children's Rights Officer	3
Area Manager	3
Resource Worker	2
Review officer	2
Field social worker	2
Who Cares? development worker	2

Administration and information systems

Although developed by academics and applied by professionals and carers, the use of LAC records requires effective administration and information storage and exchange. The centrality of this aspect was sometimes slow to be recognised. In only four of the six councils was a senior administrator included in the implementation group, and in one of these the individual was unable to attend the meetings. Other authorities incorporated headquarters administrators later.

Partly in consequence, a number of basic administrative problems were reported by senior and front-line staff interviewed. For example, in some areas blank forms were not readily to hand when needed; uncertainties existed about who should receive copies of completed forms and how; and arrangements for storage were not standardised.

In contrast, certain administrative practices were identified as helpful. These included compiling separate packs of records for different situations, e.g. emergency and planned admissions. An alternative grouping was:

- Admission pack
- Post-admission pack
- Review pack.

The original forms could be produced with colour coding so that each type of from was readily identifiable. This was expensive when mass printing or photocopying was entailed. In consequence, two of the authorities did not colour-code the records.

In all the authorities, the records were completed in writing on to blank records, not typed on disk into pro-formas. Typing support was said to be available universally to reproduce the completed versions so that they were more legible, but this entailed duplication of time and effort. Not uncommonly, considerable delays resulted before typed versions had been produced.

Making and circulating copies was another issue. Only one agency used expensive self-duplicating forms, which produce multiple copies at the time of completion. Elsewhere photocopying was generally necessary. This took up further time, especially when dealing with papers for sibling groups. Some photocopied versions were hard to make out, because of the effects of the layout, colour and handwriting on the copying.

Distribution of the records is partly a practical matter, but also raises the question of who the records are for, with associated issues about confidentiality. In certain teams, LAC records were integrated with other documents in a child's file, whereas in other places they were kept separately, partly because of their bulk. Although the training emphasised that foster and residential carers should have a copy, not all fieldworkers and clerical staff were aware of this. Some fieldworkers voiced concerns that foster homes might not have a suitable secure location for keeping records In residential units, records were generally kept in the office, where a young person was entitled to access, but copies were generally not given directly to young people, let alone parents. Social workers and carers mostly recognised that children and young people might have copies if they wished, but this seemed to be left to their initiative.

A number of fieldworkers believed that young people should not have a copy in case they lost it and let sensitive information go astray. None of the few young people spoken to by the main researcher possessed any of their LAC forms.

By and large, steps were gradually taken to deal with the administrative difficulties with the records of individuals. However, when it came to use of the information on a more collective basis for monitoring and strategic planning, the authorities had hardly left the starting blocks. Unfortunately, the format in which data were gathered on the LAC records did not correspond with any of the existing information systems in the six implementing authorities, nor with previous categories used to generate Scottish Office statistics. Disks provided by the Scottish Office had to be adapted to the authority's own software and then converted into templates. In only two authorities were information staff involved directly in working with the Implementation Group to look at ways of using the information collated from the LAC materials.

Ensuring adequate linkage between the LAC records and authority information systems required appropriate equipment, software and trained staff, but these were not available. Nowhere were fieldworkers expected to input and update their records directly on to computers. One administrative representative probably spoke for others in remarking that this was unlikely to happen in the near future:

> There is no proposal yet for social workers to put information on to the computer, as we still need to get the IT system in place. . . . and would social workers buy into this anyway?

For all these reasons, and also because of the time taken up in ensuring that case recording happened reasonably satisfactorily, no attempts had been made to collate information from the forms in any of the authorities.

The training

The Scottish Office had run its own training for key local authority personnel prior to the piloting, issued training packs and provided finance for support training. All six authorities organised training programmes, usually before staff began to use the records though sometimes alongside the introduction of the system. In several agencies young people or Who Cares? development workers contributed to the training.

The training followed a similar format in each authority, comprising two parts. The first sought to capture the hearts and minds of participants so that they would become committed to the project. This involved discussion of the philosophy underpinning the LAC materials and the relevant principles and requirements of the Children (Scotland) Act 1995. The second part was about practical use of the records, and normally included some opportunity to practice filling in a form. In all but one authority the training was carried out over two days. Interestingly, no training was provided in the use of computers to input or handle information gathered for the forms.

Staff were trained in mixed groups, including field social workers, seniors, team leaders, review officers, foster carers and residential staff. In a small number of authorities, out-of-hours staff also attended. Generally, far fewer carers attended than mangers and fieldworkers, though one agency stated that all its residential staff had been present. It was reported to be harder for residential staff and, especially, foster carers to take time away from their commitments to the children they were looking after. Attendance was also affected by staff shortages.

On the whole, training was for social work staff only, particularly in the early stages. Four agencies were able to include staff from other departments in their training, although this was once the materials were being used. Such staff included health visitors, school nurses, Reporters, and some education staff. Although a few young people participated as contributors, neither they nor their parents were invited as *recipients*, despite the vital role they are expected to have in participatory planning and decision-making.

Feedback on training

Field social workers generally reported the training itself to be very valuable and positive. They liked the content and approach. The main criticism was that the training was too short: most thought a third day was needed to focus further on how to apply the records. Many also requested a 'follow-up' or 'refresher' session once they had started to use the records. Such a session would have enabled them to check whether they were using the records properly and to raise any difficulties they were having.

The small numbers of residential staff involved in the research said they enjoyed the training experience and welcomed the opportunity to discuss issues raised by the materials alongside field social workers. Similarly, the foster carers who had been able to attend were generally enthusiastic about the experience and found the mix of staff led to productive discussions. However, a few had felt intimidated by the social workers and would have preferred to have separate sessions for themselves.

Overall it seems that the training was a useful means of preparing the workers and carers who attended for the use of LAC and engaging their commitment. However, targeting was selective, with relatively few invitations of non-social-work professionals in most areas and none to family members. Uptake was also partial, especially among carers. It is perhaps understandable that initial training did not attempt to include everyone who has a role in providing information, planning and decision-making, but the incomplete coverage had knock-on effects for the development of a sense of engagement with the new system and for partnership in general.

Views on using the LAC Records: social work staff

The interviews asked all respondents to give their opinions on how LAC was working, the perceived advantages and drawbacks. Of course, each answered from his or her own perspective, but certain common themes emerged:

- The principles underlying the system were generally approved of.
- The records were thought to be good for sharing relevant information and helping to develop focused plans.
- The AAR in particular could promote open discussion, but also included matters that were difficult to raise or address.
- The volume of questions and answers made it hard to complete the records fully and difficult to absorb their contents.

Two core tensions threaded through much of the feedback:

1. The records are useful (actually or potentially), but it is very hard to spare the time to do them justice.
2. The records can aid communication in some circumstances, but are awkward to use in others.

Each of the main viewpoints was examined in further detail. For the most part, senior staff in the authorities were convinced advocates of LAC, which presumably contributed to the positive evaluations of the training and also led to a reasonable degree of compliance in filling in forms. Nevertheless, a few team leaders were not keen on the system, and this led to resistance. Fieldworkers took encouragement when their supervisors were supportive and especially when they acknowledged the time demands in their workload or time-management systems.

Many seniors and front line workers said they liked the system in principle and felt it accorded with the new directions offered by the Children (Scotland) Act 1995. The majority saw the system as more thorough and appropriate than their previous forms of recording, though a minority did prefer the ones they were used to. Two-thirds of workers interviewed said that the records had improved their practice, helped communication with carers or young people and made shared responsibility more explicit. Nearly half also thought the forms assisted in involving parents. For instance, two said:

We're getting more information from the parents for the carer's benefit and for the social worker's benefit.

[LAC] makes it harder for parents to opt out once their child has been accommodated.

On the other hand, most social workers emphasised or complained about the large amount of time that was needed if the records were to be completed conscientiously. Ideally this would involve a number of meetings, as well as the time taken up with writing and then getting forms typed, copied and distributed. Among the remarks made were that the records were 'onerous' and 'a wearying process'.

The effort required was especially resented when workers were asked to complete records retrospectively, as they could see little or no immediate gain from this. Although there was considerable hostility to retrospective use of the forms, in a small number of cases fieldworkers indicated that going through old files allowed them to reflect on and develop a new perspective on some of the children. For one child, it triggered further investigative work in relation to health needs.

More extensive and systematic feedback about the records was obtained from evaluation sheets that were distributed. There was a considerable element of self-selection in determining which social workers took time to complete these sheets, so there can be no guarantee that the views obtained are representative. Sheets were completed in relation to 53 cases. It was requested that one sheet would be used to comment on each record used in case, but some people provided a combined response with respect to several records on one case. The types of records evaluated were as follows:

Table 8.2 Types of record evaluated	
EIR 1	19
EIR 2	15
Placement Agreement 1	16
Placement Agreement 2	17
Care plan	20
Review form	15
Assessment and action record	12
Combined questionnaire	16
Total	130

We had expected that the evaluation sheets would be completed by field social workers and this was the case with all but ten. The remainder came from care staff or resource workers whose role was to support foster carers.

For most questions the replies were broadly positive, with a minority expressing some reservations or dislike. Half said that the record achieved its purpose well or very well, and fewer than one in ten responded that it was poor or very poor in that respect (Table 8.3). A substantial number of people (43%) were neither particularly enthusiastic nor critical, however.

Table 8.3 How well does the record achieve its purpose?		
	Number	%
Well or very well	58	49.6
Satisfactory	25	21.4
Mixed views	25	21.4
Poorly or very poorly	9	7.6
Total	117*	

* 13 missing

Respondents were asked several questions about the layout and content, which produced very similar distributions. Roughly three-quarters agreed or strongly agreed that the layout was easy to follow, the questions easy to understand, the instructions clear and the questions relevant. On the same questions between 10 and 20 per cent disagreed and the rest were not sure.

Three-quarters of the evaluation sheets identified questions that had worked particularly well, and just over half highlighted at least one which had not worked well. About a quarter of the sheets identified one or more questions that had been difficult to discuss.

Approximately two-thirds thought the number of questions was just right, a third thought there were too many and one person thought there were too few. Some discrepancy is evident between responses to this question and frequent comments about the forms being too long. It may be that though the overall impression was of considerable and unnecessary length, it was difficult to identify individual questions which could be omitted. One comment lent support to this interpretation:

Too lengthy and repetitive was my first impression, but when going through the forms again there was little repetition and most information seemed to be required/useful.

Descriptions of the forms as cumbersome and time-consuming were made on the evaluation sheets, as in the interviews. One comment was: 'When do we have time to see clients?'

It was suggested that the questions were too complex and detailed for meaningful participation by children with learning disabilities, and were potentially demoralising in that they highlighted problems rather than competence.

Although opinions expressed about each particular type of form varied, a number of generally agreed features were apparent. These are briefly summarised in Table 8.3.

The following quotations demonstrate how the AAR could either help or hinder communication with children and young people, depending on factors such as their age, ability and general attitudes, as well as presumably the circumstances and the communication approach taken by the social worker:

The section on family and social relationships helped us to talk about her parents and grandparents. She hadn't done so because she hadn't wanted to upset her carers.

It's especially good for sibling groups as it deals with the individual child. It helps identify individuality.

We assume young people are vulnerable, weak, but this shows them as being far more resilient than they get credit for.'

The length is off-putting and it is very time consuming. Much of this record is inappropriate for young people with learning difficulties, as they are unable to participate in its completion.

Very difficult to fill in. Child did not want to answer many of the questions. Too intrusive and threatening for the child.

Since I've started, the young person now says she doesn't want to complete it.

At the end of the evaluation sheets, social workers were given the opportunity to make suggestions for change regarding the contents, processes and use of the information. In relation to content, the majority of comments were about the bulk of the package, with requests for 'streamlining', 'condensing' and 'shortening'. Several pointed to duplication across records and a few proposed that forms could be combined to reduce repetition. Another criticism was that it was difficult to access particular information quickly.

Table 8.4 Feedback on individual records

Essential Information Record 1   MAINLY POSITIVE FEEDBACK

Straightforward to complete and provides basic essential information in a format that is easily accessible.

Essential Information Record 2   MAINLY POSITIVE FEEDBACK

Helpful and comprehensive but time and other constraints make full completion difficult.

Placement Agreement 1   MAINLY POSITIVE FEEDBACK

Useful as a basis for detailed discussions about the child's routine and broader expectations of the placement.

Placement Agreement 2   MIXED FEEDBACK

A useful tool for reviewing and updating changes. Some concerns expressed about duplication with other records and handling sensitive information.

Care Plan   MIXED FEEDBACK

Some found this offered a useful framework, but a number of critical comments were made, especially about the lack of relevance of the questions and the separation of the plan from the child's history.

Review Form   CONSIDERABLE DISLIKE

A number disliked the way the form fragmented information and did not allow for continuous narrative. Also, the language used was not easy for children and parents to understand. Others did find this thorough and helpful.

Assessment and Action Records   MIXED FEEDBACK

The overall impression seemed to be that this was a potentially useful exercise but that there were also some practical and ethical difficulties in using them. The AAR were widely criticised for being time-consuming and cumbersome, especially where there were several children in one family. Some young people also found the layout and questions off-putting. However, some social workers reported that they were prompted to consider or discuss important issues which otherwise would have been overlooked.

Comments about arrangements for distribution and storage revealed practical and ethical concerns. Fitting the bulky forms into existing case files was problematic for some and systems for copying and distributing the forms were described as cumbersome and time-consuming. Some people objected to the waste of paper that widespread copying entailed. Others were worried about what would happen to such personal information and who would keep it. Uncertainty was expressed about systems for updating, in particular about when new forms were needed and when old ones could be amended.

Views on using the LAC records: Other perspectives

Residential staff were largely positive about using the LAC forms, even where they had not been able to attend any training. In their view, the new records provided more information than previous systems and encouraged greater recognition by fieldworkers of their role in communication and planning. They liked the emphasis on involving young people and suggested that the records would help avoid 'drift' in preparing for the future. However, some voiced concerns, largely about the age-old problem of their relationship with field social workers. They believed that some fieldworkers did not include them adequately in the use of the record or in joint assessment.

On the whole, foster carers were also enthusiastic about their experiences of using the LAC materials. They found the forms helpful since they increased the information they received about children, and this helped them engage with the child or young person. Their experience had largely been a passive one of receiving the information from social workers, but a few had employed the AAR in discussions with a child or young person. In one instance this had helped focus attention on plans for a young woman to move to independent accommodation and connect this with reflections on the past:

> She completed it herself and it was very useful for us as carers to understand more about her.

A few carers did express qualms about the volume of paperwork, and a couple were influenced by the negative attitudes of social workers who had doubts about the value of the system.

In general, both residential and foster carers saw the system as helping to involve and indeed empower young people. Some feared that field social workers would spend so much time on the forms that contact between the worker and carer or child would be reduced.

We gained insights into young people's views through a small number of individual interviews, attendance at a few meetings and, indirectly, through reports by carers and social workers. We learned of some young people who engaged with the materials enthusiastically, and of others who either wanted nothing to do with them or quickly gave up when they saw what was involved. The bulk and format was often seen as unattractive, confusing or boring. Comments were also made about intrusiveness. For instance, why did social workers need to know about their friends? More positively, some young people felt that they became more involved than formerly in developing their care plans. A few young people were said to have gained helpful insights into their past or identity through the AAR, which helped them to 'move on'. One described how the form had helped her to remember and 'sort out' some things from her past.

The research team's contacts with Reporters and chairpersons in the Children's Hearings systems indicated that very few of them were aware of the LAC system and that none had any direct experience of it. Since the hearings obtain information from social workers and hold their own reviews on children placed away from home compulsorily, the interchange between the two systems of planning and review needs further attention.

It was beyond the scope of the study to obtain feedback from other professionals. Only one of the authorities had provided information and training to a wide range of other agencies. One other had involved health professionals. Comments from social workers and managers indicated differences of opinion between them and teachers about reviews and uncertainties about how best to gather medical information from GPs or health visitors. This aspect of inter-agency contact in relation to looked-after children deserves much closer investigation (Mather, Humphrey and Robson 1997; Borland *et al.* 1998).

Records scrutiny

The LAC records for 24 children were scrutinised in detail. Two-thirds of them were placed in foster care and the rest in various types of residential care. A total of 93 records were examined, ranging from 9 Assessment and Action Records to 16 care plans and review forms.

The aims of the scrutiny were to check for such things as:

- the legibility and clarity of the information provided
- how well questions and instructions had been understood
- consistency
- gaps in completion.

The review forms were nearly always typed, but otherwise the majority of records were filled in by hand. With a couple of exceptions, legibility was good. Our broad conclusion about thoroughness was that the majority of the records had been filled in appropriately and consistently, though most also had some missing information. We identified a few difficulties in the records themselves and some problems in the way they had been completed. We suspect that these could be found in any recording system and are unlikely to be unique to LAC.

The blank records appeared deficient in a small number of respects. Certain elements of the layout and instructions on the form were unclear, over-elaborate or too cramped. When colour-coded records were used, a photocopied version was hard to read. The meaning of signatures on the forms was not clear.

With regard to the case information provided in the records, one-third of the forms (38 of the 93) had all the relevant information required and a further one-third had only minor omissions. Our judgements of the quality of the information were inevitably subjective, but in the main we thought this was good. The review forms were particularly good at giving a rounded and clear picture. A few of the AARs showed that careful discussion had taken place with young people, who in two cases had made substantial written contributions themselves.

On the negative side, one-third of the records had what seemed to be significant gaps. The ones that most often had important gaps were EIR2, PA2, care plan and AAR. On occasion, key points were missing that were essential for understanding, such as the reason why the child was being looked after or what type of placement the child was in. The Unique Reference Number for each child was provided in only 8 of the 24 cases, an omission that could lead to problems in tracking cases or aggregating information, although normally the child's name would suffice for most purposes. The use of particular names like Susan or Mr McKay meant that roles and relationships were often unclear to anyone not familiar with the case, which could include someone responsible for the child some years later.

In about half of the cases where there was more than one record, the names of the child or young person were inconsistent, usually because formal and informal names were used in different places. In five cases there were discrepancies over a child's date of birth or it was missing.

The scrutiny indicated that most of the records were completed satis-factorily, but room for improvement was apparent in both the layout and wording of blank forms and the manner in which a significant minority of records were completed.

Conclusions

Caution is needed in drawing wide conclusions from this research, as it was a time-limited study of the preliminary stages of introducing the LAC materials into Scotland. In the long run a number of the significant practical difficulties that have been identified should be sorted out, but on the other hand early enthusiasm and energy may wane. Nevertheless, it has been possible to shed light on certain of the claims of proponents and critics of the system.

Of the system's avowed purposes, the first and most obvious was to accumulate and share comprehensive information better than previously. Most respondents thought this was being achieved. The detailed evaluations and record scrutiny identified some problems with the layout and a minority of particular questions, but were on the whole positive. The records are also intended to prompt proactive planning. A number of instances were reported of issues being tackled and actions undertaken which would probably otherwise not have happened.

In terms of enhancing communication, workers and carers believed the LAC forms had helped, though many saw scope for considerable improvement. With respect to participation by young people and family members, it was clear that the care plan and review forms encouraged their involvement. The AAR appealed to some young people, but their bulk and format were intimidating or irrelevant to others. The level of detail and repetition required for the recording and assessment function of the LAC records is ill-suited to be a tool for direct work, though the issues covered are relevant. It was apparent that alternative or supplementary mechanisms are needed, including visual materials that are more interesting and accessible for children and young people.

It was beyond the scope of the study to assess the impact of the LAC system on longer-term planning and progress of individual children. An original aspiration of those who developed the system was to facilitate aggregation of data about populations of children in order to assess care career outcomes and the impact of services. This remains an important goal. It was evident that, as elsewhere, the administrative and IT systems, and the computing skills, were not yet in place to even begin that process.

How did the study illuminate the points raised by critics of LAC? Through our interviews and the evaluation sheets, we had contact with a wide range of people at different levels in the organisations. The great majority were in favour, but it must be recognised that those who were opposed could well have been less likely to have participated in the study. We found little evidence to support the view that the enterprise is misguided in its approach or represents a biased cultural perspective, though the nature of the agencies in Central Scotland meant that the viewpoints of people from minority ethnic backgrounds were barely represented in the study. The principles underpinning the LAC records were widely valued and respected. Detailed comments on the questions indicated that most people saw the great majority as relevant and useful. It may be of course that middle-class social workers simply share the assumptions of the creators of the records, but many workers in Scotland have working-class backgrounds. Also, this and other studies indicate that foster carers, who have a wide socio-economic spread, usually value the records.

We do not know whether the records appeal to parents or not, nor whether they will find that the system gives adequate attention to the structural pressures they experience. Only if and when aggregate use of the data feeds into strategic planning of responses to collective needs, including poverty, will the system be in a position to have an influence at social and neighbourhood levels.

In some areas, it was apparent that the top-down imposition of the materials was resented, but more often the system was welcomed as an improvement on previous systems. The detailed checklist approach was seen as effective in the information and planning records. It worked less well for reviews and for communications around the AAR in general, although in a number of particular cases specific questions did provide helpful reminders or give legitimacy to the broaching of sensitive issues. The study showed clearly that, while standardisation and thoroughness may be assets for record-keeping, selectivity and adaptability of timing and format should guide use of the questions in direct work with children, young people and families.

By far the most serious shortcoming was the time-consuming nature of the enterprise, which led to stress and diverted energy away from other activities. This also accounts for the fact that many records are not fully completed and errors occur. It could be helped by improved administrative systems and greater use of computer inputting, perhaps jointly with carers, young people or parents, as appropriate. Also, the strain on fieldworkers could be eased if they were more willing to share the tasks with residential and foster carers, many of whom are keen to have an enhanced role.

Our study gave guarded support for LAC in general and contributed to specific revisions that have occurred in the Scottish records, including the integration of previously separate information and placement forms. We concluded that LAC records can and will improve care planning and direct work with children and young people who are looked after away from home, though the records are not a panacea and have to take their place alongside other systems and measures. Appropriate administrative back-up and time availability is essential for effective and thorough application. Further, the materials should be used flexibly, participatively and, on occasion, selectively.

CHAPTER 9

Educating Accommodated Children

Moira Borland

Introduction

The subject of this chapter is one which has attracted increasing attention over the last decade. During the eighties, Sonia Jackson and others began to draw attention to the fact that children in public care generally did very poorly in school (Jackson 1987; 1989). Since then the reasons for this have been explored and a range of actions to remedy the situation proposed. The importance of education for looked-after children has been emphasised in inquiry reports (Utting 1991; Scottish Office 1992; Kent 1997), and a wide range of projects and initiatives have been developed to improve young people's educational opportunities. Though the importance of achieving good results in formal exams is fully recognised, a broader definition of education also applies. The aim is to equip children with general knowledge, the ability to discuss issues and the self-confidence that comes from being able to participate in school life and make progress alongside peers in both academic work and other activities such as hobbies.

This chapter is based on a review of research, policy and practice in this field, funded jointly by the Scottish Office Education and Industry Department and the Social Work Services Group. The review was carried out in 1997. Several members of the Centre of the Child and Society collaborated to complete the work in a ten-week period (Borland *et al.* 1998). Geographically we confined the scope of the review to UK material. This was partly because of time restrictions but also because differences in the care and education systems make cross-country comparison unreliable. Indeed, since much of the British material available relates to England and Wales, a degree of caution was needed in applying the findings to Scotland, which has significantly different legislation and contexts for both education and social work services. The Northern Ireland context is different again.

A difference in the use of the term 'looked after' in the Scottish and English contexts also has to be borne in mind. Whereas in England and Wales the term 'looked after' refers only to children cared for away from home, in Scotland this also applies to those subject to a Children's Panel order but supervised at home. Those in residential or foster care are 'looked after and accommodated'. The term 'accommodated' shall be primarily used in this chapter, highlighting that our focus is on children living away from home, while avoiding the cumbersome wording of 'looked after away from home'.

Perhaps the key issue to emerge from our review was that improving educational opportunities for accommodated children is a complex matter. Rather than suggesting quick remedies, the research underlines that there are barriers to be overcome at several levels, from work with individual young people to strategic planning. Collaboration between education and social work staff emerges as essential to improving the service young people are offered, change being required within and across each of these major professional groups and their associated bureaucratic divisions. The current situation can be viewed with both optimism and continuing concern. On the positive side, there is much more awareness of the importance of education for this group of children and young people, and several current policy initiatives promote action in this field. However, intransigent attitudes and practices, resource constraints and fragmented planning still present potential barriers to improving young people's experience in school.

The summary of evidence indicating poor educational outcomes for children in public care will be outlined, then recommendations to effect positive change will be put forward. Finally, some developments and examples of good practice will be discussed.

Educational attainment

Evidence that accommodated children underachieve in education has emerged from various quarters over the last 20 years, notably from national cohort studies and research on care leavers.

Drawing on information from the National Child Development Study, Essen, Lambert and Head (1976) were among the first researchers to provide evidence of the educational underachievement of children who were or had been in care. At age eleven, this group of children were performing below average, and those who had come into care before the age of seven performed worst of all.

A sequence of leaving care studies undertaken at the University of Leeds have provided ample evidence of care leavers' poor attainment and the often negative impact of this on their adult lives (Stein and Carey 1986; Biehal *et al.*

1992). Stein and Carey reported that of the young people who took part in their first study in the early 1980s, 90 per cent had no qualifications. The same was true for three-quarters of care leavers surveyed by Garnett (1992) and for two-thirds of the 183 young people who participated in a further study in the early 1990s (Biehal *et al.* 1995). Only 15 per cent of this group had a GCSE A–C grade or its equivalent and only one young person had an A level.

This compares very unfavourably with the position of most young people in the UK as assessed in the Economic and Social Research Council's '16–19' study of 5000 young people. They reported that 18 per cent of young people had poor GCSE or equivalent qualifications (Banks *et al.* 1992), compared to an average 70 per cent of the care leavers in the Leeds-based studies who had no qualifications at all.

In addition to research, the joint inspection by the Office for Standards in Education (Ofsted) and the Social Services Inspectorate provided evidence that educational outcomes for accommodated children continue to be poor (Ofsted and SSI 1995). This inspection, carried out in four English local authorities early in 1994, indicated that underachievement was more severe among secondary than primary pupils. Only a third of the 60 secondary age children achieved satisfactory standards in terms of their age and ability, and none were judged by their teachers as likely to achieve five subjects at Grade A–C in the GCSE examinations, though in 1993 this result was achieved by 38.3 per cent of their peers.

Local authorities themselves are able to add very little to our understanding of this matter. With a few notable exceptions (Humberside County Council 1995), local authorities do not routinely monitor the educational progress or attainment of children in their care. It has been suggested that this failure may be both a symptom and a contributing factor to the problem (Fletcher-Campbell 1997; Fletcher 1998).

Factors that contribute to children's poor educational experience

A range of factors have been identified as potentially contributing to this poor performance, in combination often resulting in considerable educational disadvantage for accommodated children. These include:

- pre-care experiences and adversity
- young people's experience in schools
- non-attendance
- frequency of moves

- social workers' attitudes

- care environment

- ineffective collaboration between social work and education.

Pre-care experiences and adversity

It is evident that many children who become accommodated have significant emotional and behavioural problems, while their families typically experience high levels of stress and live in poor material conditions (Bebbington and Miles 1989). It is therefore not surprising that a high proportion have long-standing difficulties at school. Two Scottish studies (Kendrick 1995a; Triseliotis *et al.* 1995) found that, among secondary school age children being admitted to care, half presented school-related difficulties including non-attendance, behaviour problems and specific learning difficulties. Indeed for many, school problems had been a major factor in precipitating admission to care.

A number of studies have tried to clarify the extent to which experiences prior to entering care account for continuing poor performance, even when children spend most of their childhood in care. Though this is difficult to establish retrospectively, there is some evidence that behaviour and emotional difficulties which may also have contributed to children being accommodated continue to depress their achievement for some time (Osborn and St Claire 1987).

A longitudinal study of children in foster care has shed further light on the complex ways in which early deprivation can continue to impact on children's educational attainment (Aldgate *et al.* 1993; Heath, Colton and Aldgate 1994; Colton, Heath and Aldgate 1995c) These researchers examined the progress of 49 foster children aged 8–14. All were in mainstream state schools in one English county and had been in care for a minimum of six months. Many had been in their placements for several years, the mean and median length being six years. Thus this was a sample of children in fairly stable circumstances, living in what is generally regarded as the optimum form of substitute care available. The foster carers were mostly judged to be interested in helping the children with their school work.

Using several standard instruments, children's attainment and behaviour were measured at the start of the study and at yearly intervals over the following two years. Their scores were compared with a control group of 58 children living in circumstances similar to those in the foster children's birth families. The findings were considered to be disappointing. Children in foster care and the comparison group were performing well below the national average, but there was no statistically significant difference between the two groups. Thus, despite being in favourable placements, there was little evidence of foster children 'catching up' while they were in care.

In tests in maths, reading and vocabulary and in all rounds of testing, the children who came into care for suspected child abuse or neglect scored significantly lower than did the other foster children. Although there was some evidence of progress in reading, the educational disadvantage of early abuse and neglect was not overcome, even when children were in long-term settled placements. Nor could their poorer educational performance be attributed to continuing behavioural difficulties. Even when there was no evidence of behavioural or emotional problems, foster children scored below the national average in reading, vocabulary and maths. In contrast, children in the comparison group with no behavioural or emotional problems reached national average levels of attainment.

This research seems to indicate that early adversity affects the ability to learn in ways we have yet to fully understand. However, it also provides evidence that specific inputs can make a difference. Additional help with reading did lead to improved scores, while children in foster homes where at least one carer was educated to A level did better on the initial reading and vocabulary tests. However, these children did not make further progress during the course of the research, suggesting that early educational intervention may be necessary to secure an 'escape from disadvantage'.

It is evident that many children who enter care are educationally disadvantaged and this is often not overcome, even when professionals take over their care and the local authority assumes a duty to 'safeguard and promote their welfare'. Indeed, certain aspects of being looked after by the local authority are thought to compound children's difficulties at school and potentially to create problems even for accommodated children who are educationally able.

Young people's experience in school

From the leaving care studies (Stein and Carey 1986; Biehal et al. 1995), surveys of young people's views (Fletcher 1993) and through young people's organisations, notably Who Cares?, a familiar picture has emerged of how becoming accommodated can affect young people's experience at school. For some young people, coming into care provides an opportunity to concentrate on school work and benefit from the support of interested carers, while for others bullying, lack of self-confidence and adjusting to change makes school an ordeal (Fletcher 1993).

Comments from young people themselves highlight their varying experiences:

> Well it was a bit of a struggle at first, but then it got better … 'cos I were used to not going to school. But then, you know, I pulled me socks up really and started going full-time. (Biehal et al. 1995)

> School is better because I've worked hard doing my homework. I've done this because I get more encouragement from my carers. (Fletcher 1993)

> You walked about the school thinking 'I wonder what they're all thinking about me.' You can't walk around the school with your head up high. (Scottish Office 1994b)

> If people know [I'm in care] I'm teased and called a 'charity scrounger', also if a teacher knows they treat me different, sympathising, asking how I am. (Fletcher 1993)

A frequent complaint that young people make is that both teachers and other pupils treat them differently. For some, additional attention from school staff gives them the confidence to make progress, but others resent the assumption that they need special treatment:

> Teachers are more involved because I'm in care. I have more confidence at school. Being in care has helped. (Berridge et al. 1996)

> Teachers were much more lenient, no work was expected of me. Being a grammar school, this kind of treatment was in a way suggesting that I was no longer good enough. Why should the grades change – after all I'd achieved A grades while being abused. (Fletcher 1993)

The key message seems to be that help should be offered as part of getting to know and understand the individual young person rather than on the basis of assumptions about what accommodated children in general need or will find helpful.

Another recurring complaint is that young people who become accommodated are assumed by teachers to be unintelligent. Inevitably this is more likely to happen when children change schools:

> Before I went into care I was in top sets and everything. They put me in bottom sets as soon as I moved into care and moved schools. (Fletcher 1993)

> I feel that the actual education is no different, but people generally tend to put you in a certain group and because of being in care, people don't expect a lot of you. It's like people in care are classed as 'thick', but there are many who have proved them wrong. (Fletcher 1993)

Although young people's experience is often that teachers treat them differently because of their care status, Berridge et al. (1996) found that all the teachers they interviewed emphasised that looked-after children did not present significantly more problems than other young people. In fact, teachers said that since the pupils in care were such different individuals, it was difficult to perceive them as constituting a discrete group. This awareness of individual difference does not support the suggestion that teachers generally have low expectations of children in care, but neither does it indicate that there is sensitivity to particular needs that may arise from being accommodated.

In the absence of detailed research on young people's experience in school, the Ofsted and SSI inspection report on provision for accommodated children provides valuable information on schools' practice (1995). First, the report revealed that children in primary schools fared better than secondary pupils. While all primary school children had access to a broad and balanced curriculum, in some secondary schools modifications to the curriculum had reduced the range of subjects studied for some children. Exclusion, poor attendance and part-time teaching had also limited opportunities to meet curricular requirements for some accommodated children.

Assessment and recording systems were being developed in most schools, but few had an effective system which could quickly map the child's progress. School records were not usually organised in a way that would give a new school a clear picture of the child's educational history and needs.

Second, the report indicated a lack of focused and timely attention to the needs of accommodated children, especially in secondary schools, where responsibility is more diffuse. In primary schools the class teacher had an overview of the child's needs, with a supportive and co-ordinating role in relation to the child. In secondary schools the identification of a key teacher was less clear. All children had access to normal guidance arrangements, but when a child faced a crisis, the personal support was sometimes not sufficiently flexible or immediate to meet the child's needs. The authors pointed out that investing time at crisis points can reduce future stress for the child and school.

Children who needed support services were not always identified early enough. Being looked after did not confer priority for additional action, and sometimes the intervention was not flexible or immediate enough to turn around a deteriorating situation.

In most schools there was insufficient guidance on the use of confidential information, only one school having an explicit policy on confidentiality. The children reported that teachers knew too much about their personal lives, and head teachers thought that staff allowed knowledge of children's circumstances to influence their expectations.

Based on their review of the schools, care arrangements and collaboration between departments of education and social services, the report's authors concluded that little has been done in practice to boost the achievement of children in care. No strategies were in place to ensure that their education was appropriately planned and monitored, so that individual educational needs continued to be overlooked.

Discontinuity

For a substantial proportion of children in care, there are barriers to even attending school. Several sources indicate that on any one day a substantial proportion of looked-after children will not be in school. Based on a one-day census, the Audit Commission (1994) reported that 40 per cent of looked-after children were not in school for reasons other than sickness. Another single day snapshot in the former local authority of Strathclyde Region reported a similar level of absence (Lockhart *et al.* 1996).

The possible reasons for poor attendance at school are many, relating to school or care environment, the young person and the inter-relationship between all three. There is no clear evidence on whether disproportionate numbers of accommodated children are formally excluded. Maginnis (1993) reported that in Lothian Region the likelihood of a child living in residential care being excluded was 80 times the average. However, other research has not found this association (Berridge and Brodie 1998; Cullen and Lloyd 1997).

Fletcher (1995) suggested that 'exclusion' in a more general sense is a feature of the lives of looked-after children. According to her, they are a stigmatised group who feel 'dumped and punished by a care system which also punishes them'. At school they feel stigmatised by the intrusive interest of teachers and social workers, the prejudice of friends or their parents and the genuine concentration problems that come with emotional turmoil. Thus the notion of 'exclusion' extends beyond the formal sanction. Fletcher warned against making exclusion procedures and the associated appeals machinery a 'specialism'. She argued that schools should develop broad-based 'inclusion' policies to ensure that looked-after children are given the same educational opportunities as other pupils.

Another characteristic of life in care is that children frequently have to move placements and schools, often more than once. Not only does changing school entail the risk of being placed in an inappropriate class, but it might involve delays in finding a new school. The work may also be somewhat different, and young people have to get to know a new set of teachers and friends. Not surprisingly, young people are critical of the frequent changes and some report feeling disorientated and unable to focus at school:

> *I didn't know what was going on inside my head because I was moving round so much and I had to start on different pieces of work.* (Biehal *et al.* 1995)

There is ample evidence that frequent moves are a feature of life in residential and foster care, and that moves are not necessarily prompted by the needs of the children (Berridge 1985; Berridge and Cleaver 1987). Francis, Thomson and Mills (1995) suggested that moves in care were more likely for children of secondary school age. Although numbers in the study were small, over a two year period 87 per cent of secondary school children in their study experienced at least one placement change but none of the primary school children did. Francis and colleagues also noted that when there were changes of placement and school, these were more likely to be prompted by school-related rather than placement issues. The authors concluded that close liaison between social work and education is needed to anticipate when difficulties are likely to occur.

Attitudes of social workers

Social workers' attitudes and actions have been widely cited as contributing to discontinuity and poor attainment in young people's education. In particular, they have been criticised for according education a low priority, for having insufficient knowledge of the education system and for having low or vague aspirations for accommodated children (Fletcher-Campbell and Hall 1990; Aldgate *et al.* 1993).

Jackson has criticised social workers for failing to appreciate the importance of education as a potential route out of disadvantage and a means of enhancing self-esteem (Jackson 1989; 1994). These criticisms were echoed by Gilligan (1997; 1998), who pointed out the paradox that while social work's defining characteristic is its emphasis on social context and experience, the profession has lost sight of the fact that, after the family, school is the most powerful influence on children's development. He argues that school is a vital source of educational and social experiences, pointing out that its benefits are in fact greatest for children living in adverse circumstances.

Evidence that social workers have not generally placed education at the top of their agenda comes from a number of studies. Knapp, Bryson and Lewis (1985) reported that though half the children in their sample were assessed as having school-related difficulties, educational improvement was a specific objective for only six of them. Of 285 objectives listed by social workers, only 16 related to education. Similar findings have been reported by Aldgate *et al.* (1993) and Francis *et al.* (1995).

From the accounts of children who have grown up in care, we know that many experienced indifference on the part of social workers and carers as far as their education was concerned (Kahan 1979; Triseliotis and Russell 1984; Jackson 1994). Jackson (1994) carried out a study of children who had grown up in care and been educationally successful. This indicated that their success owed little to the support and encouragement of social workers. Most stated that their ability and achievement had gone unrecognised by social workers and residential staff.

It might be expected that social workers' attitudes would be changing, since current guidance seeks to increase the priority accorded to education (Social Work Services Group 1997) and the Looking After Children materials provide a framework to help ensure that schooling issues are fully addressed (Ward 1995). However, as yet there is no clear evidence as to whether they are altering perspectives and practices.

Care environment

While social workers have an important case management role, it might be argued that the environment in which children live has a more immediate impact on their school experience. Residential care has been found wanting as an educationally rich environment in terms of its physical environment and general ethos, including a tendency to tolerate non-attendance (Berridge *et al.* 1996).

The atmosphere in many children's homes has been identified as not conducive to educational activities. Frequent crises and lack of private space make it difficult to concentrate on homework, while staff may not have the time to make sure notes from school are read or children given time to talk over concerns (Berridge *et al.* 1996; Jackson and Martin 1998). Residential staff have also been criticised for failing to maximise the educational potential of leisure activities such as outings or watching TV, while resources such as books, computers and even newspapers are often in short supply (Berridge and Brodie 1998). Residential staff have also been criticised for being ill-informed about education and having low expectations of children in their care. It has been argued that because many of the staff are untrained, they do not value formal education and lack the confidence to deal effectively with schools (Berridge *et al.* 1996) or to offer individual children help with homework (Bald, Bean and Meegan 1995).

One criticism frequently levelled at children's homes is that staff tacitly accept non-attendance at school, allowing it to become part of a culture to which new entrants are quickly introduced (Biehal *et al.* 1995). In a recent study, Berridge and Brodie (1998) found that non-attendance was a major concern for staff but that they were sometimes unsure how to negotiate with the school, for example over exclusions, or how to handle outright refusal to attend. The authors concluded that a clear agency policy on non-attendance was needed.

Some of the problems identified within residential care are considered to be less applicable to foster care. Foster carers usually take a personal interest in the children they care for and the potentially negative and contaminating aspects of peer culture are largely avoided (Colton 1988). There is indeed some evidence that children in foster care do better educationally than their peers in children's homes (though the latter tend to cope with older and more 'difficult' children). Biehal *et al.* (1995) found that those young people who did get qualifications had had intensive support from foster carers, having been encouraged, for example, to stay on at school for another year or to move into further education. Similarly Jackson (1994) reported that many of the educationally successful care leavers in her survey spoke warmly about receiving support from foster carers who often advocated on their behalf with education and social services. However, other research has indicated that where foster carers' own educational achievements are modest, they may expect little of the children in their care and lack the confidence to deal effectively with schools (Triseliotis and Russell 1984; Jackson and Martin 1998).

Ineffective collaboration between social work and education

Underpinning almost all the factors contributing to poor educational outcomes for accommodated children is a lack of communication and collaboration between social work and education. This emerges as a key factor at each level, from work with individual children to strategic planning across departments (Fletcher-Campbell and Hall 1990; Walker 1994). Jackson (1989) urged that in order to improve the educational experience of looked-after children, co-operation was necessary at structural, practical and attitudinal levels.

In relation to individual children, a number of studies and reports have highlighted confusion among carers, social workers and teachers about who is responsible for supporting the child's schooling in terms of maintaining contact with the school and making decisions related to his or her education (Berridge *et al.* 1996; Aldgate *et al.* 1993; Ofsted and SSI 1995). A number of studies have found that access to at least one consistent, supportive individual can greatly enhance the child's educational motivation and achievement, and mitigate the consequences of change and loss. It is therefore important, when a move is required, to identify in conjunction with the child the key people for providing continuity and support (Kahan 1979; Jackson 1989).

In terms of care planning, Francis *et al.* (1995) noted that educational issues were discussed at most reviews but seldom in great detail since an educational representative was present at only about a third of statutory reviews. Of course, many children do not wish school staff to be present at reviews when personal matters are discussed, but neither was it clear that educational plans had been more fully considered in another forum. When asked about their educational experience, young people themselves have made a plea for more effective communication between teachers and care staff to ensure that their schooling and social or emotional needs are appropriately met (Scottish Office 1994b).

At a strategic level, Fletcher-Campbell's review of policy and practice in England and Wales (1997) revealed that only a minority of authorities had a specific policy on or were actively developing practice in relation to the education of looked-after children. This is despite the issuing of joint guidance and wide dissemination of key points from the inspection carried out by Ofsted and SSI (DoE and DoH 1994; Ofsted and SSI 1995). There is little indication from studies carried out in England that highlighting this issue alone will significantly improve children's educational experiences. Instead it would appear that improving the educational opportunities of accommodated children is a complex task which needs to be tackled at different levels and which involves social work and education staff finding new ways of working together.

Frameworks for change

It is hardly a new suggestion that social work and education should plan and work closely together. The value of close links between education and social work was recognised in Scotland by the Kilbrandon report (1964), and several Scottish councils developed joint schemes to *divert* children from care during the 1980s (Kendrick 1995b). Current legislation requires local authority departments to develop a Children's Services Plan and to collaborate in certain respects in relation to individual children. However, working together has never been easy, either at front-line or management level. Since education and social work share responsibility for the education of looked-after children, their failure to join forces too often results in the child falling between them (Walker 1994; Ofsted and SSI 1995).

Table 9.1 Framework for the education of looked-after children

LEVEL	ACTIONS
National	Guidance on good practice issued to local authorities
Local Authority	Corporate policies and action plans are developed concerning the education of children looked after
	Children's Services Plans identify the educational needs of children looked after away from home and resources in place to meet them
	Management systems are in place to monitor progress and identify changes, especially when children move school
	Managerial responsibility for the education of looked after children is established in departments of social work and education, with close co-operation between the designated officers
	Accurate information is obtained about the needs and situation in each local authority
Institution: *School*	Staff are aware of agency policy and practice in relation to looked after children
	A designated member of staff is given responsibility for overseeing needs of looked after children
	A system is in place for ensuring quick transfer of information and individual support when children change school
	Assessments are made routinely to establish whether additional input is needed
	Agreement is negotiated with each young person about how personal information about them should be shared and managed within the school
Institution: *Residential/ Foster Home*	Carers are aware of the authority's policy and expectations in relation to the education of children who are looked after
	The home is well equipped with the resources children need for homework, e.g. reference books, computers, quiet space
	Carers are well informed about school practice and curriculum
	Carers talk to children about school and encourage them in their learning
	The ethos and routines of homes promote attendance at school and convey that education in important
Individual	Social workers, carers and teachers co-operate to ensure that educational needs are taken into account when planning for children
	Education is given a high priority at child care reviews
	Young people's views are taken into account in all matters which affect their education
	Parents are encouraged to take an active role in supporting the young person in their education

Source: Fletcher-Campbell (1998a, 6)

There is now broad agreement that the key to improving the service for children lies in developing frameworks and practice which encourage collaboration across social work and education. While specialist projects can demonstrate that change is possible, their limited scope and duration usually mean that only a few children benefit and that they do not alter long-standing practices among teachers and carers. There is now general agreement that change is needed across the entire school and care systems if children's needs are to be appropriately assessed and met. Based on a review of policy and practice within England and Wales, Fletcher-Campbell proposed the framework shown in Table 9.1.

Fletcher-Campbell identified *partnership, prevention* and *equal treatment* as three key principles which should underpin practice. Partnership involves staff at all levels of social work and education knowing about each other's roles and expectations, but also entails talking to children and parents and keeping elected members informed about developments. Good collaboration should aim to prevent young people looked after being further disadvantaged within the care system, prevent some of the well-documented problems arising and ensure that accommodated young people have the same educational opportunities as their peers.

Developments in practice

During the past decade, a number of local authorities have developed services to provide educational support to accommodated children (Walker 1994). Inspired by one of Sonia Jackson's pioneering projects (Jackson 1987), the most popular approach has been to develop the role of the link teacher. Though their specific tasks vary, the essential element of the link teacher's role is to act as a bridge between home and school. Tasks include helping care staff provide appropriate educational support, linking with the child's previous school, providing teaching support in the classroom and assisting children with homework.

South Lanarkshire Educational Support Service

In Scotland one of the earliest educational support services was set up in 1985 in the Hamilton district of Strathclyde regional council, transferring to South Lanarkshire council following local government reorganisation in 1996. Developments in this authority provide a good example of how improvements can be made through a combination of teaching support, planning for individual children and collaboration between social work and education at individual, managerial and strategic level. They also demonstrate the principles of partnership, prevention and equal opportunities in practice.

Introduced as part of a policy of positive discrimination for children in residential care, the initial scheme centred on the provision of two link teachers, though equally important was the establishment of a core group of workers at local level to plan and deliver the service. This comprises the educational psychologist, a child care manager from the social work department, two link teachers employed by the education department and an officer in charge from one of the children's homes. Thus the group makes links between social work and education at managerial level and across front-line staff.

Essentially, the link teacher's role is to support young people in mainstream schooling. On entry into care, information on the young person is gathered, assessed and shared with each agency in order to identify the optimum educational placement and if necessary to determine what is needed to maintain this placement. This process involves collaboration between social work staff, psychological services, the Reporter to the Children's Hearings, young people and parents.

The individualised role of the link teacher is worked out at a post-admission meeting and is negotiated with the schools or other educational establishments. In the school, the link teacher is involved in co-operative and individual teaching for the pupil and liaises with school management and teaching staff. In the children's home, tuition is given to young people awaiting placement, whilst staff are informed about the school curriculum and encouraged to become involved in the schooling process. Hence, the link teacher has two crucial roles: ensuring that the child is able to make optimum use of education and generating effective collaboration between care and education staff. In addition, there has been training for key staff from schools and careers services.

Another key element of practice in South Lanarkshire is the drawing up of an education plan for each child in care. In order to highlight the importance of this, it is written up in a separate document, not just as part of an overall plan or review form. The main aims of developing an education plan are three-fold. First, it aids joint planning by co-ordinating information from the social worker, headteacher, link teacher and care staff, parents and young people. The second aim is to develop a framework of realistic goals in accordance with individual needs. This may highlight that remedial assistance or a gradual build-up of attendance is required. The plans encompass a broad definition of education so that social, practical, creative and physical activities are considered alongside literacy and numeracy. A third and consequent aim is to boost the young person's educational attainment and self-esteem. Every effort is made to involve parents fully in the development of the plan.

Developments elsewhere

In her most recent research, Fletcher-Campbell (1997) conducted case studies in six local authorities which had developed a discrete education support service for looked-after children similar to the South Lanarkshire scheme. On the basis of interviews with young people, carers and a wide range of education and social work staff, she concluded that these services formed a vital link between education and social services. Key points about these services included:

- Arrangements for funding varied across authorities and the nature of services reflected local circumstances and need.

- Once a discrete education support service had been established, policies, procedures and documentation had undergone rapid evolution.

- Services perceived themselves as mediators between education and social services departments. The ability to move with ease between social work and education were key skills for staff in specialist support services.

- Specialist staff were keen to assist schools and carers in supporting young people who were looked after, rather than giving direct support to individual young people. They engaged in formal training of colleagues across agencies and also in a range of supportive initiatives such as homework clubs.

- Most services focused on adolescents, though referrals of primary school age children were increasing.

- The accessibility and responsiveness of the services was much appreciated by carers and teachers.

Services of this kind are currently developing in a number of authorities. The evidence from the experience in Hamilton and from Fletcher-Campbell's research is that link teachers will be most effective when their service is part of a policy of discriminating positively in favour of accommodated children and when it is supported by systems for collaboration across social work and education. In addition, it would seem to be most beneficial when link teachers adopt a developmental and communication role, focusing on improving the educational environment and links between social work and education rather than working directly with individual young people over a long period.

Equal Chances project

Indications are that the process of establishing joint working practices based on partnership is not easy. The Equal Chances project, run by the Who Cares? Trust, was set up in two English authorities with a view to developing appropriate policies, structures and practices (Fletcher 1998). The experience of this project was that this process can be difficult. Equal Chances has identified three key stages in effecting change:

- mapping need
- identifying what each school has to do differently
- setting targets for change.

In relation to identifying need, practical difficulties such as the incompatibility of computer systems can create problems. The process can also be uncomfortable, as it involves staff confronting how the system has been letting children down in the past.

When it comes to schools changing their practices, one key issue to be addressed is how information about individual pupils should be handled. Inevitably there is a tension between identifying accommodated children as entitled to special consideration and respecting their wishes for confidentiality. The approach of the project is to include young people in the policy development process and accord individual young people the right to be consulted about which information should be disclosed and to whom. Both social workers and teachers are reported to have found it surprisingly difficult to open up this kind of discussion with young people.

The third stage is for the authority to set targets for change, based on the specific problems identified by the initial mapping of need, and to monitor progress. Joint training or creating of particular posts may be a means of reaching the required standard.

This project demonstrates in practice many of the elements of the framework proposed by Fletcher-Campbell. Well-informed joint planning and reviewing is essential, while working systems should reflect both local priorities and the views of young people. Improving educational opportunities for accommodated children requires concerted action by service planners, managers and front-line staff. A consensus emerges from the literature that this is necessary if the barriers to equal opportunity in education are to be overcome.

Concluding remarks

Our review of research, policy and practice in this field indicates that while there is little cause for complacency, there are encouraging signs that accommodated children's opportunities in school can improve. The importance of education for accommodated children has been highlighted by several major reports, while government guidance specifies what good practice should entail and the Looking After Children materials provide a framework for carrying out these requirements. Current legislation requires local authorities to collaborate in planning for children, and educational support services are being developed in a number of areas. In addition, social inclusion and education are priorities in wider government policy and the introduction of 'Higher Still' in Scotland aims to increase opportunities for all children to obtain formal qualifications.

There is, however, little evidence to support the view that the factors which contribute to poor educational outcomes have been or can be easily overcome. The research by Aldgate and colleagues demonstrated that the effects of early adversity can be long-lasting, while Berridge and Brodie reported that awareness of the importance of education will not in itself change practice if demands on carers' time do not permit them to attend to school-related concerns. From Fletcher-Campbell's survey of English authorities we can see that progress in developing joint policies and practice has been slow, and the Equal Chances project demonstrates that effecting change is a difficult and time-consuming process.

Compared with a decade ago, there is now much more appreciation of what has to be in place in order to reduce the educational disadvantage of accommodated children. However, our understanding of how best to support specific groups of children remains partial. For example, we know little about how children with disabilities fare, nor do we have much understanding of the particular issues for young people who become accommodated during their teens. The educational experiences of black children in care are also little understood (Barn *et al.* 1997; *see also* Chapter 10).

It is evident that to effect general change action is needed at several levels, but it is perhaps equally important to highlight the apparently simple messages, for example that children's educational opportunities are improved when just one adult takes an active and enduring interest in their progress.

Confusion and Perceptions: Social Work Conceptions Regarding Black Children in Scotland

Satnam Singh, Vijay K.P. Patel and Patricia Falconer

Introduction

This chapter considers how traditional social work conceptions have pre-vented the needs of children and families from black and minority ethnic communities from being identified or met. It then moves on to demonstrate how these conceptions still influence the policy and practice of social workers within Scotland.

Emerging themes

Webb (1996) observed that in the last decade social work has entered a climate of increased scrutiny, suspicion and challenge. Such radical question-ing has emanated from a wide range of perspectives and interests, including government (Webb 1996); the media; feminist perspectives (Orme 1998); and anti-discriminatory perspectives (Thompson, 1997), to name but a few. One of the more pressing critiques has come from black and anti-racist perspectives, which have challenged social workers to examine and address the racism inherent within 'social work' itself (Malahleka and Woolfe 1991). This has served to shift attention away from its previously very myopic focus on those at the receiving end of racism and discrimination. Such workers have highlighted the manner in which social workers have intervened and reacted on the presenting problems, as opposed to acknowledging both the structural inequalities and strengths that the families show in coping in the face of such adversity. Below we set out a framework for a critical under-standing of the development of social work provision to black and minority ethnic communities. Within this framework, three main themes can be identified.

First, we consider 'social work' itself. Much of the early literature gave very little attention to understanding how the nature of 'social work' inevitably underpins and frames social work's response to and relations with people from black and minority ethnic communities. This position has shifted in recent years to more fully acknowledge the historical, ideological and political context of mainstream social work (Parton 1996; Payne 1997; Dominelli 1998).

The second theme is about delineating 'what' social work is responding to. In particular it is necessary to go beyond the often misleading discourses of 'diversity' and 'multiculturalism' to examine the realities of ethnicity and racism in modern British society, including Scotland where little recognition has been given to these issues.

The third theme is an examination of social work's response to individuals and groups from black and minority ethnic communities, in particular identifying the dominant discourses and approaches which over the years have been seen to both pre-empt and inform current anti-racist approaches.

Historical underpinnings: The development of social work

The purpose at this stage is to provide a theoretical framework for understanding social work as a public institution and to begin to identify how this has underpinned and will continue to frame social work's response to a 'multi-ethnic society'. Davies (1994) challenges traditional nostalgic notions of benevolent beginnings by locating social work's origins within more specific societal and economic developments of the period:

> Social work as a formal activity originated in the nineteenth century in Britain, other European countries, and the USA in response to the undesirable social consequences of industrialisation and urbanisation. (p.41)

This perspective is useful at this stage in that it treats social work as a direct product of Western industrial society and in doing so gives some acknowledgement to the dominant forces, beliefs and values which have shaped and directed its development. These are widely accepted as Christian, industrial, democratic and humanitarian values with special emphasis given to individuation, self-determination and self-help. These values were described by Midgley (1981) as being 'fundamentally underpinned by 'white' perceptions of society, human development and human psychology'. Similarly, Dominelli (1998) later referred to 'making white norms the measuring rods of life'. It is these 'norms' which have continued to dominate the development of apparently 'universal' social work knowledge, values and practice (Doel and Shardlow 1996).

In tracing social work's development, postmodern and deconstructivist critiques should alert us to the fact that there are always other voices. Cree (1995) draws particular attention to some long-standing alternative traditions in the voluntary sector. Payne (1997) and Midgley (1981) discuss the development of social work in non-Western countries and the growth of 'non-Western' social work knowledge, values and skills both within and outwith the UK. Similarly, Langlan (1998) identifies influences, even inside mainstream social work, which testify to the existence and activity of 'other' voices and discourses within what might appear to be a very conservative institution. These include the chameleon-like development of radical, social justice, feminist, black and anti-racist perspectives.

It becomes apparent then that anti-racist or indeed any other perspective cannot be easily integrated into social work; rather, it is a site of much struggle, conflict and contradiction. Failure to acknowledge this is to risk a form of social work which espouses 'the great democratic ideals of liberty, equality and justice' whilst continuing to routinely marginalise and pathologise black and minority ethnic individuals and communities. (Younghusband, cited in Bowes and Sim 1991).

Modern Britain: Multi-racial or multi-racist?

Britain has long been recognised as a multicultural society. As far back as 1968 the then home secretary used this term to describe British society. Since then numerous political statements, policy documents and reviews have underlined this pluralist conception of British society. In the 1980s the term 'multiculturalism' achieved wide acceptance and usage within Britain's public institutions and services. As Cohen and Bains (1988) observe, there has been little in the way of formal definition of exactly what is meant by this popular and contemporary conceptualisation of British society. In particular, what is to be made of the term 'multicultural' from anti-racist and black perspectives?

Official statistics demonstrate that Britain is a racially mixed society (Office for National Statistics 1994). This, at least, is supported in the literature, in which there is agreement that the British population consists of people with diverse national origins, cultural backgrounds and religious beliefs. Skellington and Morris (1992), however, point out that Britain is also a 'racially ordered' society, and there exists a vast body of literature which demonstrates that personal, cultural and institutional racism continues to ensure unequal access to and experience in every area of politics, policy, social relations, narrative and popular culture. (Gilroy 1987).

As Cohen and Bains (1988) observe, it is necessary to recognise that it is these realities which constitute the race issue in modern Britain and continue to define the everyday experience of both Britain's black and white population.

The notion of a multi-racial society fails to acknowledge the multiple and implicit forms of racism within British society. The fact that there are different peoples living in Britain does not necessarily mean that Britain is a tolerant society. Further, the concept is criticised for its covert politicisation of race, whereby the issue of race is conveniently seen to operate in a vacuum from wider cultural, social, economic and political realities. Dominelli (1998) argues that the terms 'multi-ethnic' and 'multi-racial' have been used by the white majority to obscure the real problem which needs to be tackled, namely racism:

> Conceptualising society along these lines assumes that different racial and cultural groups have already achieved equality and in doing so neglects the contradictions engendered by social divisions such as class, race and gender. Assumed equality defines racism away rather than dealing with it and obscures the necessity of … confront[ing] racism as a structural inequality and endemic feature of society. (p.55)

Dominelli concludes: 'Britain is only multi-racial in so far as it contains people with a variety of skin colours. It is not socially and politically multi-racial' (p.55). The accepted conceptualisation of British society as multi-ethnic or multi-racial is thus found to be both inadequate and illusory. In recognising the ethnic diversity of Britain's population, it at the same time negates the inequality and discrimination experienced by black and minority ethnic communities. Despite this fact, 'multi-ethnic' or 'multicultural' remain the dominant banners under which the race issue in British society is encapsulated.

The Scottish context

Whilst all of this is true for Scotland, it is also necessary to draw attention to some of the particular issues of ethnicity and racism within Scotland. As most commentators on the Scottish situation observe, race relations in Scotland have long been clouded by a presumed underlying ideology of equality and commonality amongst all peoples, which continues to be reinforced by popular Scottish history and culture. McCluskey (1991) comments that Scotland has long regarded itself as culturally separate from England, and in doing so has been keen to shed any part in its history of empire, colonialism and imperialism. This has helped to sustain an idealised view that 'Scotland has good race relations' and that 'there is no racism here'. This perception, whilst attractive, is clearly challenged by evidence from Race Equality Councils, the Commission for Racial Equality (CRE) and the black and minority ethnic communities.

The overall proportion of the population from black and minority ethnic communities is seen to be significantly lower than it is in England, and partly as a result race has hardly featured on the Scottish political agenda. The 1991 Census suggested that 1.3 per cent of the Scottish population identified itself as being from an ethnic minority community. A variety of bodies have used these figures to demonstrate that the black and minority ethnic communities are small, and have inferred from this that issues around racism, racial harassment and service delivery are less relevant in a Scottish context. The Commission for Racial Equality (Scotland) indicated that the global figure is inaccurate and misleading, because the Poll Tax and immigration legislation led to a number of people not taking part in the census. Moreover, as Bowes and Sim (1991) point out, this general picture conceals local concentrations of black people, principally in the urban centres of Glasgow and Edinburgh where even the official figures show populations closer to 3–4 per cent (Office of Population Census and Survey 1991). In any case, the size of the relevant communities does not mean that exposure to racism is any less. The experience of employment, education and criminal justice services for black and minority ethnic communities in Scotland is broadly similar to that documented for England. Most Scottish local authorities have been seen to ignore the needs of black communities and individuals on account of their 'low numbers'. As a result, no account is taken of their particular experiences or needs, so the non-white population is expected to 'fit in' with existing (white) services (McCluskey 1991).

Despite the limited attention being given to the issue of race in Scotland there is much to suggest that the experience of both personal, cultural and institutional racism is just as ingrained in the fabric of Scottish society as it is in the rest of Britain. Furthermore, the long-standing pattern within Scotland of relating to and explaining race purely in terms of biology and/or numbers has been increasingly seen as a powerful force in sustaining racist ideology in Scottish society (Gilroy 1987). Miles and Muirhead (1986) concluded over a decade ago that 'racism in Scotland [remains] a matter for further investigation'.

Social work's response

Tracing social work's response to Britain's black and minority ethnic population is a task which can prove both difficult and elusive. Braham, Rattansi and Skellington (1992) suggest that this is largely due to the fact that social work's 'response' has, for the most part, been absorbed within the wider ideals of social work itself – those of liberty, equality and justice amongst all peoples, regardless of race or colour. Connelly (1989) observes that this underpinning ideology of universalism has been gradually eroded over the years, revealing, at best, an intrinsic 'colour blindness'. This realisation, arising largely from black struggles, has gradually forced the issue of social work's response onto the mainstream agenda.

So what should social work be responding to? We can identify a number of areas and suggest that social work should be:

1. responding to an ethnically and culturally diverse British population (Office for National Statistics 1994)

2. responding to a racially ordered society, in which the effects and impact of racism continue to ensure that black people experience a different reality from that experienced by the dominant 'white' majority, as revealed in access to employment, housing, health and social services (Cohen and Bains 1986)

3. responding to and challenging institutional racism, not least within the institution of social work itself (CRE 1989).

These three aspects can be seen to constitute the current social work task in relation to a 'multi-ethnic' Britain. They are clearly outlined in the Central Council for Education and Training of Social Work (CCETSW) Paper 30:

> Social workers need to be competent to work in a society, which is multi-racial and multicultural. CCETSW will therefore seek to ensure that students are prepared not only for ethnically sensitive practice but also to challenge and confront institutional and other forms of racism. (CCETSW 1991, s.1.18)

It might be assumed that this has long been the social work task, since the very same tenets can be seen to underpin the Race Relations Act 1976. As Thompson (1997) observes: 'One aspect of the relationship between racism and social work that is often not appreciated is that the foundations of anti-racist practice are actually enshrined in the [1976] legislation' (p.72).

The 1976 Race Relations Act is generally considered as the first formal recognition and response to the racial inequality and discrimination within British society.[1] However, not until recently has the Act become widely

---

1   It should be noted however that the 1976 Act was the third Race Relations Act in just over a decade.

recognised for its explicit anti-racist approach. The 1976 Act makes dis-crimination on racial grounds unlawful and places a statutory duty on local authorities '*to make appropriate arrangements to ensure that their functions are carried out with due regard for the need to eliminate unlawful discrimination and to promote equality of opportunity and good relations between persons of different racial groups*' (s.71).

However, the journey between the 1976 Race Relations Act and the present day belies the proactive anti-racist intentions and foundations of that Act. For example, studies particular to Scotland document a very low awareness among managers of statutory duties under the Race Relations Act (Cadman and Chakrabarti 1992). This belies the image of social work's response as following an apparently progressive development from an assimilation approach through multi-culturalism and ethnically sensitive practice to finally arriving at the present anti-racist approach (Cheetham 1982; Dominelli 1998). What emerges, however, is a less 'progressive' picture of social workers continuing to ignore the needs of black and minority ethnic communities and individuals.

Dominelli (1998) identified that 'White peoples efforts' to overcome the weaknesses of the assimilation approach led to the development in the 1980s of 'multicultural' and 'ethnically-sensitive' approaches. These were seen to herald the 'embodiment of equality' between different 'races' and cultures, drawing on a model of equal opportunities coupled with cultural diversity and mutual tolerance (Cheetham 1982). Whilst such approaches sought to recognise cultural strengths and encourage understanding of 'cultural differ-ences', they have been heavily criticised by black perspectives for failing to acknowledge the inequality existing between different ethnic and cultural groups in Britain. Furthermore, such approaches have been criticised as being a 'diversionary activity' which has ultimately blamed those at the receiving end of racism instead of the social relations enforcing it (Gilroy 1987).

The most recent approach that emerged from these failings has been anti-racism, which has been predominantly recognised within the literature as being the official social work response for the 1990s and beyond (CCETSW 1991). Dominelli (1998) states that the overriding emphasis of an anti-racist approach is on change, at both a personal and an organisational level: 'Anti-racist perspectives focus on transforming the unequal social relations shaping social interaction between Black and White people into egalitarian ones' (p.80).

These approaches have demanded often vigorous and shifting attention in the social work literature and, as was alluded to earlier, are generally regarded as representing three key stages in the 'progressive' history of social work's response to ethnic diversity in Britain. Whilst there is some basis for this conception there is also much to suggest that social work's response, particularly in practice, has been far from progressive.

Research evidence in relation to children's services

Having considered the conceptions, how do these operate within a Scottish context? Research was undertaken by the authors in response to growing concerns expressed by many people in a range of settings about the inadequacy of services for black and minority ethnic children. A number of forums pointed to both scarcity of provision and inequality of access. These included:

- A conference organised by Strathclyde Regional Council Social Work Department in 1993 in association with Strathclyde Community Relations Council, 'Ethnic minority issues in Child Care'.
- The Scottish Black Workers Forum child care workshop in 1993.
- A conference of the Scottish Black Workers Forum in 1994, 'Lift As We Climb'.

Interest in this issue was reinforced by the fact that the Children (Scotland) Act 1995 introduced new duties for local authorities to pay due 'regard to a child's religious persuasion, racial origin, and cultural and linguistic background'. This responsibility was already present in the Children Act 1989, applying to authorities in England and Wales, and it reinforced the provisions of the 1976 Race Relations Act.

Whilst some social workers were trying to do this previously, there was little in terms of guidance which had supported or empowered staff in meeting such needs. The 1995 Act was therefore a significant milestone in the provision of services to Scotland's black communities in that it enshrined in social work statute the specific duties to identify, assess and meet the needs of black and minority ethnic children.

Purpose and design of the study

The purpose of the study was twofold:

1. To try to establish the actual numbers of black and minority ethnic children receiving statutory and non-statutory services.
2. To assess how local authorities and voluntary agencies provide services to children and families from black and minority ethnic communities.

To help provide a broader picture, within the appropriate context, it was necessary to consider the state and nature of policies in relation to both personnel and service provision.

The study was undertaken by a partnership comprising Barnardos Family Placement Services (FPS), the Scottish Black Workers Forum (SBWF) and Children in Scotland. Each of these organisations has an interest in services for children from black and minority ethnic communities. Barnardos FPS provide Adoption & Fostering services to some of the most disadvantaged and vulnerable children in Scotland. The Scottish Black Workers Forum is a network of black workers within the personal social services and community education throughout Scotland. Children in Scotland is a major research and development organisation working towards improving services for all children in Scotland. The partnership reflected a diversity of knowledge and also actively demonstrated the principle of agencies working in partnership, which was central to the 1995 Children (Scotland) Act.

A standardised questionnaire was designed to focus on three areas: children, policy and service delivery. This was sent to a total of 64 agencies:

Table 10.1 List of respondents	
All the local authorities	32
A sample of voluntary agencies from the main cities:	
Glasgow	3
Edinburgh	3
Dundee	3
Aberdeen	3
Inverness	3
Voluntary organisations from rural Scotland	12
Large national voluntary sector child care organisations	5
TOTAL	**64**

The voluntary organisations from each of the cities were selected on the basis that one was working exclusively with black communities, one exclusively with the white community, and one with mixed groups. By selecting the sample in this way it was possible to obtain a reasonable level of representation and a snapshot of the 'state of play' at that time.

A total of 33 questionnaires were returned (51.5%). Nineteen were completed by the local authorities (57%) and 14 by the voluntary organisations (42%). It should be noted that the majority of responses were from agencies in the main cities.

Findings in relation to children and services

Fifty-three per cent of the local authorities and 77 per cent of the voluntary organisations said that they monitored the numbers of black and minority ethnic children who use their services. These results raise a number of important considerations. First, there is a considerable divergence in practice between the local authorities and voluntary organisations in relation to monitoring. Second, local authorities who have the statutory responsibility of providing services to promote the welfare of children in need are doing so with very inadequate information about the users of the service. This would serve to evidence the point made by Gilroy (1987) about unequal access. It raises the question of how the duty to pay due regard to a child's religious persuasion, racial origin, and cultural and linguistic background can actually be met if mechanisms for recording and monitoring are not in place.

As far as results on practice issues are concerned, a total of 718 black and minority ethnic children were receiving services from the agencies that responded. Local authorities worked with 141 cases (19%); the rest (81%) were involved with voluntary child care agencies. This marked difference is only partly explained by the fact that some of the voluntary organisations had a specific remit to work with black and minority ethnic children.

Six hundred and sixty children were receiving home-based services and supports. The voluntary sector was much better at having staff from black and minority ethnic communities working with the children. In general, the voluntary sector is the main provider of community-based services to black children and families. A question worth exploring is whether the higher uptake is related to the presence of staff from black and minority ethnic communities or the location of such projects. In this respect, therefore, the role of the voluntary sector in both prevention and support work should not be underestimated.

There were few cases involving children being looked after or accommodated away from home. Eight were in residential settings and 18 in substitute family placements. None of the children in residential care had any contact with staff from black or minority ethnic communities. Only two children were placed within a black foster family, so the great majority of black children in substitute family based care were living with white families. Anecdotal evidence would suggest that these white families are often in fairly rural areas themselves. As a result there is far less potential for children to have contact with their community of origin and carers will find it harder to promote their heritage. Research, as yet unpublished, by de Lima has highlighted the increased barriers preventing people from black and minority ethnic communities living in rural communities from maintaining their social networks and identities.

The lack of black residential workers and black foster families is an important issue in terms of children having access to someone who may have a better understanding of racism and the feelings that it engenders. Recent research evidence continues to confirm the importance of same-race carers in promoting the welfare and resilience of black children (Thoburn, Norfurd and Rashid 1999). Black child care workers in Scotland have reported instances of residential units being unable or unwilling to deal with racist behaviour from staff or young people.

Given the lack of appropriate services it may be worth considering models developed in Manchester (Bibini) and London of residential units specifically for young people from black and minority ethnic communities. Such resources are geared up to provide a variety of support which can promote and support a child's heritage. Initiatives in Scotland such as Khandan (Barnardos) have highlighted that with appropriate resources, carers from black and minority ethnic communities can be recruited.

It is clear that black children looked after are at a disadvantage, and serious questions are raised as to how the needs arising from that child's racial origin, religious persuasion, and linguistic and cultural background are being assessed and met. Irrespective of where children are residing, it is important to know how issues of children's heritage are being supported. As part of the questionnaire, respondents were asked: *How are staff encouraged or helped to meet racial, cultural, linguistic and religious needs of black and minority ethnic children?* There was little difference between the comments of local authority and voluntary sector respondents. Among them were:

> *Staff would be briefed on issues*
>
> *Equal opportunity policy through training*
>
> *General race awareness training*
>
> *Anti-racist training for unit heads who have copies of 'Care for children from ethnic minorities'.*

It was encouraging to see that some respondents are recognising the importance of children's racial, religious, cultural and linguistic needs. The responses demonstrated, however, that there is little differentiation between concepts such as the impact of racism, cultural difference and cultural deprivation. Ideas of equal opportunities were confused with multiculturalism and anti-racist practice. At best this suggests willingness, at worst culpable neglect. It further raises questions of the nature and relevance of the training that has been provided. Does it come back to practitioners operating in a 'colour-blind' manner?

Staffing issues

In relation to information about personnel working with black and minority ethnic children, the picture is slightly better, with 88 per cent of local authorities and 79 per cent of voluntary organisations monitoring the ethnicity of their staff. The higher levels of monitoring of personnel for local authorities may be due to the fact that this is a process undertaken in relation to human resources in general rather than to inform social work policy and practice. The data from local authorities highlighted that monitoring was seen as an exercise to gather statistical information primarily for personnel departments. However, there was little indication from any of the responses as to how this monitoring actually relates to policy, provision or planning. In only two instances did they suggest that monitoring might be used to inform future recruitment policy or practice: 'to inform future appointments'; 'to ensure staff group reflects authority population'.

The responses from the voluntary sector were not significantly different, although a slightly higher number gave stronger indications that monitoring was used to inform future policy and practice. Given the lack of interface between monitoring of ethnicity and policy and practice, it is natural to question what purpose monitoring actually serves. The results would confirm a widely held belief among black workers that any monitoring undertaken is tokenistic and merely pays lip-service to the requirements arising from the 1976 Race Relations Act.

The survey revealed that a total of 65 staff from black and minority ethnic communities were working directly with children in the 33 agencies, an average of two per agency. Local authorities employed 21 (32%) and the remaining 44 (68%) were employed in the voluntary sector. The majority of black staff (92%) were employed at a basic social worker level equivalent or below. Only four were in a senior social worker equivalent capacity, and only one in a senior management position.

Further examination of the figures for the voluntary sector showed that out of the 44 staff from black and minority ethnic communities, only one was employed at a senior social work grade. Six of the 44 were in full-time posts with permanent contracts, 12 were on part-time contracts, 22 (50%) were employed on a sessional basis and three were on full-time temporary contracts.

In the light of the above information it is easy to see why agencies say that they do employ staff from black and minority ethnic communities, whilst black workers are acutely aware that there are inadequate numbers of staff from black and minority ethnic communities to support families effectively. Given the current low numbers of both black staff and carers, it is hard to see how the guidance from the Scottish Office that '*background should be catered for within placement, with carers, or one or more staff members sharing the child's religion and heritage*' (Scottish Office 1997b) can be satisfactorily met.

Agency policies

In their replies to the questionnaires, 61 per cent of local authorities and 50 per cent of the voluntary organisations said they had policies relating specifically to service delivery, with similar numbers having specific policies relating to the needs of black and minority ethnic children. The responses in relation to supporting children demonstrated the lack of connection between policy and practice, e.g. '*equal opportunities policy through training*'. This statement begs some answers to the following questions: Does that lead to children being supported? And how are equal opportunities defined? This reinforces the point made earlier by Dominelli about how certain concepts can obscure the real problem. Experience throughout the UK has shown that for meaningful change to occur, initiatives must be supported from the top by clear policies which can be monitored, and cannot just rely on the goodwill and commitment of practitioners on the ground.

Policies on their own are of little value. They are of course an important starting point and provide a mechanism by which service delivery can be measured. But to be effective, policies need to be fully integrated with appropriate monitoring and reviewing procedures.

Subsequent developments

Since the research was undertaken there have been a number of developments, especially in the political arena. There is a new Scottish Parliament, with a powerful committee structure. The Consultative Steering Group has suggested that the new structure will mean committees will be able to include non-MSPs in their membership. They will also be the main means by which individuals, organisations and communities of interest can engage with the parliament (Common Purpose Scottish Conference 1998). This structure, if agreed, will provide two benefits: a clearer and easier route for communities to engage with the decision-makers; and a more accountable body.

Whilst the new parliament is potentially a very exciting development, there are weaknesses to the structure, especially in the field of race equality. The Scottish Parliament can legislate in a number of areas but not equal opportunities (which includes race equality), which is reserved for Westminster. The Parliament does have the much weaker power to debate and monitor policy. It should also be noted that there are no MSPs from a black and minority ethnic community.

Difficulties and uncertainties may arise at the interface between the two parliaments. This was illustrated by the responses to the Stephen Lawrence inquiry. The inquiry has led to a lot of media attention and, more importantly, some reflection on the nature of racism in British society. It is worthwhile quoting from two relevant sections of Lord McPherson's inquiry report:

> If racism is to be eliminated from our society there must be a co-ordinated effort to prevent its growth. This need goes well beyond the Police Services. Just as important, and perhaps more so, will be similar efforts needed from other agencies, particularly in the field of education. (McPherson 1999 46:34)

The inquiry examined the nature of 'institutional racism', which was defined as:

> the collective failure of an organisation to provide an appropriate and professional service to people because of their colour, culture or ethnic origin. It can be seen or detected in processes, attitudes and behaviour which amount to discrimination through unwitting prejudice, ignorance, thoughtlessness and racist stereotyping which disadvantage minority ethnic people. (McPherson 1999 6:34)

There have been a number of initiatives stemming from the inquiry. It is unclear how these and future race equality initiatives apply to Scotland. For example, will the targets set by the Home Secretary for recruitment of police officers from black and minority ethnic communities be applicable? Real fears were expressed that once again Scotland's black and minority ethnic communities would miss out. 'What we wanted to see here was a full-scale implementation – not a delay, not another advisory group' (A. Anwar quoted in the *Scotsman*, 15 July 1999).

It is worth noting that the Scottish parliament has accepted that institutionalised racism does exist in Scotland (Jim Wallace, Deputy First Minister, quoted in the *Scotsman*, 13 July 1999). This is just as well, as research into structural inequalities does demonstrate institutional racism as defined by Lord McPherson:

Pakistanis and Bangladeshis are easily the poorest groups in the country. High unemployment among men; low levels of economic activity among women; low pay; and large family sizes: these all contribute to a situation in which 60 per cent of Pakistanis and Bangladeshis are poor. This is four times the poverty rate found among white people. The new, more detailed, data confirms the previous survey's estimate that Pakistani and Bangladeshi households were four times as likely to be 'poor' as white households. Pakistanis and Bangladeshis were much, much more likely to be poor than any other ethnic group. (Berthoud 1998).

Many families own poor quality housing in inner city areas, and lack resources to improve or maintain it. Without loans or grants for house maintenance or improvement, these homeowners are unlikely to obtain good quality accommodation outside the social rented sector. (Bowes, Dar and Sim 1998)

Many Pakistani experiences of council housing were negative, and many families had suffered harassment. Ten households in our sample had given up secure council accommodation to move to other, sometimes less secure, tenures in safer areas. (Bowes *et al.*1998)

Implications

There is a real need for more detailed research into the needs of black and minority ethnic communities and, especially, children. Research from Child-Line highlighted that black children 'endure blatant unrelenting openly racist harassment and bullying on a daily basis' (McLeod 1996). Anecdotal evidence would also suggest that issues of conflict within families and across generations are leading to young people becoming homeless. Additionally, families with disabled children are not receiving the same service as their white counterparts. These issues need to be investigated and accurate figures obtained for policy and practice considerations in order for us to move towards fair and appropriate service provision.

There are a number of questions needing to be answered:

- Do the categories for children in need and the priorities set out by local authorities reflect the issues and realities for black children and young people in Scotland?
- Are the assessment procedures appropriate?
- How have black families been consulted?
- What are the low numbers of take-up within statutory settings indicative of?

- Is it about black and minority ethnic communities not being aware of services? Are needs being met elsewhere?

- Are black children somehow protected by virtue of being members of black families, despite poverty, poor housing and other structural disadvantages? Garbarino (1999) would suggest that within a US context, race is a risk factor. Within a Scottish context, do the lower levels of delinquency reflect families from black and minority ethnic communities being better able to support their children?

The research does enable some recommendations to be made.

Policy

The Scottish Office has provided clear direction through the three volumes of guidance notes to the Children (Scotland) Act 1995. Local authorities and voluntary organisations need to develop and review their current policies on all aspects of service delivery. Procedures need to be developed to ensure that policies do lead to action. This is in line with a report by the Race Equality Unit, which recommended:

> Managers and practitioners will be greatly assisted by developing clear policies at corporate and directorate level. These should address equal opportunities and employment, service provision, and inform procedures and practice. Policies need not be dogmatic rather they should set standards and establish guidelines that enable staff to make appropriate decisions. (Barn, Sinclair and Ferdinand 1997)

Monitoring

There needs to be a directive from the Scottish Office requiring ethnicity to be recorded. The Looking After Children forms (*see* Chapter 8) do give attention to ethnic identity, but to be effective, information has to be recorded and analysed. The information should be published regularly and made available in a variety of formats. This information also needs to feed into the formulation of Children's Services Plans.

Training

Despite the emphasis placed on anti-racist and culturally sensitive practice there is still a long way to go before practitioners will be skilled and confident enough to take on some of the work. The Scottish Office has published a handbook for practitioners, but that in itself will not be enough (Scottish Office 1998b). Existing training on the Children (Scotland) Act 1995 has touched on issues relating to black and minority ethnic children and there is a need for further training at all levels.

Conclusion

It is evident from the research findings that existing social work conceptions do not allow for adequate provision of services to families from black and minority ethnic communities. In order for that to change, whilst practitioners need to consider their practice, much more leadership and work is needed at a strategic level.

There has been much hype about a 'New Scotland', a Scotland that will be more accountable to the people and focus more on their needs. We hope that comes to pass, but in order for it to do so the parliament needs to provide a clear lead on developing and pursuing the race equality agenda. Without it families from black and minority ethnic communities will continue to be 'invisible' within social work. We need to be able to move on from a state where 'the response of social service departments to the existence of multi-racial communities has been patchy, piecemeal and lacking in strategy' (Association of Directors of Social Services (ADSS) 1978). Our research findings, along with the work of Barn et al. (1997), would suggest that that statement is still true in Scotland.

The recommendations from the research set out one potential starting point: it is, as Lord McPherson stated, 'incumbent upon every institution to examine their policies and the outcome of their policies and practice to guard against disadvantaging any section of our communities.' (McPherson 1999 46:70) We would also add, in looking to the future, that far more proactive work needs to happen, especially outwith the central belt of Scotland.

The impetus for the research arose from a concern for the needs of Scotland's black children. The results of the research reinforce the analysis that social work has a long way to go if it is to provide any meaningful support to black and minority ethnic communities. It also needs to be carried out in a context which acknowledges the perceptions and realities that black and minority ethnic communities face on a day-to-day basis.

PART III

Child Protection

From Childhood to Adulthood: The Outcomes of a Twenty-year Follow-up of Children who Failed to Thrive

Dorota Iwaniec

Introduction

The most basic needs of humans throughout their lives are fairly simple: we need to breathe air and gain nutrition. From the moment of birth, when babies are encouraged to take a breath and cry for the first time, it is clear that they can usually satisfy these needs by themselves. However, for the nutrition requirement they will need a lot of help. Newborn babies and children rely on others, notably their parents or other care-givers, to provide the nutrition they need to survive. Childhood is a busy time with many things to learn and much growing up to do, both physically and psychologically. In secure environments, fuelled by adequate nutrition, children will thrive, growing healthily and happily.

But nutrition alone will not facilitate positive psychosocial growth. It is now a cliché that a baby needs a close, confident and caring physical and emotional contact with the parents, be it mother, or mother surrogate, or father, in order to grow and develop vigorously and fulfil its potential. The absence of such continuing nurturance and physical intimacy can bring about anxiety in the child, fretting and disruption of biological functions. It is now recognised that infants deprived of their accustomed parental care, such as body contact, good-quality interaction and stimulation, may develop a profound depression (sometimes referred to as 'anaclitic depression') with consequent lack of appetite, wasting and even marasmus, leading to death (Spitz 1945; Bowlby 1969). One of the indices of basic trust and security in an infant is stable feeding behaviour. In order for eating to be nutritionally beneficial and enjoyable, it requires conditions that denote a relatively benign and calm state of psychosomatic harmony. Indeed, it was suggested as early as the beginning of the seventeenth century by Dr Harrington that the secretion of the digestive juices might be induced by pleasurable emotions and inhibited by unpleasant ones. As he put it:

> Use three physicians still, First Doctor Quiete, next Doctor Marryman and Doctor Diet'. (Harrington 1608/1920)

Researchers investigating failure-to-thrive children and their carers, and practitioners dealing with such cases, will find this quotation very poignant, as it sets a scene that is often absent in the lives of those children.

Until the first part of the twentieth century the condition of a wasted body was called marasmus and was always associated with some known or unknown physical disease. Only a few decades ago, when growth began to be studied scientifically, was it realised that what we now call failure-to-thrive is not a clear-cut disease but a symptom (or more accurately a syndrome) which may have many causes. The aetiological factors are complex and varied; they include inadequate nutrition, malabsorption, chronic infection, major structural congenital abnormalities, and metabolic and endocrine defects. However, there are some infants and young children who fail to thrive in whom none of the above factors are obvious and whose present management and well-being is problematic.

While most children grow and develop satisfactorily, some lag behind, and their well-being causes concern. These children are described as failing to thrive; they are significantly smaller than their peers and can be expected to have poor outcomes. They can be found in all social classes and levels of society. Without help one can expect their physical growth, cognitive progress and emotional development to be affected.

Children who fail to thrive as infants are found to be at high risk of developmental delays, personality problems, abuse and neglect, and even death. The effects of early malnutrition may be extensive given the rapid period of growth, particularly brain growth, which occurs during the first five years of life (Wynne 1996). Slow weight gain in infancy can also lead to subsequent stunting of growth. If successful intervention does not take place at an early stage, failure-to-thrive may lead to the distortion of the parent–child relationship, serious attachment disorders, disturbed behaviour and developmental impairment. These effects may be long lasting, persisting even into adulthood, as the results of the follow-up presented here indicate.

The aim of this chapter is to share with readers the author's research findings accumulated over the last 22 years. Although literature on failure-to-thrive based on various research projects and practice experience is quite extensive, there are only a few long-term follow-up studies available and this is the first one of 20-year duration. The rest of the chapter will cover:

- an overview of failure-to-thrive
- findings of other follow-up studies
- findings and discussion of the current study.

An overview of failure to thrive

Failure-to-thrive is defined as failure to grow, in terms of weight and height, and develop in a healthy and vigorous way. It is conceived as a variable syndrome of severe growth-retardation, delayed skeletal maturation, and problematic psychomotor development, which are often associated with illnesses, nutrition inadequate for normal growth, acute feeding difficulties, disturbed mother–child interaction and relationship, insecure attachment, family dysfunctioning and poverty (Iwaniec, Herbert and McNeish 1985a; Frank and Zeisel 1988; Drotar 1991).

The condition may result from organic illness or psychosocial causes (i.e. the failure of the child's environment to provide appropriate nurturing), but further complexities occur when organic and non-organic factors combine. This combination is more common than was thought, and is apparent when treatment of what had seemed to be a clear-cut organic condition does not produce the expected improvement (Frank and Zeisel 1988). Iwaniec (1995) pointed out that a child who fails to thrive because of illness might also be rejected, neglected, and severely deprived of attention and care, so that the effects of the illness are exacerbated by parental maltreatment.

Failure-to-thrive is generally defined in terms of growth. When children are undernourished they fail to gain weight. After a while their growth in length also falters. On growth charts they drop below the third or fifth percentiles of weight or height. Most children are diagnosed as FTT when their weight or height percentiles are low; others are diagnosed when their growth crosses percentile lines downwards. Undernutrition also impairs brain growth, so the head circumference is measured as well.

The hypothesis of a psychological aetiology for the non-organic failure-to-thrive syndrome has its roots in the extensive literature on the effects of institutionalisation, hospitalism and maternal deprivation in children. Some of the best early documentation of the failure-to-thrive syndrome was that of Spitz (1945), Talbot et al. (1947) and Widdowson (1951). In the late 1950s and 1960s studies of growth-failure and developmental delay similar to those previously carried out on institutionalised children were replicated on infants and young children living at home. Researchers such as Coleman and

Provence (1957), Barbaro and Shaheen (1967), Leonard, Rhymes and Solnit (1966), and Fischhoff, Whitten and Pettit (1971) postulated that maternal psychopathology, family dysfunction and inadequate nurturing were the major aetiological factors contributing to failure-to-thrive. They found that the mothers under investigation were depressed, angry and helpless, had low self-esteem and felt isolated, generally presenting a constellation of psychological features conducive to inadequate mothering, including limited ability to perceive and assess accurately the environment, their own needs, and those of their children (especially nutritional needs). Alcoholism, marital problems, unemployment and poverty were found in many cases.

Bullard *et al.* (1967) argued that failure-to-thrive is a result of emotional neglect demonstrated by lack of interest in the child, absence of physical contact (such as holding, cuddling, smiling at, and playing and communicating with the child) and being insensitive to the child's signals of hunger and lack of emotional nurturing. The children they studied came from middle-class families where material standards were high, and they argued that FTT is not always linked to poverty.

Pollitt, Eichler and Chan (1975) conducted a control study of social development, emotional adaptation and functioning of mothers of failure-to-thrive children. Results indicated that mothers of FTT children did not show overt psychopathologies. The largest differences between groups were found in the scores drawn from the mother–child interaction check-list. Mothers in the experimental group showed less frequent verbal and physical contact and were less positively reinforcing and warm. Substantial differences were also noted in maternal affection, described as 'inoperant' in many of the index mothers. Similarly, Iwaniec *et al.* (1985a), when comparing FTT with two control groups, found that mothers of FTT children did not differ significantly from the norm in their personality structures. However, significant differences were found in mother–child bonding, feeding difficulties, mother–child interaction, children's behavioural style, and lack of help and support for the mothers. Many of these mothers showed a sense of helplessness and despair when trying to feed the child, quite often straining an already fragile relationship. Serious interactional problems have been found in FTT children and their mothers (Pollitt and Eichler 1976; Herbert and Iwaniec 1979; Skuse 1989; Hanks and Hobbs 1993; Iwaniec 1995; Raynor and Rudolf 1996). These authors reported maladaptive maternal reactions to rearing difficulties created by various behavioural styles in their children. Active, vigorous, irritable, hypertonic, stubborn, demanding and aggressive children showed severe disturbances in relationships with their mothers, involving considerable struggle and anger, especially during feeding.

Mother–child interaction was tense, anxious and often hostile, which had a negative reaction on child food intake and subsequent refusal of food. Quiet, lethargic, withdrawn, undemanding children seldom experienced inter-action, had little physical and emotional contact, and were often overlooked and ignored. Pollitt and Eichler (1976) and Iwaniec *et al.* (1985a) found that many FTT children were temperamentally 'difficult'. This suggested that a child's behaviour might contribute to the distortion of parental perception and attitudes towards the child, and, consequently, negatively affect the parent–child relationship and interaction, in some cases leading to maltreat-ment. This two-way process in parent–child transaction is often overlooked or considered irrelevant when planning intervention.

Many researchers identified inadequate caloric intake and problematic mother–child interactions during feeding/eating as a major contributory factor to poor growth (Iwaniec 1983; Skuse, Wolke and Reilly 1992; Hampton 1996). However, inadequate calorific intake has many roots and tends to differ from case to case. The range is wide, starting from a child's difficulties in feeding, for example poor sucking, vomiting, swallowing or falling asleep while being fed, to a parent's difficulties in introducing solids, lack of understanding of children's nutritional needs, or knowledge about what to feed, when and how. Many mothers are found to be depressed, socially isolated, inexperienced in child rearing, lacking access to help, advice and support, or living in adverse social and economic circumstances. Other features are present in some though not all cases. These include dislike, rejection and neglect of the child; life habits, such as alcohol or drug abuse; mental health problems; and deliberate starvation of the child. Munchausen's syndrome by proxy is increasingly linked to growth failure that results from administration of laxatives/medication to induce vomiting, or from the child starving by fabricating that he/she is ill or is allergic to many food items. A strong statistical association has also been found between maternal eating habits and attitudes to food (i.e. anorexia and bulimic tendencies) and non-organic failure-to-thrive in children. As we can see, aetiological factors are complex and varied. Comprehensive assessment is essential in order to establish what the contributory factors to failure-to-thrive are and how the problem is maintained.

Psychosocial short stature

Children who are defined as having psychosocial short stature (formerly called psychosocial dwarfism) are those who are exceptionally short and remain stunted for a considerable time, although there may be no obvious organic reason for this. Weight is normally below that expected for the height. The child might appear well-nourished, but that may be deceptive because neither weight nor height is normal for the chronological age (Skuse 1989). It is believed that children exposed to severe stress and emotional adversity may be stunted in growth and that functioning of growth-hormone secretion could be arrested. Once the child is removed from the stressful environment growth and development quickly accelerate, but if returned to the same environment a marked deterioration becomes evident and behaviour worsens (Iwaniec 1995; Skuse *et al.* 1996).

This disorder has been known of for many years and extensively studied. Some investigators hypothesise the existence of a physiological pathway whereby emotional deprivation affects the neuroendocrine system, which regulates growth. Some researchers (Talbot *et al.* 1947; Patton and Gardner 1962; Powell, Brasel and Blizzard 1967; Apley *et al.* 1971; Green, Deutsch and Campbell 1987; Blizzard and Bulatovic 1993) favoured a theory of emotional influence on growth, with secondary hormonal insufficiencies as the main cause of psychosocial short stature. Whitten (1976), on the other hand, concluded that such children were simply starved and therefore did not grow. Skuse *et al.* (1996) found that a proportion of short-stature hyperphagic children live in stressful social circumstances, have growth-hormone insufficiency and possess a special vulnerability that is genetically determined.

Children of short stature may be divided into two groups: hyperphagic and anorexic. Hyperphagic children are those who present excessive and unusual overeating behaviour such as having a high hunger drive, drinking excessively, hoarding food, searching for food during the night, eating non-food items, scavenging food from waste bins, eating other people's leftovers, eating voraciously, gorging and vomiting. Additionally, they are poor sleepers, present acute conduct problems, have disturbed toileting behaviour (smearing faeces, urinating in inappropriate places, encopresis), poor attention-span, and severe problems in social relationships both at home and at school. Attachment behaviour at home is grossly insecure, avoidant or ambivalent/anxious, or disorganised. In short they are unloved.

Anorexic children are very poor eaters, have little appetite, show faddiness and refuse to eat. When pressed to eat they heave, store food in their mouths, and chew and swallow with difficulty. They tend to be anxious, apprehensive, withdrawn, passive and unable to stand up for themselves. Relationships with other family members are poor and marked by fear and apprehension. While at school they tend to be excessively quiet and uninvolved, unable to concentrate, and are often bullied by other children.

These authors suggest that acute stress affects hormonal functioning and that the excessive eating of these children is a reaction (a compensatory measure) to cope with stress. They also suggest that excessive appetite is not simply a response to food restriction, but is much more associated with acute stress. They further propose that children of short stature of the under-eating (anorexic) group are stunted because of chronic nutritional deficiencies.

Follow-up studies

There are few systematic long-term studies of growth and development in non-organic failure-to-thrive children (NOFTT). The longest follow-up, of 13 years, is that by Oates and Yu (1971), who found a difference in growth between former FTT children and the control group when the relationship between the height ages and weight ages of the children were compared with their chronological ages. Six out of the fourteen children of NOFTT were one or more years below their chronological age, in comparison with only one child from the control group. Equally, statistical differences were found between groups in weight ($p<0.04$). Former FTT children were significantly behind in language, reading age and verbal intelligence with reference to the comparison group. They also scored lower on a social maturity rating. In another study, Oates, Peacock and Forest (1984) found that youths who had been admitted to hospital for failure-to-thrive 16–18 years earlier scored significantly lower on a cognitive measure than a matched comparison group.

Drotar and Sturm (1988) found that children with weight below the fifth percentile scored on cognitive functioning within the normal limits when investigated between one and nine months, but at three-year follow-up the average score dropped to one standard deviation below the mean. The cumulative effect of neglect and failure-to-thrive on cognitive functioning has been found by numerous researchers. In a study by Singer and Fagan (1984), even after extended hospitalisation NOFTT infants manifested persistent intellectual delays at a three-year follow-up examination.

Reif et al. (1995) reported the following findings at five-year follow-up of 61 FTT children and a comparison group matched for age, sex, social class and ethnic affiliation. Children with a previous history of failure-to-thrive were found to be shorter and, in particular, lighter in weight. Birthweight percentile and maternal height of children with failure-to-thrive were lower than those of matched children from the control group. They also had more learning difficulties and evidenced developmental delay. The degree of growth retardation and the duration of follow-up had no significant effect on the outcome. In contrast, birthweight, maternal height and social status and, to a lesser extent, paternal parameters were good predictors of the catching-up capabilities of these infants in terms of weight and height. Children who caught up faster had better school performances and came from families of higher socio-economic status. Reif *et al.* concluded that failure-to-thrive is a multifactorial process involving biological, nutritional and environmental factors, and that all these components should be considered in long-term follow-up and management.

Catch-up growth in NOFTT children seems to be greatest among those who receive intensive psychological and social intervention early on. High-risk families in particular seem to benefit from frequent home visits focused on parenting skills training, dealing with maternal depression and providing practical help and support (Chatoor, Hirsch and Persinger 1997). Grantham-McGregor *et al.* (1994) have demonstrated that when malnourished children were given sufficient food on a daily basis at school, their cognitive development accelerated and school attainments increased. Additionally, when the treatment programme was extended to home-base intervention and included stimulating activities for children, there was a positive impact on children's growth, development and academic performance. These improvements were sustained for 14 years even though the home visits stopped after three years.

The present study

Background and aims

In 1977 an in-depth study of non-organic failure-to-thrive children and two control groups began. There were two major objectives guiding that study: first, to identify possible causal factors of non-organic failure-to-thrive; and second, to develop and to test the short- and long-term effectiveness of treatment and intervention strategies for this client group. The findings of the original investigation of this controlled study and the effectiveness data were published at the five-year follow-up stage (Iwaniec *et al.* 1985a; Iwaniec, McNeish and Herbert 1985b). The results from the initial investigation indicated several problem areas: mother–child feeding difficulties; disturbed mother–child interaction and relationship; maternal anxiety, low self-esteem, depression and poor self-control; and conduct problems (notably coercive or non-compliant behaviour) among the children. Some children exhibited emotional problems such as fear, depressive reactions or severe inhibitions. At a more macro-level the families of FTT children were more disadvantaged in their socio-economic conditions and experienced significantly more acute disharmony in marital relationships. Comparison of the index group with two control groups revealed statistically significant differences in all these areas.

The non-organic failure-to-thrive group and additional 27 cases referred between 1978 and 1979 for assessment and treatment have been followed up in the same way until 1998. Thirty-one out of the possible 44 cases were available at the final follow-up. The aim of the long-term follow-up was to find out what happened to those children over the intervening 20 years, and whether early failure-to-thrive negatively affected them physically, emotionally, socially and educationally in the long run. An assessment could also be made of whether intervention and treatment had a positive and lasting effect on their lives. Additionally, the follow-up explored former FTT subjects' experiences as children, their perceptions of early difficulties, and current situations in various areas of their lives.

Subjects and methods

The sample comprised 31. There were 16 males and 15 females ranging in age from 20 to 28 years, with a mean age of 21.6 (*see* Table 11.1).

Table 11.1 Gender and household circumstances of the sample		
Gender	**No.**	**%**
Female	15	48
Male	16	52
Partnership		
Single	22	71
Living with partner or married	9	29
Parental status		
Have children	8	22
Single parents	3	10
No children	20	68
Household circumstances		
Living with parents	10	32
Living with extended family	4	13
Living on their own	7	23
Living in institution	1	3
Living with partner or married	9	29

Semi-structured and open-ended interviews took place with adults who had failed to thrive when young. Whenever possible their parents, adopters or foster carers were interviewed too. Respondents were asked about what had happened in the years since initial investigation; whether early problems had

had lasting effects on the subjects' lives and functioning; and how helpful or effective intervention had been.

The results presented in this chapter are mostly based on qualitative data to give the reader a picture of the young adults and the history of their experiences. Quantitative methods were also used to obtain demographic and growth data. Validated questionnaires were used to assess attachment and a sense of well-being. This data is only partly presented in this chapter as the final analyses are not concluded yet.

A selection of suitable and valid tools for data collection is achieved if the selected methods will provide information and measures appropriate to what the researcher intended to find out and measure. It is worthwhile to point out that the methods of data collection and the process has been worked out with two mothers of the former FTT subjects, who were familiar with research methodologies and had experience in research. Collaboration and consumer participation proved to be invaluable, as it enabled me to choose important areas of investigation and devise questions which would reflect and uncover some hidden issues that might otherwise have been missed.

Long-term outcomes

The most striking findings to emerge from this study were the correlations between the age of a child at referral point, time of catch-up in weight and height, improvement in mother–child relationship, and long-term outcomes. Children who were referred for medical investigation and psychosocial assessment and intervention during the first year of life (16 subjects – 55%) and who made satisfactory progress in terms of increased nutritional intake with subsequent growth improvement have done well on both a short- and long-term basis. Significant positive results were identified in relation to physical growth, notably height, cognitive development, educational attainment, psychosocial stability and maturity, secure attachment to partners and other significant people, and a sense of well-being generally.

On the other hand, children with a long history of failure-to-thrive (15 subjects – 45%) referred for assessment and intervention between three and seven years of age, and whose improvement was slow or unsatisfactory if they remained at home, had disappointing outcomes. This was especially apparent with respect to height, educational attainment, cognition, employment, social adjustment, emotional stability, attachment and a sense of well-being. These 15 subjects were classified as psychosocial short stature, eight falling into the hyperphagic group (overeaters) and seven into the anorexic group (under-eaters).

Six subjects out of these 15 were removed from neglectful and abusive homes. They achieved better outcomes than the nine remaining at home. Two subjects who were adopted at three and five years respectively have done well both professionally and personally, had better educational attainments, and were taller than their parents. Children who were fostered (three subjects) at the age of four, five and seven had poorer educational achievements and employment, as did one subject who was accommodated with his father at the age of 11 years.

Nine out of 15 who remained at home (three on the Risk Register) developed behavioural and emotional problems such as delinquent behaviour, running away from home, aggression, inability to concentrate, and disruptive and attention-seeking behaviour. Seven of them were statemented for special education.

Six subjects had, on average, three to four episodes of respite foster care. During their stays with the foster parents their weight, height and head growth accelerated, they became more alert, and bizarre eating, disturbed toileting, self-harming and destructive behaviour diminished. On their return home their growth and development slowed down and their behaviour worsened. At the moment their height is below the average of the general population in spite of their parents being tall. They are also thin and underweight.

Psychosocial short stature subjects reported being badly treated as children by their mothers and siblings. They reported being deprived of food, often isolated from the rest of the family, locked up in their rooms, and persistently criticised and rebuked; furthermore, there was little affection and attention shown to them when living at home. They felt that they had better relationships with their fathers, although the latter appeared to be uninvolved. The marital relationship of FTT children's parents in three-quarters of the cases was problematic, and marked by more serious frictions and quarrels in almost half of the sample. FTT children felt that their mothers were very domineering, cold and unsupportive. Marital breakdown took place in seven families between closure of the case and the final follow-up. Frictions in those families were obvious at the time of assessment and intervention, but were only admitted and dealt with in two cases. Ex-husbands and wives stated that ill-treatment of the FTT child was often the triggering factor for quarrels and fights. Withdrawal of food as punishment for any misbehaviour was common and frequent in cases of psychosocial short stature. The following statements would demonstrate the seriousness and consequences of such parental behaviour on a child's actual nutritional intake and physical growth.

I was sent to bed without having tea at least three or four times a week if I was lucky. I was so hungry I could not sleep.

No amount of crying and screaming and saying that I was hungry would do no good, the door was locked and that was that.

If I did eat quickly and made a mess, she would take plate away from me, and ask me to get out from the table. I had to sit still and watch the others eat.

Of course I have hidden food even under the carpet – wouldn't you if you were hungry all the time?

I felt so miserable that I often cried myself to sleep.

I did break things and smashed my toys and scratched myself until blood started to run. I don't know why, I guess I was hurting inside – I guess I wanted to let my mum know I wanted someone to see how unhappy I was. No one believed me anyway.

Self-confidence and self-esteem

All subjects were asked how they currently feel about themselves and how confident they are when dealing with other people in personal or work matters. They were asked to give answers to 12 questions covering various aspects of self-evaluation.

Fifty per cent felt positive about themselves in terms of their achievements at school, higher education and work. They were also satisfied with the relationships within their families during childhood and adolescence and current contacts with parents and siblings. Their sense of belonging was deeply rooted in the parental home. They found it easy to form romantic and friendly relationships and were able to deal with conflicts, disagreements or difficulties with relationships in an assertive and confident manner. They were securely attached to their partners and friends and in seven cases to their children.

Thirty per cent reported a lack of self-confidence when dealing with other people. They were often bullied at school, and found it difficult to assert themselves at work or in their personal relationships. They tended to give up an idea or request easily and to their disadvantage, even when they had power or were in a position to protect their interests and rights. They were often manipulated, undermined and used, and, although they were aware what was happening, were unable to stand up for themselves. Those subjects associated their difficulties with their experiences as children and the way they were treated by their parents, siblings, peers or teachers. The following statements indicate those subjects' perceptions and beliefs:

I was often told that I was stupid and thick, I guess this is the reason why 'I doubt myself'.

If I said that I want something or this is what I saw or heard, I was ignored or told that I was wrong.

It does not matter how much I tried to be friendly with kids at school, they did not want to play with me, told me that I did this and that which was not true. I did not know how to convince them and how to fight back. I just gave up and felt miserable.

I have this feeling inside me – I don't know how to describe it – that makes me feel I am not good enough, nervous to say that I am right, or this is the way things have to be done.

I will lie in bed thinking that my boss is unfair and I have to do far more than others, and promise myself that I must 'put the cards on the table' with him. I go to work next day and do nothing.

The lack of self-esteem is also evident in difficulties with making decisions or taking an appropriate course of action, for example applying for a better job or initiating a new relationship. There is a prevailing inferiority complex and an urge to be associated with people of importance (as they see it) to improve their image and to be seen as being wanted and appreciated.

Twenty per cent stated that although they do not feel confident and often agonise about what decision to make, what to say and what to do, they hide their feelings, thoughts and behaviour in order to portray themselves as strong and decisive. For example:

It is such a hard job to pretend how strong you are, when inside you are not, but people think I am. If they only knew how hard it is. I am glad though I can do that.

Relationships with significant people

One of the major difficulties experienced by some of the subjects is in the area of attachment to significant people. Thirty-five per cent reported often feeling insecure in their relationships with partners or friends. They tended to react even to minor disagreements or frictions with anxiety and fear of being rejected, unwanted and abandoned. They tended to cling to people who showed them some interest and affection, and were inclined to attach themselves to partners who are emotionally volatile and vulnerable. This sense of insecurity had been evident throughout their lives at home, at school, with friends and in personal romantic relationships. They tended to anticipate difficulties, even when there was no reason to feel anxious. The sense of insecurity was also demonstrated in active avoidance of sharing their problems, difficulties or ideas with partners, boyfriends or girlfriends out of fear of being seen as weak, inadequate or not worth being associated with.

The same pattern of behaviour was identified in relation to parents, siblings and peers in childhood and adolescence. One in five tended to be aggressive and pushy in order to hide their internal fear and apprehensions.

The current relationship with their parents has been described as good or much better than it was in childhood in 68 per cent of the 31 cases. This was true for siblings in 55 per cent of the cases. In the cases where early relationships were problematic the situation seemed to change for the better when they left home or when they became parents themselves. There were some totally unpredictable outcomes in two cases. Both subjects were severely rejected by mothers, resulting in serious behavioural and emotional problems. They were removed from home at the ages of five and eleven respectively and made considerable progress once away from the stressful and abusive situation. Contacts with their mothers were infrequent and poor in quality until they established their own homes and had their own children. The relationship with and attitudes towards the mothers warmed up with the arrival of the child. As one of them stated:

> I never thought I would want to see or have anything to do with my mother again. She was always hitting and screaming at me. I was much happier when I went to live with my father and his new wife. Now that I have a baby I know how tough it is to cope when she cries or does not want to eat. I must have been a difficult child to look after and she found it hard to look after me. Mind you, I would never hit my baby, but I understand my mother, she must have been under a lot of pressure. What is gone is gone, she helps a lot now.

The results are not so optimistic if we look at subjects classified as psychosocial short stature and referred after prolonged difficulties at home: 10 out of 15 subjects continue to have poor relationships and contacts not only with parents but with siblings as well. Lingering indifference, alienation and detachment is apparent and appears to be insurmountable. This is particularly the case for those who were fostered out. These subjects were not given an explanation as to why they were in care while their siblings remained at home, why they were singled out and what they had done to deserve such treatment. Some of them felt that their attempts to get closer to their mothers as they grew older were not reciprocated and encouraged. They felt guilty, confused and abandoned in spite of the good relationships they had with the foster families. Greater openness and full explanations are required to eliminate an unnecessary sense of guilt and utter confusion which has prevailed over the years.

In contrast to the confused and alienated subjects who were fostered, those who were adopted said they were fully aware of the reasons for this and appeared to be reconciled to the fact that they were adopted. Their relationships with adoptive parents, extended family and people they mixed with were described as normal. The subjects felt they were much loved, wanted and cared for. Adoptive parents stated that they were honest and open with them. In spite of some serious emotional and behavioural problems that those children presented when adopted, such as bizarre eating behaviour, difficulties in concentrating, attention-seeking, and in one of the cases soiling and wetting, they gradually settled down and behaviour improved considerably within the first two years.

Physical growth, psychosocial and educational attachments

At the time of the follow-up, 19 subjects are slightly smaller than their siblings or parents: men between 5 ft. 4 in. and 5 ft. 6 in., and women between 5 ft. 1 in. and 5 ft. 3 in.. The mean height for all subjects is 5 ft. 6 in., while their parents' mean height is 5 ft. 4 in.. Most subjects managed to achieve average height and were able to catch up in terms of physical growth.

Twenty subjects appear to have appropriate weight for height, and look well. Nine are underweight for their height, while two are exceptionally thin – 8 and 8½ stones respectively (both men). Two are obese – 15 and 16 stone respectively (both women).

Eating behaviour

Currently there are no very serious eating problems. One subject became anorexic at the age of 16 but reports that after two years of treatment she recovered and is fine now. Seven tend to eat a lot when under stress and two consume large quantities of food. Four lose appetite when stressed. Six dislike big meals and prefer snacks, liking to nibble rather than eat. Twelve really enjoy food and eat well and healthily. Eating behaviour appears to be determined by mood rather than hunger and good appetite or eating needs and routines of eating.

Education and employment

Intellectual cognitive ability appeared to be impaired in 40 per cent of the cases. School attainments in those cases were poor or very poor. Six subjects had not passed any exams such as GCSEs; seven were moved to special education due to their slowness in learning and maladjusted behaviour. Five subjects are semi-literate and four have considerable difficulties with reading and numeracy in spite of finishing secondary education. All these subjects were exposed for a considerable time to inadequate nutrition and extremely poor intellectual stimulation. They experienced acute emotional maltreatment in the form of rejection for several years. Poor cognitive development and subsequent school performance might be directly linked to malnutrition and poor brain growth, and problematic, painful relationships with mothers.

Table 11.2 Education history		
	No.	%
Secondary school	16	51.61
Special school	8	25.81
University	2	6.45
Professional courses or colleges of further education	5	16.13
Total	31	100.00

Table 11.3 Employment status		
	No.	%
Employed	10	32.26
Unemployed	7	22.58
Still in education	7	22.58
Occasionally employed	7	22.58
Total	31	100.00

Difficulties with maintaining employment are apparent where the ability to read and act upon written information and instructions is necessary. Six subjects had had between seven to ten different jobs since they left school. These findings are in line with other shorter-term follow-up studies showing that children who failed to thrive exhibit significant deficit in cognitive development, not only during the early stages of their lives but also later on (Oates and Yu 1971; Drotar and Sturm 1988; Achenbach *et al.* 1993). This study shows that prolonged under-nutrition and psychosocial neglect in infancy and early childhood seriously curtails cognitive development if action is not taken to move the child to a caring and stable environment or when home intervention is not available or infrequent and of poor quality.

Two subjects who were diagnosed as severe psychosocial short stature were adopted at the ages of four and five years respectively and have done very well personally and professionally. Both have finished higher education, are in successful jobs and have stable marital relationships, and one has a four-month-old baby, thriving and well cared for. Resilience is apparent here, demonstrating that children can successfully recover from very serious deprivation and maltreatment if they are rescued and provided with high-quality nurturance, attention and affection.

Time of intervention seems to be of major importance for positive outcomes. One subject was not removed from a well-known abusive situation until he was 11 years of age. Although his physical growth in terms of height accelerated rapidly, and his withdrawn and depressive behaviour, as well as his bed-wetting (once he had moved to live with his father), vanished, his educational attainments were very poor. In spite of finishing secondary school, he is semi-literate. As he said:

> I can't read properly and I don't know how to spell. Good job my partner helps me with forms. I can do some number work. I had to give up jobs in the garage as I could not do papers and read things. Window-cleaning is fine as you do not have to mess with papers.

Another subject said:

> I always wanted to go to the army, but I only lasted there three months. Once they found me out that I can't really read, they would not have me. I tried different jobs, thought I could do it. I don't want to be just a labourer. I keep trying.

Other findings

One subject developed manic depression at the age of 21 and was treated in hospital for six months. In spite of having finished a university course, she is unable to maintain any employment. Another person was committed to care at the age of 13 years, when it was discovered that the mother starved the child deliberately by fabricating that the child had a widespread allergy to food (Munchausen's syndrome by proxy). This child grew quickly in a new foster home (five inches and one and a half stone within three months), became alert, sociable and outgoing, and his school work improved vastly. Cases of Munchausen's syndrome by proxy are more frequent than we are led to believe, and require that particular attention be paid to any signs of irrational illness.

Acute anxiety, what could be described as post-traumatic stress disorder, was identified in four subjects. These subjects were acutely rejected by their mothers and often siblings. Their attachment to primary carers was classified as insecure/anxious or avoidant. Severe emotional reactions are triggered off by related or unrelated loss, or fear of being abandoned by a person they care for very much, e.g. a boyfriend or girlfriend. These subjects tend to suffer severe panic attacks, insomnia, loss of appetite, loss of weight, flashbacks and extreme fear of being rejected. All of them sought help from their GP and were prescribed tranquillisers when in a particularly bad state. They tend to react to stress with heightened anxiety, especially when the problem is linked to the possible loss of a relationship. Two subjects also reported having experienced these symptoms at school when there was a drift and a danger of losing much-cared-for friendships. They stated that they can link these feelings to being unwanted and rejected at home. They recall similar sensations from their childhood and adolescence.

Interviews with subjects' parents

All mothers, and two-thirds of fathers, were interviewed to find out how they feel now about the child and how they view the help which was available to them. Four mothers still feel angry that their worries, concerns and persistent requests for investigation of possible organic causes for failure-to-thrive were not taken on board for a long time by the medical profession. Subsequently, organic causes were discovered and eliminated by surgery or medication, so that the children began to grow and their relationship with the parents improved as well as their school work. These parents feel that they were treated as neurotics, and were often told that the children were perfectly healthy, thus implying that their treatment of the children was poor.

Over 60 per cent of parents stated that their early difficulties in terms of child-rearing and their relationships have improved considerably due to the support and therapeutic help provided by the social worker/researcher and, in ten cases, paediatric services. They particularly appreciated a hands-on approach, eg. helping them to feed the child and showing them how to play, talk and deal with difficult behaviour. They felt that developmental counselling, eg. developmental quizzes, helped them to understand what children should do at a certain age and when and how to help them to catch up. Provision of day nursery, family centre or daily minder was highly appreciated and identified as being very helpful. They appreciated being treated with dignity and that there was a balance in addressing children's needs as well as theirs, with the obvious understanding that the child's welfare would come first if a conflict of interest arose.

Conclusions

Some important messages emerged from this study. Although the sample is small and there is a need to be cautious about generalisation, it is nevertheless suggestive and in line with earlier and shorter-term follow-up studies.

Earlier identification, well devised treatment/intervention, and implementation of helping strategies in partnership with parents led to improved intake of food, weight gain and mother–child interaction. All subjects referred and dealt with during the first year of life managed to escape adverse consequences, in contrast to those who came to professional attention after prolonged difficulties.

Optimistic expectations that problems would disappear without serious consequences and reluctance to take appropriate action when failure-to-thrive persisted were too often apparent amongst all professions involved with failure-to-thrive children. Yet prolonged malnutrition affects children's cognitive development, which directly affects their school performance and consequently employment. It also affects people's problem-solving abilities, and the ways in which they perceive and deal with various issues in their lives. A second disadvantage for those who did not get early intervention appears to be reduced ability to build and maintain secure and lasting relationships. These findings are currently being analysed.

Failure-to-thrive can have serious and long-lasting consequences as outlined in this chapter, but equally it can be resolved quickly and effectively if attended to seriously at the onset of the presenting problems. Early identification of poor weight gain, withdrawn and detached behaviour, inadequate intake of food and problematic mother–child relationships should inform professionals that they need to step in so as to prevent further harm.

Implications for policy and practice

The results indicate that some changes could be made at the decision-making, service-provision and policy-making levels.

1. Early intervention is essential to prevent escalation of negative parent–child interaction and relationship and to prevent poor growth and development. Failure-to-thrive, when attended to earlier on, had no effect on the child's growth, development, social adjustment or educational attainments. Neither parents nor subject remembered early difficulties.

2. Family support in terms of service provision and direct therapeutic input is required at an early stage of failure-to-thrive.

3. Parental concerns and complaints regarding poor feeding and inadequate weight gain should be taken seriously, dealt with and monitored until satisfactory weight gain for the child's chronological age is established and maintained for at least six months.

4. Repeated parental visits to the doctors regarding worries about the child's poor physical health should be investigated, as in some cases the medical reason for failure-to-thrive was not recognised, risking a false presumption that the care was inadequate or neglectful parenting.

5. Regular monitoring of children's growth (weight, height and head circumference) should be mandatory for all children. Many children were not referred for assessment and treatment until they were between three and six years of age, in spite of health visiting records indicating growth failure. A growth and development chart is a good instrument for identifying problems early and responding to them quickly.

6. Children who are identified as severe psychosocial short stature should be removed from stressful and abusive environments. The prognosis of problem solving at home is extremely poor.

7. Full psychosocial assessment is essential when failure-to-thrive is persistent. There are many reasons why children fail to thrive. The assessment of problems and needs has to be done comprehensively and acted upon promptly. A care plan addressing all aspects of identified difficulties should be devised on a multidisciplinary basis and tasks allocated to appropriate professions.

8. A multidisciplinary approach to assessing and helping those children and their families is essential. Social workers, health visitors, GP, paediatricians and dieticians are usually involved. Day care services such as family centres, day nurseries and community centres can help the child and parents.

9. Most serious cases of failure-to-thrive, especially those where rejection and emotional maltreatment is present, need to be conferenced promptly and an appropriate care plan put into action urgently. Those cases need to be monitored and followed up for a considerable time, as the relapse rate is high.

10. Family support seemed to benefit the child and the family. Clear goals for intervention worked best when a contract of mutual obligations was written down and negotiated with both parties. Loosely defined support does not work.

CHAPTER 12

Visual Signals in Child–Child and Adult–Child Communication: Implications for the Use of the Live Link with Child Witnesses

Gwyneth Doherty-Sneddon,
Sandra McAuley and Ozlem Carrera

Introduction

Understanding the development of communication skills is central to being able to communicate effectively with children. Adults must be aware of both children's abilities and their limitations in order to do this. When investigating communication skills one must consider both verbal and non-verbal phenomena, and how these interact to produce a set of efficient communication strategies. It is important for professionals assessing what a child understands or knows to assess the information which children send in their non-verbal behaviour. In this vein, Rich (1968) pointed out the importance of both the non-verbal signals that the child sends and those sent by the professional when interviewing children. He emphasised the wealth of information available in behavioural cues that may never be expressed verbally by a child who either does not have the verbal ability, or is embarrassed or shy. Such issues are extremely relevant for children called to give evidence in courts of law, the experience of which is often reported as extremely stressful for children (Davies and Noon 1991; Goodman *et al.* 1991).

Research has found adults to be, on the whole, practised communicators who adjust their communicative strategies to cope with different communication media and therefore maintain their task performance regardless of the availability of visual signals (for example, Chapanis *et al.* 1972; Williams

1977). However, the presence or absence of visual signals has been found to affect the process of communication. Boyle, Anderson and Newlands (1994) found that while the same level of task performance was maintained regardless of the availability of visual signals, significantly more words and turns were required for pairs of adult subjects to accomplish a problem-solving communication task in an audio-only context than through face-to-face interaction. Such findings have suggested that communication involves not only the words which are spoken as part of an interaction but also a vast array of other audio and visual signals, e.g. the pitch and intonation of the voice; gaze; gesture; posture; and changes in facial expression (Ekman and Friesen 1969; McNeill 1985; Goldin-Meadow, Wein and Chang 1992).

Children may be particularly dependent upon non-verbal signals in their communication attempts. One important aspect of the non-verbal channel is gesture. Goldin-Meadow *et al.* (1992) found that, when explaining their reasoning on conservation tasks, children transmitted information via hand gestures that they did not verbalise. When children attempted to convey difficult material, they often transmitted some of it by using gestures alone, suggesting that at some level they understood the material but could not yet verbalise it. Further evidence that gesture is an important source of inform-ation, for adults as well as children, comes from the work done by Cassell, McNeill and McCullough (1994). They followed up work by McNeill (1992), who showed that there is a close semantic and pragmatic relationship between gesture and speech. Cassell *et al.* demonstrated that this is taken into account by listeners, with information transmitted via gesture being incorpor-ated into listeners' mental representations.

Children's communication: A referential approach

The referential communication model developed by Glucksberg, Krauss and Weisberg (1966) has been used in many studies of children's communication skills. The basic form of this involves one person describing an object to another person in such a way that the second person can pick out the target object from an array of possible referent objects. The number of correct choices is then taken as a measure of communicative outcome.

Pechman and Deutsch (1982) found that the use of pointing gestures in the accomplishment of a referential communication task changed with age. Four year-olds used such pointing when referring to distant objects sur-rounded by other potential targets, making pointing ambiguous. In contrast, nine-year-olds and adults preferred to name referents in such contexts, although they were just as likely to use pointing when referring to near referents or if the context was less potentially ambiguous. This suggests that it is not just isolated linguistic or non-verbal skills that are lacking in young children, but pragmatic knowledge about how to use such communicative tools effectively.

A general conclusion from work in this area is that referential communication improves with age. Explanations for the poorer referential abilities of younger children range from language limitations (Asher and Wigfield 1981) to cognitive restrictions (for example, Glucksberg *et al.* 1966; Asher and Parke 1975). It is therefore predicted that if visual signals are less cognitively demanding, and children are able to represent knowledge in gesture before verbalising it (as discussed above), then visual signals will play a particularly important role in the communication attempts of young children.

The experiments discussed in this chapter show that young children's communication abilities are affected by their access to visual signals. We have shown that for some tasks access to visual information is beneficial to children's abilities. In contrast, decreased access to visual cues may be beneficial in other types of communicative situation. We report five studies, the first of which compared six- and eleven-year-olds' performance with adult performance on a collaborative communication task in both face-to-face and audio-only contexts. The second study investigated the referential abilities of three- to four-year-olds, using an adaptation of the original Glucksberg and Krauss task (Glucksberg *et al.* 1966). The motivation behind the second study was to investigate whether the impact of visual signals on communicative outcome would be greater for subjects with more limited linguistic abilities. The third study investigated how the visual channel influences the efficiency of interviewing these young children. The final two linked studies (4a and 4b) looked at the impact of live video links compared with face-to-face interviewing of child witnesses.

Video mediated communication

Video-mediated communication (VMC) refers to a class of remote communication systems which includes visual access for speakers and uses video phones, live closed-circuit television (CCTV) links and desktop video conferencing. An important question arises: can video-mediated visual signals be a substitute for those found in face-to-face interaction? A number of studies have illustrated that in many ways they cannot. For example, Doherty-Sneddon *et al.* (1997) found that video-mediated conversations did not carry the efficiency benefits that had previously been found in face-to-face interactions (Boyle *et al.* 1994). Other studies have reported that VMC provides an intermediate level of support that lies between face-to-face and audio-only communication (Rutter, Stephenson and Dewey 1981; Olson, Olson and Meader 1995).

Heath and Luff (1991) reported that many non-verbal actions did not achieve the same performance significance during VMC as they did in face-to-face interaction. For example, iconic and illustrative gestures appeared to have little communicative significance when performed via a video link. The authors suggested that one reason for this may be that because of our familiarity with television we have become insensitive to screen-based images in terms of communicative commitment. Furthermore, these problems may have arisen because many gestures function within the peripheral vision of the recipient, and the screen exists as only part of that peripheral vision. Only gross changes of screen configuration attracted attention, while smaller ones went unnoticed. Finally, Heath and Luff proposed that technologies may actually distort the shape of gestures and thereby affect information transfer. Similarly, Sellen (1995) suggested that the critical difference between remote interaction (either audio-only or video-mediated) and face-to-face interaction may be the distortion of certain conversational acts, such as perceiving how one is being received. This occurs either because of the complete loss of certain signals or because of the relative impotency of the signals that are transmitted. Such effects may be important in determining the degree of satisfaction reported by users of the technology.

One reason why VMC is not equivalent to face-to-face interaction is that there may be a novelty effect. Doherty-Sneddon *et al.* (1997) found that some of the differences associated with video-mediated communication (compared to face-to-face or audio-only interaction) with adult users were related to novelty effects. For example, they found that VMC where eye contact was possible involved more speech than VMC where eye contact was not possible. The authors suggested that a TV which 'looks back' is very novel indeed. Participants will be used to seeing images on screens but not images which look right back at them. Around three times as much 'non-task' conversation occurred in VMC when eye contact was possible than in face-to-face interaction. This suggests that the video technology has a social influence on users, for example making them more likely to joke with one another. The following extracts give examples of the non-task conversation found in the interactions.

1 *Instruction Follower.* Its pukka all this equipment isn't it?

   Instruction Giver. Yeah, it's excellent.

2 *Instruction Follower.* Oh for goodness sake, its going to take me ages. Just have a sleep or something.

An important difference between technology-mediated and face-to-face conversations is a reduction in the range of communication cues available in the latter. For example, in telephone conversations facial expressions and gestures of speakers and listeners are not available. In video-mediated interactions such cues are often degraded and sometimes absent. Rutter (1987) proposes that it is the aggregate of communication cues available that determines the feeling of 'psychological distance' within a given interaction. It follows that in video-mediated conversations, where access to visual communication signals is reduced, the psychological distance experienced by those involved will be increased.

Children's video-mediated communication: Studies of the live link

One specific application of VMC is the live video link (live links) installed in many UK courts to facilitate the giving of evidence by child witnesses involved in crimes of violence or sexual assault (Davies and Noon 1991; Murray 1995; Flin, Kearney and Murray 1996). The live link allows the child to give evidence from a room remote from the main courtroom, so avoiding the need to confront the accused or enter the sometimes intimidating atmosphere of the courtroom.

Video links may have negative or positive effects on evidence quality for different reasons. Negative effects may result from the attenuation of visual communication. Earlier we described the importance of visual signals in children's communication and the evidence for the attenuation of visual communication in VMC. From the findings in these two research areas we would predict some information loss in live link testimony. In contrast, a positive influence may result from a decrease in social and emotional pressure when psychological distance between the child and questioner is increased. This chapter proposes that the influence of the live link is dual-edged in these ways.

The social and emotional benefits provided by the live link may *facilitate* the giving of evidence. There is evidence that providing social support and decreasing intimidation increases the accuracy of children's reports (Goodman *et al.* 1991). One important factor in children's testimony is their ability to deal with leading and misleading questions. Baxter (1990) concluded that children's suggestibility is a situational factor which can be exacerbated by stress. Carter, Bottoms and Levine (1996) found that children interviewed by a warm, supportive interviewer were more resistant to misleading questions about the event than were children interviewed in an intimidating manner. Saywitz and Nathanson (1993) reported an experimental study comparing 8- to 10-year-olds' evidence given either in a mock courtroom or at school.

Children questioned at court gave less accurate accounts and rated the experience as more stressful than those interviewed at school.

Stress and intimidation are reduced in live link testimony in a number of ways. Flin et al. (1990) reported that the main fear children have prior to testifying is of seeing the accused in court. Furthermore, those children most worried about seeing the accused were rated as having most difficulty in answering the prosecutor's questions. Using the link means that the child does not have to confront the accused. Another way in which stress is reduced is by distancing the child from the questioner. There is considerable evidence that video-mediated communication involves an increase in 'psychological distance' (Rutter 1987). Because of this, the link should improve testimony.

A number of studies have evaluated the use of the live link. On the whole, significant emotional benefits are found. Cashmore and De Haas (1992) reported that children showed no direct benefit from use of the live link but did benefit from the right to choose how they gave their testimony. Davies and Noon (1991) found that, compared with testifying directly in open court, the live link reduced stress in child witnesses and improved the quality of their evidence. Live link children were rated as more fluent and audible; they were rated as happier and were more likely to be judged competent to swear the oath. However, the researchers also reported that live link testimony took significantly longer than the open court (50 minutes versus 24 minutes); that the judicial assessment of competence took longer with the live link (three minutes versus two minutes); and importantly, that judges were found to be less empathic to the live link witnesses. According to Flin et al. (1996), both prosecution and defence lawyers agreed that the use of the live link enabled some children to give evidence who would otherwise have been unable to testify. Flin et al. also reported that there are communicative problems associated with the use of video links. For example, children failed to understand questions more often across the link, and provided less detail and were less resistant to leading questions. In contrast, an experimental study of seven- to eight- and ten- to eleven-year-olds by Westcott, Davies and Clifford (1991a) found that the quality of responses to open-ended questions did not differ between face-to-face and live link interviews. In addition, Davies and Noon (1991) found that independent raters evaluated children as more resistant to leading questions in live link questioning compared with open court. One aim of the current work was to investigate the impact of the live link on children's actual resistance to misleading questions in an experimental setting.

Goodman et al. (1998) carried out an experimental study using mock court trials. Children were witnesses to an event, and lawyers and jurors were played by actors. The study had ecological validity, since the 'trials' were carried out in a real court house. The study compared the outcomes and testimonies of two age groups of children (six- and eight-year-olds). The children either testified in open court or across a live link. The results showed that younger children (six years) were *more* resistant to misleading questions in the live link condition than in the open court condition. This suggests that children are more comfortable disagreeing with an adult when there is some distance between them. When testifying across the link the younger children were as accurate as the older ones, suggesting improved quality of evidence in the mediated condition. This American study is therefore in agreement with the 'ratings' data from England provided by Davies and Noon (1991), but in disagreement with the Flin *et al.* study carried out in Scotland.

In this chapter we report the results of five experimental studies investigating children's communication in different communication media. The first two studies illustrate the facilitating role of visual communication signals in child–child interaction (the first with school-aged children, the second with pre-school children). The latter three studies are investigations of adult–child communication, with adults interviewing children (about neutral events) in face-to-face, audio-only, and video-mediated interaction. Studies 1 and 2 illustrate the way in which visual signals can affect children's communication. Study 3 reports differences between face-to-face and unseen adult–child communication. Studies 4a and 4b report data comparing children's evidence given in either video link or face-to-face contexts.

Study 1: Visual signals in problem-solving communication tasks with primary school-aged children

The first study investigated the development of the role of visual signals in children's communication. Church and Goldin-Meadow (1986) proposed that non-verbal signals require less processing capacity and that, furthermore, they are used in place of verbal messages when children express knowledge or information that they are on the verge of understanding fully, i.e. knowledge that is within their 'zone of proximal development' (Vygotsky 1962, first published 1932). Shatz (1977) suggests that communicative development involves the learning of 'information-handling techniques'. As these become better learned, tasks become easier and require less processing capacity. Communication tasks therefore present greater problems to younger children than older ones, and non-verbal signals are likely to be more prevalent in their communication.

The Map Task (Brown *et al.* 1984) was the preferred assessment tool for this study, since a large corpus of adult Map Task dialogues with which to make comparisons was already available. The Map Task involves two people randomly assigned to the role of Instruction Giver or Instruction Follower. Each is given a schematic map of the same location. The Instruction Giver's map has a route through the location while the Instruction Follower's map does not. The aim of the task is for the Instruction Giver to tell the Instruction Follower about the route so that he or she can reproduce it on his or her map as accurately as possible. Participants are informed that there may be differences between the maps (some discrepancies between the maps were incorporated into their design in order to produce points of communicative difficulty). A useful feature of the Map Task is that it provides an objective, quantifiable measure of communicative success. By calculating the area (in cm^2) between the original 'correct' Instruction Giver route and the route that is drawn by the Instruction Follower, a map deviation score is produced for each dialogue.

In the present study six-year-olds were taken as the younger group, since pilot work had shown that this is the youngest age group with which the Map Task is an appropriate communication task. The eleven-year-old age group was chosen because it was expected that there would be significant developmental differences between this age group and the six-year-olds. The Map Task is a demanding one for children as young as six years of age, particularly since the map features have written labels. This may affect comparisons between older and younger children. However, the emphasis in the present study was on the differing ways in which children of different age groups deal with face-to-face and audio-only communication, and it was this comparison that was of primary importance.

Twenty six-year-olds and 24 11-year-olds from Glasgow primary schools took part in the study. Two pairs of maps were used each consisting of an Instruction Giver and an Instruction Follower map (see Figure 12.1). The maps were identical in terms of complexity to maps used by Boyle *et al.* (1994) for adults. The only difference was that the present maps had features that were labelled with words which young children would find easier to read. For example, a feature labelled on the children's maps as 'birds' was called 'pelicans' on the adult maps. It was predicted that the younger children would fail to adapt to audio-only communication in the way that the adults had done in the study by Boyle *et al.*

Results

The younger children, on the whole, performed less well than the older children on the task. The six-year-olds' Instruction Follower routes deviated from the Instruction Giver routes around 37 per cent more than the

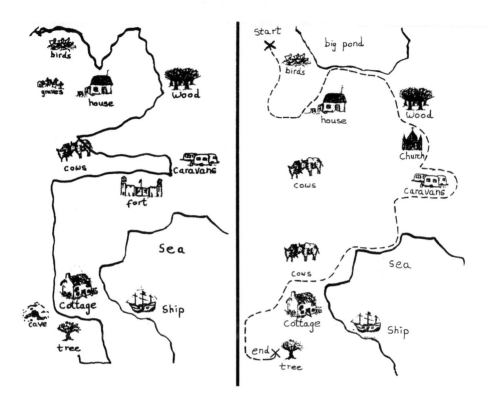

Figure 12.1 Instruction Giver and Instruction Follower maps
The right of the figure shows an Instruction Giver map and the left shows a completed
   corresponding Instruction Follower map.

eleven-year-olds' (mean deviation score for six-year-olds $= 306$ cm^2; mean
for eleven-year-olds $= 223$ cm^2). Furthermore, this was only the case in the
audio-only interactions: in face-to-face communication the six-year-olds
attained performances equivalent to those of the eleven-year-olds. The
younger children's performances were significantly worse in audio-only
interaction than both their own face-to-face attempts (face-to-face $= 252$cm^2;
audio-only $= 360$cm^2) and the eleven-year-olds' performances (audio-only
$= 203$cm^2). A full account of the results of this study is given in Doherty-
Sneddon and Kent (1996).

So, six-year-olds communicated as effectively about the Map Task as
eleven-year-olds when interacting face-to-face, but they did not adjust to the
audio-only context in the way that eleven-year-olds did, and their task
performance suffered. Boyle *et al.* (1994) reported that the mean score for
adult subjects on this task was 61 cm^2 and that there was no change in task

performance between face-to-face and audio-only communication. Adults, therefore, perform this task better than either group of children and, like the eleven-year-olds, do adapt to audio-only interaction.

The younger children used more communicative gesturing than both older children and adults, and did not abandon this non-verbal strategy in the audio-only context. In contrast, although the eleven-year-olds used communicative gestures in face-to-face conversation, they did not use this form of communication in the audio-only context. This shows that while the older children were sensitive to the change in communicative medium and acted upon this, the younger children did not have the communication skills available to do this.

The following is an extract from a face-to-face Map Task dialogue between six-year-olds. The italicised words represent speech that was accompanied by communicative gesture. The speech marked by * represents non-verbal vocalisations which were used to add effect to the gestures they accompanied.

G = INSTRUCTION GIVER; H = INSTRUCTION FOLLOWER

> Turn 1 (G): Ehm, now do three straight lines.
>
> Turn 2 (H): Straight?
>
> Turn 3 (G): Uh-huh.
>
> Turn 4 (H): *Like this?*
>
> Turn 5 (G): *No.*
>
> Turn 6 (H): *Like this, like this?*
>
> Turn 7 (G): *No* * 'dunk' 'dunk' * *straight down the way.*
>
> Turn 8 (H): *Down?* Then **do do do* *.*
>
> Turn 9 (G): *No just* three *lines straight down the way* just three.

This example illustrates how poor the verbal attempts could be, and how poor the comprehension of the listener could be. The Instruction Giver wanted the Instruction Follower to draw three straight lines vertically down. He did not at first specify that the direction was down. In Turn 4 the Instruction Follower showed that he had misinterpreted the instruction to mean horizontal straight lines when he accompanied his utterance with a gesture indicating a horizontal line straight across. In Turn 5 the Instruction Giver said 'No', and gestured straight lines vertically down the way, but had not yet verbalised the downwards information. The Instruction Follower then asked 'Like this, like this?' while gesturing curving lines first vertically down and then horizontally across. The Instruction Giver repeated his instruction in Turn 7, this time verbalising that the lines were to be drawn downwards, and again accompanied the utterance with gestures designating straight lines vertically down the way. The Instruction Follower was still confused and accompanied his utterance 'Down?' with a downwards gesture, but accompanied 'do, do, do' with horizontal curvy gestures. The exasperated Instruction Giver then repeated his instruction, accompanying his verbal utterance with vertical downward gestures, and for the first time verbalised all the relevant information.

Study 2: Visual signals in problem-solving tasks with pre-school children

The purpose of Study 2 was to investigate whether the face-to-face benefit found in Study 1 for the six-year-olds would be found with younger children using a different task. Earlier pilot work at Glasgow University had found that pre-school children could not cope with the Map Task. A simpler referential task, the Shape Description Task, was used.

Twenty-six three- to four-year-olds from a playgroup in the psychology department took part. The Shape Description was a variation of the referential task designed by Glucksberg et al. (1966). The stimuli used were carefully designed in order to present the children with a task which would be communicatively challenging, but which they could achieve with some effort. The children were randomly assigned the role of Instruction Giver or Instruction Follower. The Instruction Givers were provided with a set of five blocks stacked in an opaque dispenser. The Instruction Followers had an array of 13 blocks in front of them, which were hidden from the view of the Instruction Givers by a screen. Each block had an individual design on one of its faces (see Figure 12.2 for examples of these designs). The designs were chosen on the basis that the correct referent would not always be readily identifiable, as some ambiguity would exist between two or more blocks in the Instruction Follower's array. The different shapes and colours meant that children of this age would find describing them a fairly demanding but not impossible task. Five of the Instruction Follower's blocks matched exactly the designs on the five blocks that the Instruction Giver possessed. The task involved the Instruction Giver removing his/her blocks from the dispenser one at a time and describing them to the Instruction Follower so that he/she could choose the correct matching block from their array.

The children were brought to the testing room in pairs. They were introduced to the task by the experimenter using practice blocks on which were pictures of farmyard animals. This was done to familiarise the children with the task itself without giving them practice at describing the kinds of

Figure 12.2 A set of Instruction Follower blocks used in Study 2.
The top row shows the target referents (the Instruction Giver's blocks match these five).
   Below these are the filler blocks, which are similar to the targets but differ in, for
   example, the colour or an element of pattern. There is one filler which is not related to
   the target blocks, in this case the cross to the right of the figure.

shapes they were about to use in the test proper. The children were informed
that the Instruction Follower could pass blocks that they thought were
correct through the 'flap screen' so that the Instruction Giver could check
whether the intended block had been selected. When the experimenter
judged that the children had grasped the principle behind the task, the test
proper began. All of the pairs completed versions of the task in both
face-to-face and audio-only conditions, with order of presentation counter-
balanced across the sample.

Results

The four-year-olds' communicative performance was significantly affected
by the presence or absence of visual signals. The same children's face-to-face
performances were on average 57 per cent better than their audio-only

performances. It appears that, as for the six-year-olds in Study 1, visual signals play a central role in the communication of four-year-olds. Both of the younger age groups showed increases in verbal material in the audio-only context (18% more words for six-year-olds and 35% for four-year-olds; 22% more turns for six-year-olds, and 33% for four-year-olds). This corresponds to the increased length of audio-only Map Task dialogues between adults reported by Boyle *et al.* (1994). A full account of the results is given in Doherty-Sneddon and Kent (1996). The increase in dialogue length in the audio-only context reflects an increase in verbal effort when non-verbal communication is not possible. Young children therefore make some adjustments to audio-only interaction. This contrasts with the lack of adaptation in gesturing behaviour found in Study 1.

Study 3: The role of visual signals in adult–child interviews

Studies 1 and 2 both investigated the role which visual signals play in child–child task-oriented interaction and illustrated face-to-face benefits, particularly for younger children. We wished to see whether visual signals would have similar effects in adult–child interactions. Furthermore we wished to move away from referential and problem-solving dyadic communication to the more applied, communicative situation of an adult interviewing a child. It was likely that visual signals would play a rather different role during an interview situation than in a task-oriented interaction. In the performance of a communication task (as in Studies 1 and 2), the task itself gives some structure to the interaction. Furthermore, there are task materials which have to be attended to. Such considerations may override aspects of visual signal functioning, for example in regulating interaction. In an interview the more social functions of visual signals may have greater importance. For example Kleinke, Staneski and Berger (1975) found that interviewees gave longer responses and rated their interviewers more highly when the interviewers gazed relatively frequently compared with when gaze frequency was low.

Twenty of the pre-school children who had taken part in Study 2 took part in Study 3. A staged incident paradigm was used, i.e. an unexpected event was arranged about which children were later asked to recall details. This method is commonly used in empirical studies of recall during interview (e.g. Geiselman *et al.* 1984; Saywitz, Geiselman and Bornstein 1992). Early in the day a research confederate, dressed as a clown, visited the playgroup. The confederate was given a set protocol of things to do, which were as follows:

1. Say hello.

2. Juggle some coloured balls.

3. Inform the children that it was the clown's birthday but that all her friends had forgotten.

4. Ask the children to sing Happy Birthday to the clown.

5. Give all the children a colourful sticker.

6. Shake hands with each child.

7. Say goodbye.

Later the same day the children were interviewed individually about the events that had taken place that morning. This was done either face-to-face across a table, or with a screen between the interviewer and the child. The interview continued until the interviewer had elicited all of the information about the clown's activities from the child. The interview followed a semi-structured format. The interviewer had a set of questions about the different elements, which ranged from very general open questions to specific questions. The criterion for ending an interview was that all seven events were recalled accurately. The measure of communicative success used here was therefore how many questions and conversational turns (defined by changes in speaker) it took to reach that criterion. The children's responses were videoed as an aid to evaluation.

Results

No difference was found between the face-to-face and audio-only interviews in terms of the number of questions that were required to elicit the desired information. However, it took significantly more conversational turns to elicit the same amount of information in the audio-only context (mean = 38.4) as in face-to-face interaction (mean = 27.4). One reason why the face-to-face interviews were shorter was the children's use of non-verbal responses (with no verbal accompaniment). In the audio-only condition these responses had to be spoken. The following is an extract from a face-to-face interview.

Interviewer:	Did anything special happen at playgroup today?
Child.	A clown.
Interviewer:	A clown? {*child nods*} Yes, OK. Did the clown do anything?
Child:	Juggled.

Interviewer:	Juggled. Did the clown talk to you? {*child nods*} What did she talk about?
Child:	Happy birthday.
Interviewer:	About happy birthday, yes. Anything else happen after that? Did the clown ask you to do something?
Child:	No.
Interviewer:	Did the clown ask you to sing happy birthday? {*child nods*} Yes? OK.

The extract illustrates an important difference between the face-to-face and the audio-only interviews. The child uses nodding without any verbal accompaniment on three occasions. The mean number of 'non-verbal only' responses made in the face-to-face condition was 4.7 per interview. The mean number in the audio-only condition was 0.4 per interview. The information carried by nods and shakes of the head in the face-to-face interviews was therefore replaced by verbal utterances in the audio-only context.

It therefore took fewer conversational turns to elicit the same amount of information from a child in face-to-face interaction compared with audio-only interaction. This suggests that visual signals facilitate interaction for children. The interviewer gained 'yes', 'no' and even 'don't know' responses from the children in a non-verbal format only in face-to-face interaction (approximately every fourth turn was of this nature in the face-to-face interviews). This propositional information had a significant impact on the communicative process both in terms of the information it supplied and in terms of the structure of the verbal dialogue. This highlights that important information is lost if audio-only recordings of face-to-face interviews are relied upon.

Discussion of Studies 1, 2 and 3

The first three studies showed that young children do not communicate as effectively when visual signals are not available. This contrasts with adults and older children, who maintain the same task performance in both face-to-face and audio-only communication. It appears that this was due in part to the younger children transmitting non-verbally a significant amount of information that was not expressed verbally. In Study 1 the use of gesture to communicate information was found to be most prevalent for the younger subjects. Furthermore, younger children may continue to attempt to use non-verbal communication in audio-only settings. While children increased the amount that they said in audio-only interaction, the increased verbal material did not benefit their performance. In Study 3 non-verbal answering of questions was found to be a frequent strategy used in the face-to-face interviews. It was replaced by verbal answering in the audio-only interviews.

The results support previous claims that non-verbal communicative strategies are easier for young children (for example, Feyereisen and de Lannoy 1991; Goldin-Meadow *et al.* 1992). Given that young children have various linguistic and cognitive limitations (Asher and Wigfield 1981), the face-to-face benefit for young children may have been due to two aspects of the communicative process. First, the speaker found it easier to convey information non-verbally and conveyed information in his/her visual signals which was never expressed verbally. Second, the young listeners may have found it easier to process visual signals than they did verbal messages; for example, a shape drawn in the air may give them a more comprehensible representation of an object than a verbal description of that object. When the verbal descriptions are opaque the listener's difficulties will be compounded. We are not suggesting that children are better decoders of non-verbal information, indeed there is evidence that young children are less skilled non-verbal communicators than adults (Doherty-Sneddon 1995). What is claimed is that, relative to linguistic expressions, gestures and other visual signals may be easier for children.

It has yet to be shown that young children have the ability to alter their communication strategies in response to different communicative media and styles in the way that many adults can. In his book on how to interview suspected child abuse victims, Jones (1992) advises the interviewer that 'direct gaze fixation is often too intrusive for children' (p.38), and that techniques should be employed which avoid this. The present results suggest that this may not help to elicit information from young children, since they seem to be especially dependent upon the informational cues in visual signals. Similarly, Otteson and Otteson (1980) found that children's recall of stories was better when the adult reader gazed at them while telling the story compared with when gaze did not occur. Study 4 investigates specifically the impact of decreasing 'interviewer intrusiveness', while preserving visual access between the child and interviewer, on children's evidence quality.

Studies 4a and 4b: Video link versus face-to-face adult–child interviews

A specific application of the findings of Studies 1–3 relates to the use of video-mediated interviewing in court. As discussed above, there is evidence that video-mediated communication is not equivalent to face-to-face interaction for adults, and indeed may be more similar to audio-only communication (O'Connaill, Whittaker and Wilbur 1994; O'Malley and Langton 1994; Doherty-Sneddon *et al.* 1997). The first three studies showed that visual signals have a particular importance in the communication of young children. The question that must be answered is whether the visual signals provided by video links are an appropriate substitute for face-to-face interaction.

The last two studies (4a and 4b) involved comparisons of interviews carried out via either high-quality video links or face-to-face interaction. We were interested to compare in both conditions:

- how accurately children recalled a sequence of events (correct information; incorrect relevant information; task-unrelated information)
- what level of specificity of questioning was required to elicit the information
- what communication strategies the children employed to express information (e.g. relying on entirely non-verbal versus verbal expression; the suggestibility of children to misleading questions)
- the demeanour of the children (confidence; nervousness; happiness and truthfulness).

Our focus was on the way in which the different modes of testimony affected communication strategies and how this influenced the quality of information given. The literature suggests that there may be both positive and negative effects of video mediation, and this study was directed at identifying which aspects of VMC are responsible for those effects.

We predicted that there is a 'communicative cost' associated with the use of video condition in that visual and social cues will be attenuated. However, this attenuation may be advantageous to this type of communication, i.e. an unfamiliar adult questioning a child. The increase in the psychological distance between adult and child resulting from video mediation will decrease the intimidation felt by the child, resulting in more accurate and efficient 'testimony' and a decrease in susceptibility to misleading questions.

The participants were 32 six-year-old and 32 ten-year-old children from primary schools in the Stirling area. The children came to the University of Stirling for the experimental sessions in pairs and were collected by the experimenter in a University car. A sequence of events was staged upon their arrival. The experimenter 'found' a ball and a box in the car and told the children that she did not know to whom they belonged ('someone else using the car must have left them there'). The children then accompanied the experimenter to 'Fred's' room. They were told that Fred took care of lost property. He was not there and so the experimenter left a note for him. Each pair of children experienced the same sequence of events. Later they were interviewed individually and asked about the events and various details surrounding them, e.g. the colour of the note paper, the picture on the wall in Fred's room, the name of the corridor where Fred's room was, whether the experimenter dropped the ball and so on.

Three interviewers took part in the study. They were all postgraduate psychology students at the University of Stirling. They received a half-day training in the interview procedure and were given some practice sessions. They were also given guidelines and outlines of interview procedure. Each pair of children was interviewed by the same person, one child in the face-to-face condition across a table, the other child across the video link. Each interviewer therefore carried out equal numbers of face-to-face and video-mediated interviews.

A phase approach was adopted based on the Memorandum of Good Practice (Home Office with Department of Health 1992) for practitioners involved in interviewing children. Interviewers were instructed to work through the phases using questions necessary to elicit the required information. The phases and their order were as follows:

PHASE 1: ESTABLISH RAPPORT

The goal of this phase was to relax the child so that they felt happy about talking with the interviewer.

PHASE 2: NARRATIVE REPORT

The children were asked to provide, in their own words, an account of the relevant event. Interviewers were instructed to use open-ended prompts to keep things going (e.g. 'What happened next?'; 'Can you remember anything else that happened?') and to acknowledge what the child was saying.

PHASE 3: QUESTIONING

1. Open-ended questions were used to pick up some of the points raised in the free narrative, e.g. 'Can you tell me more about the ball?'

2. Specific, non-leading questions allowed extension and clarification of previously provided information, e.g. if a child had already mentioned a ball but had not specified a colour: 'What colour was the ball?'

3. Closed questions gave the child a limited number of alternative responses, but preferably more than two; e.g. 'Was the ball, blue, brown, or another colour, or can't you remember?'

In addition children sometimes provided spontaneous information, and those were referred to as 'Explains' (from a system of conversational analysis described in Carletta *et al.* 1997).

The video condition was achieved using 'video-tunnels' (Smith *et al.* 1991). Each of these consisted of a colour monitor mounted in a wooden box behind an angled half-silvered mirror. A second, fully silvered mirror was fixed above the half-silvered mirror and angled so that light reflected from the first mirror would reflect off the second into a video camcorder located behind the box and above the TV monitor. Because of the half-silvered nature of the first mirror, Subject A, looking directly into the video-tunnel, was able to see an image of their partner (Subject B) on the monitor. With correct positioning of the camera, subjects were able to make direct eye-contact with each other.

MISLEADING QUESTIONS

Following the main part of the interview, the children were asked a series of leading questions, three of which were true (positive response correct) and three which were false. The true questions were controls. The misleading questions were as follows:

1. The blue car you came in today is really comfortable isn't it? (correct answer is that it was a red car)

2. It's really fun coming up in the lift in this building isn't it? (correct answer is that the children did not come in a lift)

3. The cartoon you watched with Sandra was really funny wasn't it? (correct answer is that they did not watch a cartoon with Sandra)

Analysis, results and discussion of Studies 4a and 4b

The six-year-olds' interactions were coded for gesture. Gestures which were pictographic or iconic (McNeill 1985; Argyle 1996) were marked onto transcripts of the interviews. The use of gesture was infrequent and was not responsible for a large amount of information transfer. There were individual differences in gesturing behaviour: one child used 51 in his interview, while the majority of children used only one or two. Given that the frequency of such gestures was expected to decrease further with the older children (for rationale *see* Goldin-Meadow *et al.* 1992), gesture coding was not carried out on the older sample. Four of the interviews were gesture coded by an independent judge who agreed with *all* of the gestures coded by the original coder.

In several ways the video condition interviews were the same as those carried out face-to-face, resulting in the same total amount of correct information and the same questioning style. The video condition was therefore comparable to face-to-face interviewing in these respects. It did not result in decreased efficiency of the interview process. This contrasts with Davies and Noon (1991), who report that elements of the judicial process took longer over the live link, suggesting decreased efficiency.

Differences which were evident suggest that children were better able to disagree with adults in the video condition: they were less likely to answer incorrectly in response to closed questions (probably because they were less inclined to guess) and were more resistant to misleading questions. Video interviews resulted in 47 per cent *less* incorrect information than face-to-face interviews. The impact of visibility on resistance to misleading questions occurred only for the younger children, the older children having a higher level of resistance regardless of condition. The younger children were 62 per cent *more* resistant to misleading questions in the video condition than in the face-to-face. Furthermore, interviewers spent more time managing younger children in the video condition. We propose that this was partly to do with ensuring that the child stayed on camera but also because the children were more relaxed in the video condition. Initial impressions from the videos of the interviews and the reports given by the interviewers backed this up. The results are reported in full in Doherty-Sneddon and McAuley (in press).

Study 4b was therefore carried out to determine whether or not the younger children were more relaxed and confident in the video condition. Video excerpts were analysed in two different ways: adult observers rated the children's demeanour, and the children's smiling behaviour was coded by an experimenter. It was expected that children in the video condition would look more confident, relaxed and happy than children in the face-to-face condition. Furthermore, we expected that video condition children would smile more often and for longer than those in the face-to-face condition, as Ekman and Friesen (1969) report that false smiles tend to be shorter than genuine smiles.

Thirty-six adult observers (students and staff of the University of Stirling) took part. Half were male and half were female. The observers watched 30-second vignettes of the children who had taken part in the interview study. As the effects of the video condition were most marked for the younger children, the video clips were of the six-year-olds. The vignettes were extracted from the same point in the interview for each child. Each adult viewed children from either the face-to-face *or* the video-mediated condition.

While viewing the videos the adults completed a questionnaire relating to each child's demeanour. Each child was rated on confidence, nervousness, happiness, and how likely it was that they were telling the truth (a scale from -3 to +3 was used with -3 being 'not at all nervous' and +3 being 'very nervous'). In addition, each child's smiling was marked onto the interview transcripts by an experimenter. The frequency of smiling and mean length of smiling (in terms of the number of words the smile extended over) was measured.

Children in the video-mediated and face-to-face interviews were rated as equally happy and truthful. While the difference between conditions for ratings of confidence was not significant, there was an increase in confidence ratings for the children in the video condition (means: video = 1.00; face-to-face = 0.68). Similarly there was a trend for children in the video-mediated condition to look *less* nervous than those interviewed face-to-face (means: video = -0.48; face-to-face = -0.02). Furthermore, video-mediated smiles were found to be longer than face-to-face smiles, and the children smiled 52 per cent more frequently during the video condition than in face-to-face interviews.

The differences that emerged between the visibility conditions reflect a positive impact on evidence quality: less incorrect information was produced in the video condition interviews; more information was given in response to open questions (Dent and Stephenson (1979) report that children's evidence is more accurate when elicited with general questions than with more specific questioning); and younger children were more resistant to misleading information. The finding that the younger children were more resistant in the video condition contrasts with those of Flin *et al.* (1996), but is in agreement with Davies and Noon (1991) and Tobey *et al.* (1995). We suggest that these effects are due to a common underlying cause – an increase in psychological distance that results in decreased intimidation and increased confidence.

Previous work with adults shows that video mediation increases the psychological distance between interlocutors (Rutter 1987). Doherty-Sneddon *et al.* (1997) provide support for this in their finding that adult subjects gaze far more at one another in video-mediated interactions than in face-to-face interaction, illustrating that the normal rules about gaze frequency and duration do not apply in mediated conversations. Argyle (1996) proposes that a number of factors, for example, close proximity, intimacy of questions and high frequency of eye gaze, can decrease the psychological distance between people. This may cause anxiety if either party is not comfortable with this. It makes sense to expect similar effects in children of the ages investigated here, as children are sensitive to social norms about gazing from a relatively early age (Scheman and Lockard 1979). On this view, Westcott *et al.* (1991a) propose that 'distancing the child from the questioner may serve to ease communication…'. Furthermore, face-to-face interaction with a stranger asking questions is likely to be intimidating for children. Taken with previous research showing the informational benefits to decreasing children's stress while they give evidence (Carter *et al.* 1996), this would suggest informational benefits when psychological distance is increased through video-mediated interactions. We suggest that informational benefits are evident in the increased resistance to misleading questions and the decreased likelihood of production of incorrect information.

Negative effects found using the link appear minor compared with the positive benefits, but nevertheless deserve consideration and are indeed informative. One potentially negative impact of the video condition was that interviewers had to expend more effort managing the younger children, who were more likely to move off camera and who were on the whole more restless in the video condition. One reason for this is inherent in the system: the camera angles only have a limited field of view and both parties have to stay within that. This finding supports Davies and Noon's (1991) suggestion that both lawyers and children should be allowed some experience of the link prior to trial. Furthermore, this underlines the importance of careful con- sideration of camera angles when setting up such a system – a wide angle shot will give greater leeway. Using a wide angle shot brings other costs, such as an increase in peripheral visual information, which may be distracting, and a decrease in size of the image of the speaker, again causing an attenuation of visual cues. Westcott *et al.* (1991b) discussed some of the issues of wide versus close-up shots, for example the use of close-up to minimise the perceived differences in credibility due to age. They concluded that style of shot does influence credibility, but that its impact is complicated by other factors such as age and gender. They argue that care must be taken in the design of equipment.

Another negative effect of the video condition was the loss of gestural information. While younger children did not use pictorial and iconic gesture frequently, most of them did it at some point during the course of their interview. Sometimes such gestures were the only articulation of certain pieces of information (with no accompanying verbalisation of the inform- ation). Given this, it is conceivable that certain information (perhaps key to the testimony) could be lost over the link. Again, this should be addressed by those involved in the trial procedure. At the very least, camera angles should be set appropriately and judges, jury and lawyers should be made aware of the potential drawbacks of gesture-only information, particularly from younger witnesses or those describing difficult information (Goldin-Meadow *et al.* 1992).

Finally, there was some evidence for an attenuation of visual feedback cues in the video condition. The older children were more forthcoming in their free narrative recall in face-to-face interaction than when using the video link (it should be noted that the total amount of information in these narratives is still a small proportion of the total amount elicited). Doherty-Sneddon *et al.* (1997) report data illustrating the link between visual signals in face-to-face adult interaction and the delivery of feedback information allowing interlocutors to monitor one another's comprehension. Furthermore, they found that only some communicative functions provided by face-to-face visual signals were served in video-mediated interaction. It may be that the children picked up visual feedback cues (such as nodding and smiling) from the interviewers better, or the interviewers were more confident about their understanding of what the child was saying in the face-to-face condition than in the video condition. Either of these effects may make the children more likely to produce better narrative recalls by facilitating the flow of interaction. Our finding that very little task-relevant information is produced during the narrative recalls agrees with Davies and Noon's (1991) finding that children were generally unwilling to recount incidents spontaneously and required prosecutors to facilitate the giving of their evidence through questions.

In many ways, therefore, video condition interviews did not differ from face-to-face interviews. Our results suggest that where differences do occur, *primarily* they have a positive impact on evidential quality. It is suggested that such effects are mediated by an increase in children's confidence under the video link condition. Negative effects include the attenuation of visual cues, although such informational loss is more than outweighed by the benefits afforded by increasing children's confidence.

Conclusions

From these studies we have drawn four main conclusions. First, visual communication signals are important in children's communication. These findings have implications for professionals responsible for assessing, communicating with or interviewing children, particularly young children. Information which is not present in speech is, at times, articulated in gesture and other non-verbal signals. The likelihood that this will happen is partly dependent upon the nature of the information that is being expressed and the ability of the speaker to express it. Nevertheless, non-verbal communication should be recognised as a potentially important channel of information. Second, young children may be less able to adapt to different communicative settings. It may be of benefit to allow children to practice and prepare for using novel communication media.

Third, our results suggested that children were more relaxed in the video link condition. In face-to-face interaction the child is co-present with their interlocutor. If the relationship between child and communicative partner is fairly symmetric, non-intimidating and supportive then the non-verbal information the child *receives* (such as gesture and feedback cues) may well be of benefit. However, if the balance of the interaction is unequal the physical co-presence of the communicative partner may well augment feelings of anxiety. Our fourth conclusion is that the quality of children's evidence is improved when the psychological distance between the child and the questioning adult is increased. In the video condition children gave less incorrect information and were better able to disagree with the adult interviewer. Such effects are likely to be augmented in real trial situations, which are often stressful and intimidating. The live link is likely therefore to facilitate accurate testimony.

Acknowledgement

This work was supported by an ESRC grant (R000236467) held by Gwyneth Doherty-Sneddon and Vicki Bruce of the Department of Psychology, University of Stirling, and Anne Anderson of the Department of Psychology, University of Glasgow. Some of the work was supported by an internal research award from the University of Stirling.

CHAPTER 13

Law, Policy, Practice and Research in Child and Family Social Work

Malcolm Hill and Dorota Iwaniec

Law, policy and practice

This book set out to share recently completed research findings concerned with services for children and their families. The concluding chapter will highlight some of the key points that have emerged.

Although the studies were all carried out in Scotland or Northern Ireland, they relate to issues which are common across the UK and indeed elsewhere. The 1990s saw the consolidation of a common set of principles covering child care in all the jurisdictions of the UK, although Scotland has distinctive elements, notably in relation to juvenile justice. Among the core guiding concepts are:

- paramountcy (of children's welfare)
- partnership (with parents)
- participation (by children)
- joint planning at strategic and case levels.

New concepts have been introduced. Some represent an attempt to reframe thinking about services and practice. Thus, 'family support' services are intended to have a more positive and wide-ranging application than their predecessors, 'preventive' services (Chapters 4 and 6; Tunstill 1996). Conversely, the duties to take account of children's religious, racial, cultural and linguistic backgrounds can be seen as a reaffirmation of principles embodied in the much earlier Race Relations Act 1976 (Chapter 10).

As noted in Chapter 2, the new children's legislation of the 1990s sought to redefine the relationships between children, parents and statutory bodies. For instance, the notion of parental responsibilities has been clarified. The emphasis has changed from parents exercising their rights to parents ful-

249

filling their responsibilities, even following separation if that occurs. However, the broad principles and specific sections of legislation can provide only a general framework. The detailed practice decisions have to be made at more local level, using professional judgement. Although the law and resources set constraints on action, they also provide a springboard for creativity (Chapter 2). This should apply to those responsible for overall service provision as well as individual practitioners working with a particular family.

A number of chapters illustrate how new legal concepts need to be interpreted, or indeed how they may risk misinterpretation. Agencies in Northern Ireland have been slow to use the new terminology much (Chapter 6). This may represent simply a time-lag effect, a reluctance to shift thinking positively or perhaps a justified guardedness about the value of some of the 'new' concepts, such as children in need. The broad and vague depictions of children in need found in the legislation and guidance mean that wide variations exist in their operationalisation (Chapter 4). This illustrates how discretion can give scope for local self-determination, but can also result in inconsistencies between different areas (Asquith and Adler 1981).

Taking account of children's views has been an important legal duty for some time, but was reinforced by a number of factors during the 1990s. The UN Convention on the Rights of the Child, ratified by the UK in 1991, includes a wide range of rights – to safety, provision, protection and so on. Most attention probably has been paid to participatory rights, however (Franklin 1995). Much thought and effort has been put into optimising contributions to decision-making by young people who are in residential or foster care (Hill 1998). Studies in this book have emphasised the importance of attending to children's individual wishes, since what suits one child may be diametrically opposed to what is desired or acceptable to another (Chapters 8 and 9). Compared with the arrangements for looked-after children, participation by disabled young people in their transitions from school is underdeveloped (Chapter 7).

The Children Act 1989 introduced the 'No Order' principle to England and Wales. This has often been characterised as meaning 'minimum inter-vention'. Skinner argued in the Scottish context that this should *not* be taken to mean providing only a minimal service or only assisting families where a child is thought to be at risk (Chapter 2). Instead, he suggests, support should be provided at the appropriate level, which may be quite extensive, though with the minimum degree of intrusiveness necessary for the sake of the child's welfare.

Sometimes the legislation has made compulsory what was already a developing practice. Children's Services Plans were first encouraged by

Government Circular in England and Wales (Sutton 1995), but then incorporated as legal duties across the UK (Chapter 3). In contrast, the Looking After Children materials represent an interesting example of a policy– practice innovation that has been encouraged top-down by central government, but on a voluntary negotiated basis (except in Northern Ireland). One of the reasons the materials have proved attractive to managers and many practitioners is that they seemed to fit well with the principles of the new legislation, which in turn are well regarded (Chapter 8).

Planning and co-ordination of services

The need for different agencies to co-operate and the difficulties of doing so have been long-standing themes in the history of child welfare. Lack of inter-departmental co-operation under the Poor Law was one of the reasons for establishing Children's Departments after 1948, while the Maria Colwell Inquiry in the 1970s identified inadequate information-sharing and co-ordination as a significant factor in the failure to prevent Maria's death. Later inquiries identified similar difficulties in inter-agency co-operation (Parton 1985, 1991; Hill 1990). As a result strenuous efforts were made to improve collaboration among child protection services in the ensuing years (Heywood 1978; Hallett and Birchall 1992; Stevenson 1999). For instance, in cases of child neglect a wide range of social, health, day care and educational support services are usually involved (Chapter 11).

The issue acquired a new edge in the second half of the 1990s with the developing commitment to corporate responsibility. In England, Wales and Scotland this meant that local government departments were expected not simply to co-ordinate their services but to plan jointly and take shared ownership of children's needs and problems. The first priority of local authorities when devising Children's Services Plans was to engage all chief officers in the strategy and decision-making committees (Hearn and Sinclair 1998; Chapter 3). Many authorities developed joint departmental agree-ments on children in need (Chapter 4). On the other hand, in the early stages of introducing the LAC materials, departments and agencies other than social work were little involved (Chapter 8).

In Northern Ireland the organisational context is different since social services are provided by health and social services boards and trusts, but similar efforts to improve co-operation have been made. Here, social services' aims and priorities defined in Government papers are set within a health framework, so tend to be more universal, e.g. promoting health and well-being. On the other hand, specific targets tend to be geared towards medical considerations (Chapter 2). HSS boards are required to commission services through collaboration. An integrated Children's Services Plan is required for each board area and automatically includes health, unlike in Great Britain (Chapter 4). Health, police and education were the main agencies that child care managers reported having agreements or protocols with. Many care managers recognised difficulties in inter-agency co-operation. The most common problem was a lack of clarity of roles and responsibilities, followed by agencies not fulfilling their responsibilities and pushing their own agenda within limited resources (Chapter 4; *see also* Chapter 3). Recent guidance in Northern Ireland stresses inter-professional assessment of risk and need (Chapter 5).

Two of the key traditional departments with specific responsibilities for children are education and social services (or social work). Differences in remit and outlook have meant that teachers and social workers have often acted independently or taken different views (Bruce 1983; Borland *et al.* 1998; Gilligan 1998), though good collaborative schemes have also been developed (Kendrick 1995b). All the evidence suggests that improving inter-professional and inter-agency co-operation in this field is difficult and often slow. Co-operative mechanisms are necessary at structural, practical and attitudinal levels (Chapter 9).

Transition planning for disabled young people still tends to be carried out separately by education and social work in many areas (Chapter 7). Whereas social workers have been criticised for ignoring educational issues for looked-after children (Jackson 1989), young people with disabilities said that their personal independence and social needs were neglected because of a focus on formal education. Transition planning should be multi-dimensional, with regular assessment, review, and planning of education, vocational prospects and personal preparation for adult life. Different agencies and professionals need to come together to co-ordinate their contribution to the transition plans of disabled young people.

With respect to looked-after children, several studies have concluded that change is needed across the entire school and care systems if children's needs are to be appropriately assessed and met. Many children who enter foster or residential care have school difficulties as well as home-related problems, but often their educational disadvantage is not tackled effectively. A stimulating and supportive home environment is important, but usually extra tuition or teaching is needed. The appointment of link teachers is an effective mechanism, especially when they combine direct educational input with advocacy, information-sharing and liaison. However, they must be supported by joint policies and commitment at front-line and senior management levels (Chapter 9). The principle of open sharing among professionals can run into conflict with children's rights to confidentiality and privacy. Hence it is helpful to have separate education and care plans in order to tackle the distinct issues and minimise confidentiality problems (Chapters 8 and 9).

The changing relations between the statutory and voluntary sectors were illuminated by the study of Children's Services Plans (Chapter 3). Tisdall, Monaghan and Hill found that co-operation between the two was hampered by the lack of comprehensive information held by local authorities on voluntary agencies. Also, the latter did not act in a concerted fashion, nor offer a single contact point at local or national levels for local authorities to relate to. The emphasis on corporate and inter-statutory co-operation meant that voluntary agencies had little input in the early stages and at strategic levels, though selected agencies did make significant contributions to detailed plan development in working groups. Some local authorities saw voluntary service-providers' need to gain money to sustain and develop services as incompatible with offering 'neutral' input to represent service users' views or interests.

Several studies described in this book have shown how co-operation requires careful thought and planning, together with a substantial time commitment (Chapters 3, 7 and 9). This has major resource implications for both agencies and individuals. They need to balance the opportunity costs, in terms of service delivery that may be lost when time is devoted to liaison and meetings, against the improvements that joint assessment, planning and work can bring.

Diversity and discrimination

Following the example of the Children Act 1989, the Children (Scotland) Act 1995 introduced duties for local authority social workers to take into account the religious, racial, linguistic and cultural backgrounds of children in need and looked-after children (Chakrabarti et al. 1998; O'Hagan 1999). In part this entails ensuring that children have the opportunity to pursue the traditions of their community of origin and to develop a positive identity. More than that, it requires constant vigilance and questioning of assumptions deeply embedded within social work and wider society concerning what is normal or correct (Chapter 10). The LAC materials include prompts to social workers and carers about language, culture and identity, though they have also been criticised for imposing white, middle-class norms (Chapter 8).

A survey in Scotland by Singh et al. (Chapter 10) revealed the low level of social workers' knowledge on the Race Relations Act. Ethnic monitoring was far from universal, so data about staff and users is lacking. Respondents were sometimes confused about the difference between multiculturalism and anti-racism. Black staff were nearly all at basic grade level; many were sessional. It appeared that in many agencies staff lacked the knowledge and understanding to respond appropriately to the needs and wishes of black and minority ethnic children.

Children of minority backgrounds should be able to benefit from universal services like any other children, but may require particular provision or sensitively tailored practice. Similar considerations apply to other groups. For instance, looked-after children may well gain from special educational arrangements, but then feel stigmatised by being singled out. Inclusive practices within mainstream schooling are generally preferable, but may not respond sufficiently to a child's disadvantage (Chapter 9). The dilemma between integration and dedicated services is also apparent in relation to some disabled children (Chapter 7).

Children in need and family support

The category of 'children in need' was introduced to indicate that segment of the child population who have the main claim on social work services. Whereas the thrust of previous legislation had been on preventing reception into care or court appearances, 'children in need' represented a shift to the promotion of health and development (Chapter 4). The so-called 'refocusing' policy shift of the mid-1990s (Chapter 1) stressed that the category 'children in need' should not be restricted simply to children at risk. In particular, qualifying for the child protection register should not be the main criterion for service receipt, since this bars others who need help, as well as those who could avoid registration if given adequate support (Colton, Drury and Williams 1995a; Hardiker 1999).

In Northern Ireland, McCrystal (Chapter 4) found that a majority of managers thought the formal definition of children in need was adequate for practice, but significant numbers did not. Those working in the disability field were pleased that children with disabilities had been given clear recognition in the 1995 Order. Managers claimed to be taking into account a variety of factors when deciding whom to include as a child in need. The focus on risk was less than had been found in English and Welsh studies (Department of Health 1995). Thirteen indicators prepared by the government were widely used, but it was not clear if these added anything to existing practice (Chapter 4).

So far, most authorities have relied on existing data to assess the numbers and types of children in need in their areas. Within social work, 'need' has traditionally been defined in individualistic terms according to basic welfare deficits and rights to services. Percy (Chapter 5) suggests that a health economics approach provides a more helpful basis for assessing needs at the population level. This takes account of availability of resources, the capacity to benefit from services, and comparisons with other people in similar positions. It becomes necessary to assess the interaction between need (problems in the context of services and resources), demand (often mediated by others, not self-expressed) and supply.

Reliance on official records is inadequate for calculating the extent of need for various reasons. They are often partial and do not include hidden and unidentified need (Chapters 4, 5 and 6). Information tends to be most readily available on children who are looked after, on the child protection register or disabled (Carr-Hill, Rice and Smith 1999). Capture–recapture methods or small area utilisation modelling can be used to overcome this drawback. The later method connects with the concept of comparative need sketched by Bradshaw (1972) to supplement felt, expressed and expert-defined need. It is assumed that areas with roughly the same demographic characteristics should have similar levels of need. Other ways of assessing need include carrying out local surveys and using proxy indicators, but each has its advantages and problems.

Children's Services Plans offer a way forward for systematic needs assessment, though early evidence is that the data included are extremely generalised and often derived from service-use information rather than being needs-based (Chapters 3 and 5). The LAC records have potential for aggregating detailed information on need, but at present they are confined to the relatively small population of children placed away from home, though the Department of Health plans to adapt the materials for children in need (Department of Health 1999). According to Wheelaghan and Hill (Chapter 8), incomplete completion and inadequate use of IT are likely to remain major obstacles to collation of the information for some time to come.

Unlike the phrase 'children in need', the term 'family support' is not part of the legislation. Like partnership (with parents), it has become an ideal commonly aspired to in practice as expressing the spirit rather than the letter of the law. Family support conveys the role of services made available by a range of statutory and voluntary agencies, for children in need in the broadest sense. A survey of Northern Ireland agencies found no consensus about the meaning of family support. The services varied from the universal to the highly targeted (Chapter 6). Service providers did not make explicit their underlying assumptions about welfare delivery or levels of prevention, nor link their purposes to the legislation on children in need. Their views of need centred largely on poverty and family difficulties.

Some have used the idea of family support to cover services used on a voluntary basis, in contrast to those imposed by statutory order to protect children. Higgins (Chapter 6) concluded that child protection and family support are not opposites or alternatives, but rather grade into each other. Similarly, studies of children who failed to thrive have shown that recovery is often crucially dependent on a mix of family support services (Chapter 11).

Assessments for family support should take into account the diversity of family and household forms in modern Britain (Muncie *et al.* 1999). It is important to consider cultural differences, for example with respect to marriage, parenthood or health (Singh 1997; Humphreys, Aktar and Baldwin 1999), but also to guard against stereotyping and to recognise the impact of racism (Chakrabarti *et al.* 1998). Similarly, in families with a disabled child, it is necessary to acknowledge the implications both of the impairment and of social barriers. Also, 'family' should not be confined to parents and/or an identified child, since siblings and others may well have important needs, for example in relation to a child with autism (Newson and Davies 1994).

Disabled children and young people

Children with disabilities are one of the core groups identified under the 'children in need' category. They and their families are entitled to access services that will promote the child's welfare and to receive information about those services (Chapter 7). In Scotland, an additional group are 'children adversely affected by disability'. This reflects a growing concern with children assisting parents who have come to be known as young carers (Dearden and Becker 1998), although this approach has been criticised for disregarding parental and family roles (Keith and Morris 1995).

A wide range of general purpose and specialist agencies exist to meet the needs of children with physical or sensory impairments or learning difficulties. Among the challenges faced by relevant organisations and professionals are:

- balancing service provision with public (re-)education roles in order to modify stigmatising, excluding and disabling attitudes and practices (Oliver and Sapey 1998; Shakespeare 1998)
- moving from a 'deficit' model of disability to a strength-based empowerment approach
- co ordinating plans and actions in the spheres of education, health and social welfare
- taking a life-span perspective, particularly to avoid disjunctures at crucial stages such as entry to school and leaving school.

The present legislation emphasises that children's services should consider the long-term welfare of children. In the past, the transition to adulthood has often been problematic for disabled children, often resulting in the loss of previous supports and segregation in special training or sheltered employment arrangements. Monteith (Chapter 7) argues that disabled young people are entitled to the same opportunities as all young people to have their stage-linked needs met. Assessment and services must be holistic and not hamstrung by conventional service orientations. In Northern Ireland, HSS trusts are required to carry out an assessment of disabled children before they leave school in conjunction with education and other relevant agencies. Elsewhere in the UK, this is done by local authorities.

Research has shown disabled young people to be more vulnerable than others to isolation, low income, poor self-esteem and restricted lives. A survey carried out in Northern Ireland showed that nearly all young disabled adults were still living in the parental home and very few were in fully-paid work: most were in education or job schemes (Chapter 7). Consequently, the great majority were reliant on some form of benefit and/or parents for money. Most did have independent control over their money, however. Many were participating in mainstream clubs and social activities, though a number attended special clubs for disabled young people. The majority had similar aspirations to able-bodied people about marriage and having an independent household. Some of the means of achieving these goals (including employment, income and housing adaptations) were often not present. Evidently, their basic employment and material circumstances have to be addressed if they are to make the transition to adulthood in the ways they wish and most others achieve.

Looked-after children

The most extensive responsibilities of statutory social welfare agencies (local authorities or boards and trusts) relate to children looked after away from home. Among the duties are to:

- provide 24-hour accommodation with good-quality care
- safeguard and promote the child's welfare
- take account of the child's views
- encourage parents to maintain contact and exercise their continuing responsibilities
- nurture a child's identity and heritage.

Over the years, systems of assessment, planning and reviews have developed to try and ensure that children's needs are thoroughly examined and responded to. Government guidance stipulates minimum frequencies for cases to be reviewed. The Looking after Children system of records has been developed to assist these processes (Ward 1995). One of the main aims of proponents of the system has been to make available a set of key prompting questions, which should ensure that all of a child's main needs are considered and appropriate action taken. Perhaps inevitably, this has resulted in quite bulky, standardised documents, which some workers in some contexts find difficult to use. However, the evaluation of the Scottish pilot revealed considerable support for the records (Chapter 8). The questions were mostly seen as appropriate and helpful, though a minority found some unhelpful, irrelevant or intrusive. Few users identified items that could be readily omitted. In certain cases, use of the records had facilitated discussion among social workers, carers and young people about sensitive or previously neglected issues.

One of the seven dimensions of the LAC materials is education. Just like disabled children, looked-after children normally have poor education records and tend to be very disadvantaged in the labour and housing markets when they make the transition to adulthood (Chapter 9). The main reasons for this are:

- pre-care experiences and adversity
- young people's experience in schools
- non-attendance
- frequency of moves
- social workers' attitudes
- the care environments
- ineffective collaboration between social work and education.

Innovative projects developed in the 1990s to improve education–social work collaboration give promising pointers to elements needed in a co-ordinated strategy (such as joint planning at strategic and case levels; employment of link teachers). The academic and social significance of education also needs to be emphasised in leaving care programmes (Biehal et al. 1995). Additional educational input at home or at school has been found to assist. Borland (Chapter 9) highlights the importance of matching action to individual needs and wishes. What suits one young person may be resented by others.

Black children accommodated in Scotland usually live in otherwise all-white families or residential units, apparently with little contact with other members of their community of origin. This casts doubt on the current capacity of local authorities to take account of their religious, racial, cultural and linguistic backgrounds as required by statute (Chapter 10). Evidence from England indicates that children of minority ethnic backgrounds gain in confidence and a sense of belonging when they are placed in settings with positive black role models and confidants (Barn *et al.* 1997).

Child protection

In many ways the British child protection systems established since the mid-1970s have been a success. Many early problems, such as professionals' failure to recognise abuse, share information or act together, now appear to be quite rare (Birchall and Hallett 1995). The inclusion of parents in case conferences and the growing use of family group conferences have helped reduce animosities and misunderstandings, although inevitably tensions remain (Thoburn *et al.* 1995; Marsh and Crow 1998). Nevertheless, difficulties remain, and one of the core criticisms has been that children have suffered a form of 'secondary' abuse through being caught up in investigations and court processes whose primary aim has been to gather good evidence, not to meet children's needs for help, reassurance and information (McGee and Westcott 1996; Hill and Tisdall 1997).

A unique 20-year follow-up study by Iwaniec (Chapter 11) has shown how children can nonetheless be significantly helped by intervention, especially if it occurs early enough. She examined children who fail to thrive, i.e. they are small and weak as a result of an eating disorder closely associated with quality of parenting and attachment. The outcomes for such children can be very poor. Children placed away from home on abuse or neglect grounds have the poorest educational record (Chapter 9). In the Iwaniec study, lack of maternal warmth, poverty and social isolation were usually crucial factors. Although the children appeared to have had somewhat better relationships with their fathers, this did not seem to have compensated, since the mothers were the main carers. A combination of help was provided on an intensive basis, including parental skills training, dealing with maternal depression and giving practical help and support.

The follow-up interviews revealed that when families were referred early, received treatment and responded well, the children had very good long-term outcomes (Chapter 11). They had reached average height and weight, relationships with their mothers had significantly improved and eating behaviour usually was within the normal range.

When treatment was offered at a later stage, it was less effective. Similarly, adoption studies show that when attachment problems are entrenched, it is harder to achieve full recovery (Howe 1998). Iwaniec also found that those who had extended difficulties and were removed from home did better than those who remained at home (Chapter 11). Again this echoes earlier findings (Tizard 1977). Though numbers were very small, those fostered experienced more security and clarity about their status, whereas most in foster care were still confused and hurt (cf. Triseliotis and Russell 1984; Hill et al. 1989).

A small number of parents were bitter that their claims that there were organic reasons were discounted for some time but eventually shown to be true. Most parents valued the help given, especially those who received a mixture of practical and non-practical assistance.

Currently, children's evidence is often necessary to secure convictions of adult abusers. It is important to understand children's competencies and limitations in communication to optimise the value of their evidence in different forms. Such understanding can also inform preparation for children and indeed wider direct practice with children. A series of linked studies by Doherty-Sneddon et al. (Chapter 12) illuminated various aspects of this issue. Younger children tended to use gestures both as a sole means of communication and to support their verbal utterances. Moreover, a number of them appeared not to realise that their use of non-verbal communication was less appropriate or effective in certain contexts, such as when screens and live video links were used. They were also much affected by visual information, which is reduced in evidential situations.

Experimental laboratory studies suggested that the video link situation does result in some loss of communicative efficacy for young children. This seems to be offset by other gains. Children were more relaxed and more able to disagree with a questioner over the video link than in face-to-face circumstances. It is also known that some children would not have given evidence otherwise. Children gave relatively little information in free narrative and needed considerable prompting (Chapter 12).

These studies have implications beyond the child witness context. They suggest that, unless workers have much time to build up a relationship of trust, reliance on free recall and open-ended methods (whether for investigation, assessment or direct work) will result in slow progress. Young children's gestures should be closely attended to. It is helpful if children can practice how best to communicate in unfamiliar contexts.

The role of research

The rationale for this book as a whole and the individual studies on which it is based is that it is valuable for policy-makers and practitioners to learn from research. This position has gained growing support from government bodies (Chapter 2).

One of the catchphrases of the late 1990s was 'evidence-based practice'. In many respects this is an approach we support. Indeed, it is almost 'self-evident' that the activities of professionals, managers and others ought to be based on careful consideration of the best evidence available. As Sinclair (1998) observed,

> 'Too often policies about service provision are based on well-meaning beliefs or assumptions about what is best for children, rather than on evidence of the wants or needs of children or that a particular way of meeting need will have the desired effects – or indeed, that this effect will be in the long-term interests of the child' (p.170).

However, there are twin dangers. First, it may too readily be assumed that evidence should be the only or overriding factor, so that decision-making risks becoming merely a technical exercise. In our view, it is also vital to be clear and critical about the goals, principles and values that guide practice. Otherwise, research findings may be misapplied. For instance, critics of the permanency planning movement argued that research implications were often selectively distorted (Harding 1996; Kelly 1998). Some of the early interpretations of children's attachment needs and processes made in the 1950s were later shown to have little validity (Rutter 1981; Schaffer 1990; Burman 1994), though other core ideas have been very usefully developed and applied in child and family social work (Howe 1995; 1996). The debate about same-race or transracial placements has been as much about values as 'facts' (Chapter 10; Hill and Shaw 1998). Studies can of course help to illuminate the manner in and extent to which legal or policy principles are put into practice and the range of perceptions and views germane to a particular issue (e.g. Chapters 4 and 6).

Second, the idea of 'evidence' may be defined too narrowly. Sometimes this is identified with the theme of 'What works?', i.e. which services or interventions are effective (Alderson *et al.* 1996)? This is an important question, but it can also lead to oversimplified thinking. In particular, it seems to invoke the idea that A works and B does not work. Very possibly A may work better than B in the majority of cases, but for some people, in certain circumstances or at different times, B may 'work' better than A. Chapter 11, for example, showed how the same kind of help provided at a later stage in the evolution of problems related to neglect was less successful than earlier intervention. It is also necessary to unpack the question of what is meant by 'works'. As Chapter 12 showed in relation to children's communication, a situation of restricted interaction (a video link) can have benefits on some levels, but drawbacks on others. It may be possible to weigh up the advantages and disadvantages in that instance, but in other circumstances that may be more difficult. Short-term gains may differ from the long-term outcomes, while the perspectives of different informants are often contradictory (Sweeting forthcoming). The implication is not to abandon attempts to assess effectiveness, but to take a complex and pluralistic approach to relevant evidence.

The randomised control trial (RCT) is often seen as the prime mechanism for establishing whether an intervention works or not (MacDonald, Sheldon and Gillespie 1992). Subjects are randomly allocated to the intervention under investigation or a comparison group which may receive no service or a routine service. When rigorously conducted this approach leads to helpful and definite conclusions. For example, support has been repeatedly documented for positive results from structured pre-school programmes and behavioural approaches to certain externalising problems (Webster-Stratton and Herbert 1994; Herbert 1998; Roberts and Macdonald 1999). However, practical and ethical concerns mean that such trials are hard to achieve (Fuller 1996). Rightly or wrongly, many interventions, projects and individuals adapt their work to particular situations. This flexibility may accord with service users' wishes and needs, but the absence of consistency or stability can mean there is no unified intervention to evaluate in accord with the experimental paradigm of the RCT. Even when a trial is well conducted, it can be difficult to know which elements or combination of elements in a programme were most crucial. Consideration also needs to be given to people who cannot access or drop out of an otherwise successful programme (Hill 1999b). For all these reasons, it is often helpful to engage in pluralistic evaluation, which gathers information from a range of sources on a number of levels. As McCoy states, both qualitative and quantitative approaches are needed (Chapter 2).

Systematic, external evaluations are crucial to strengthening the basis for services and decisions. However, empirically based practice (or policy) should be more than this. Broad definitions indicate that individuals and agencies ought to be actively assessing their own work. Practitioners can develop their research-mindedness in many ways, ranging from user surveys to single-case designs (Cheetham et al. 1992; Cheetham and Kazi 1998; Iwaniec and Pinkerton 1998). Social work and other agencies have now developed an array of performance indicators and other measures to monitor their work (Connor and Black 1994). The information that can be produced and collated is crucially reliant on the quality of recording. Unfortunately, agency record and information systems do not often lend themselves to aggregation and, in any case, are often imperfectly completed (Chapters 5 and 8). The dearth of adequate data has been noted in relation to ethnic monitoring and the education of looked-after children, for example (Chapters 9 and 10).

This book has also illustrated that empirical knowledge is required on matters other than evaluation of interventions. Also vital is information on the extent and nature of needs and problems and evidence about causal, protective and vulnerability factors (Chapter 5). Experimental research can refine understanding of crucial elements in social interactions, though it is important to check how far conclusions are applicable in real world (ecological validity) (Chapter 12). It is hard to develop services, especially on a co-operative basis, without a sound understanding of the objectives and perceptions of key stakeholders (Chapters 3 and 6). This must include service users, even when they are difficult to trace or have communication difficulties (Chapter 7). An even greater challenge to researchers is to identify emerging issues of the future, which may be particularly difficult if most efforts are put into assessing responses to current problems or needs (Chapter 2).

General conclusions

The studies reported in this book have served to illuminate important elements of recent policy and legislation in relation to children and families. On the whole there is a consistency between the legislative principles and the research implications. For example, both stress the importance of early intervention, co-operation between professionals and family members, systematic planning and joint work. Several studies point to the need for multiple interventions which combine material and psychosocial support and intervention.

The research also indicates gaps between the aims and achievements of child care policies. In many areas, the resources do not suffice to fulfil aspirations. This applies not simply to the availability of services (as in relation to family support) or their appropriateness (with respect to disabled or black children), but to staff time (e.g. the LAC system). A theme threading through this book, and indeed policy and research texts for several decades, is the actual or potential value of agencies and professionals co-operating more closely. Yet this also requires much time and careful thought if it is to happen effectively. Without additional assistance, smaller organisations in particular may find it hard to divert scarce staff resources from their core activities to take on consultation and collaborative roles.

Statutory services were criticised in the early 1990s for their excessive focus on 'child protection', by which was meant investigations of suspected intra-familial child abuse. Families with significant needs were often left unaided when risk was not considered or not substantiated (Gibbons *et al.* 1994). Some people hoped that 'children in need' would prove a more inclusive basis for allocating services. It is undoubtedly important to prioritise the use of resources and have dedicated provision for particular needs. Just as important, though, is to have effective, universally available services. These are more inclusive for those who would otherwise be stigmatised (e.g. disabled children and vulnerable families).

Research and services for children and families are both constantly evolving. Each should inform the other. Openness of professionals and policy-makers to evidence is high as the new millennium starts. In order to justify the faith that others may place in it, empirical enquiry needs to be systematic, critical and pluralistic.

The Contributors

Moira Borland is Senior Research Fellow at the Centre for the Child & Society, University of Glasgow. Her main research interest is provision for children looked after away from home.

Ozlem Carrera was a part-time research assistant as vacation work during undergraduate study in the Department of Psychology, University of Stirling.

Gwyneth Doherty-Sneddon is Lecturer in Psychology at the University of Stirling. She took up this post in 1994 while completing her Ph.D., titled 'The Development of Conversational and Communication Skills', at the University of Glasgow. Her current research interests include the development of children's verbal and non-verbal communication skills, the communicative impact of video mediation, and the processing of facial cues.

Patricia Falconer is project worker with Barnados Matrix project, specialising in early intervention work with children at risk of offending.

Kathryn Higgins is Research Fellow at the Centre for Child Care Research, The Queen's University of Belfast. Her research interests and publications focus on the areas of family and child care, particularly family support, adolescent drug use, injecting drug use and HIV infection. She also has an interest in methodological issues related to researching hidden populations. She is currently Co-principal Investigator on the Belfast Youth Development Study.

Malcolm Hill is St Kentigern Professor and Director of the Centre for the Child & Society, University of Glasgow. He has carried out research and teaching on children's issues for the last 20 years.

Dorota Iwaniec is Professor of Social Work and Head of the School of Social Work, The Queen's University of Belfast. She is also Director for the Centre for Child Care Research. Dorota is well known for her work with children who fail to thrive, and on emotional abuse and neglect of children – areas in which she has published widely, including her book, *The Emotionally Abused and Neglected Child: Identification, Assessment and Intervention* (1995). Prior to her appointment at The Queen's University of Belfast she had been working as a social worker in different capacities for 20 years.

Sandra McAuley is a full-time research assistant in the Department of Psychology, University of Stirling. Previously she was at the University of Nottingham Trent, working on a Ph.D. in Education.

Kevin McCoy is a chief social work inspector in Northern Ireland.

Patrick McCrystal is Research Fellow at the Centre for Child Care Research, The Queen's University of Belfast, where he is engaged in work on the risk and protective factors associated with adolescent drug use. He has recently completed work on children in need. Patrick previously worked as Research Officer at the School of Education, University of Ulster, and at the Health and Health Care Research Unit, The Queen's University of Belfast. His research interests are in child care and vocational education.

Bernadette Monaghan has a law degree from Trinity College, Dublin and an MSc in Legal Studies (criminology) from Edinburgh University. She is a senior manager with the criminal justice charity, Sacro (Safeguarding Communities, Reducing Offending). She also worked on multi-agency crime prevention initiatives set up by the former Lothian Regional Council and the Scottish Office Safer Cities Programme. She was a member of the Children's Panel for nine years. Her research interests include crime prevention and community safety, young offenders, domestic violence and drug and alcohol abuse.

Marina Monteith is Research Fellow at the Centre for Child Care Research, The Queen's University of Belfast. She previously worked in the Northern Ireland Housing Executive and also in Human Resource Planning and Policy Research in the NHS North Thames region. Her current research interests include the transition to adulthood for young disabled people, the provision of social services for disabled children and their families, and stability in the care careers of looked-after children. She is currently principal investigator for a research project on multiple placements and the extent of stability in the care careers of younger looked-after children in Northern Ireland.

Vijay K.P. Patel is Consultant with British Agencies for Adoption & Fostering in Scotland, specialising in addressing the needs of black children who are looked after. He is also an Associate Lecturer with the Open University School of Health and Social Welfare.

Andrew Percy is Research Statistician at the Centre for Child Care Research, The Queen's University of Belfast. He is currently Principal Investigator on the Belfast Youth Development Study, a five-year longitudinal survey of adolescent drug use. His research interests include population needs assessment, methodological innovations in the survey research, and the longitudinal study of adolescent behaviour.

Angus Skinner is the Chief Inspector of Social Work Services at The Scottish Executive. After having obtained his social work qualification in London in 1973, he returned to Scotland and worked with Lothian Region Social Work Department, including six years as an Area Officer in Pilton, Edinburgh. In 1991, after three years as Deputy Director, Borders Region, Social Work Department, he took up his post at the Scottish Executive. Since then he has been responsible for the publication of several reports. *'Another Kind of Home' a Review of Residential Care* (1992) and, *A Secure Remedy: A Review of the Role, Availability and Quality of Secure Accommodation or Children in Scotland* (1996). *A Commitment to Protect* was published at the end of 1997.

Satnam Singh is Senior Practitioner with Barnados Family Placement services in Edinburgh, with the lead role for the Khandan initiative, a family placement service for black and minority ethnic children. He is also an associate lecturer with the Open University School of Health and Social Welfare.

E. Kay M. Tisdall currently holds the posts of Lecturer in Social Policy, University of Edinburgh, and Policy and Research Manager, Children in Scotland – the national membership agency for organisations working with children. She previously worked at the Centre for the Child & Society, University of Glasgow.

Suzanne Wheelaghan was Research Fellow in the Centre for the Child & Society, University of Glasgow. She has also worked in the housing field and residential child care.

References

Achenbach, T.M., Howell, C.T., Ooki, M.F. and Rauh, V.A. (1993) 'Nine year outcome of the Vermont Intervention program for low birth weight infants.' *Child Development 61*, 1672–1681.

Alderson, P., Brill, S., Chalmers, I., Fuller, R., Hinkley-Smith, P., MacDonald, G., Newman, T., Oakley, A., Roberts, H. and Ward, H. (1996) *What Works?* Ilford: Barnardos.

Aldgate, J., Heath, A., Colton, M. and Simm, M. (1993) 'Social work and education in foster care.' *Adoption & Fostering 17*, 3, 25–34.

Aldgate, J., Tunstill, J., McBeath, G. and Ozolins, R. (1994) *Implementing Section 17 of the Children Act – The First Eighteen Months.* London: HMSO.

Alwin, D.F. (1991) 'Research on survey quality.' *Sociological Methods & Research 20*, 3–29.

Anderson, E.M. and Clarke, L. (1982) *Disability in Adolescence.* London: Methuen.

Apley, J., Davies, J., Russell Davis, D. and Silk, B. (1971) 'Dwarfism without apparent cause.' *Proceedings Royal Society of Medicine 64*, 135–138.

Argyle, M. (1996) *Bodily Communication.* London: Routledge.

Armstrong, D. and Davies, F. (1995) 'The transition from school to adulthood: aspirations and careers advice for young adults with learning and adjustment difficulties.' *British Journal of Special Education 22*, 2, 70–75.

Asher, S.R. and Parke, R.H. (1975) 'Influence of sampling and comparison processes on the development of communication effectiveness.' *Journal of Educational Psychology 67*, 64–75.

Asher, S.R. and Wigfield, A. (1981) 'Training referential communication skills.' In W.P. Dickson (ed) *Children's Oral Communication Skills.* New York: Academic Press.

Aspinall, P.J. (1996) *Predictors of Child Abuse and Neglect. Review of Research Literature Relevant to Family Functioning and Child Care in Northern Ireland.* London: South East Institute of Public Health.

Asquith, S. and Adler, M. (1981) *Discretion and Welfare.* London: Heinemann.

Association of Directors of Social Services (ADSS) (1978) *Multi-racial Britain: the Social Services Response.* London: Commission for Racial Equality.

Audit Commission (1994) *Seen But Not Heard: Co-ordinating Community Child Health and Social Services for Children in Need.* London: HMSO.

Baker, A.W. and Duncan, S.P. (1985) 'Child sexual abuse: a study of prevalence in Great Britain.' *Child Abuse and Neglect 9*, 457–467.

Bald, J., Bean, J. and Meegan, F. (1995) *A Book of My Own.* London: Who Cares? Trust.

Banks, M., Bates, I., Breakwell, G., Brynner, J., Emler, N., Jamieson, L. and Roberts, K. (1992) *Careers and Identities.* Milton Keynes: Open University Press.

Barbaro, G.J. and Shaheen, E. (1967) 'Environmental failure-to-thrive: a clinical view.' *Journal of Paediatrics 71*, 639–644.

Barn, R., Sinclair, R. and Ferdinand, D. (1997) *Acting on Principle.* London: BAAF.

Barnardos (1996) *Transition to Adulthood.* Essex: Barnardos.

Baxter, J.S. (1990) 'The suggestibility of child witnesses: a review.' *Applied Cognitive Psychology 4*, 393–407.

Bebbington, A. (1996) *Synthetic Estimation Methods for Resource Allocation Formulae.* PSSRU Discussion Paper 1203/3. Canterbury: University of Kent at Canterbury.

Bebbington, A., Turvey, K. and Janzon, K. (1996) *Needs Based Planning for Community Care.* PSSRU Discussion Paper 1206/2 Canterbury: University of Kent at Canterbury.

Bebbington, A.R. and Miles, J. (1989) 'The background of children who enter local authority care.' *British Journal of Social Work 19*, 349–368.

Beecham, Y. (1999). *Report to the Department of Health on Costing Child Care Services.* Canterbury: University of Kent at Canterbury PSSRU.

Beecham, Y. and Knapp, M. (1995) 'The cost of child care assessment.' In R. Sinclair, L. Garnett and D. Berridge (eds) *Social Work and Assessment with Adolescents.* London: National Children's Bureau.

Bell, M. (1999) 'The Looking After Materials: a critical analysis of their use in practice.' *Adoption & Fostering, 22*, 4, 14–23.

Belsky, J. (1993) 'Etiology of child maltreatment: A developmental-ecological analysis'. *Psychological Bulletin 114*, 3, 413–434.

Bemrose, C. and Mackeith, J. (1996) *Partnerships for Progress: Good Practice in the Relationship Between Local Government and Voluntary Organisations.* Bristol: The Policy Press.

Berridge, D. (1985) *Children's Homes.* Oxford: Blackwell.

Berridge, D. and Brodie, I. (1996) 'Residential child care in England and Wales. The inquiries and after.' In M. Hill and J. Aldgate (eds) *Child Welfare Services. Developments in Law, Policy, Practice and Research.* London: Jessica Kingsley Publishers.

Berridge, D. and Brodie, I. (1998) *Children's Homes Revisited.* London: Jessica Kingsley Publishers.

Berridge, D., Brodie, I., Ayre, P., Barrett, D., Henderson, B. and Wenman, H. (1996) *Hello – Is Anybody Listening? The Education of Young People in Residential Care.* Luton: University of Luton.

Berridge, D. and Cleaver, H. (1987) *Foster Home Breakdown.* Oxford: Basic Blackwell.

Berthoud, B. (1998) *Incomes of Ethnic Minorities.* Essex: Institute of Social and Economic Research, University of Essex.

Biehal, N., Clayden, J., Stein, M. and Wade, J. (1992) *Prepared for Living?* London: National Children's Bureau.

Biehal, N., Clayden, J., Stein, M. and Wade, J. (1995) *Moving On: Young People and Leaving Care Schemes.* London: HMSO.

Birchall, E. and Hallett, C. (1995) *Working Together in Child Protection.* London: HMSO.

Blizzard, R.M. and Bulatovic, A. (1993) 'Psychological short stature: a syndrome with many variables.' *Bailliere's Clinical Endocrinology and Metabolism 6,* 3, 637–712.

Borland, M., Pearson, C., Hill, M. Tisdall, K. and Bloomfield, I. (1998) *Education and Care Away from Home.* Edinburgh: SCRE.

Bowes, A., Dar, N. and Sim, D. (1998) 'Too white, too rough, and too many problems'. University of Stirling.

Bowes, A. and Sim, D. (eds) (1991) *Demands and Constraints: Ethnic Minorities and Social Services in Scotland.* Edinburgh: SCVO.

Bowlby, J. (1969) *Attachment and Loss, Vol. 1.* London: Hogarth Press.

Boyle, E.A., Anderson, A.H. and Newlands, A. (1994) 'The effects of eye contact on dialogue and performance in a co-operative problem solving task.' *Language and Speech 37,* 1–20.

Bradshaw, J. (1972) 'The concept of social need.' *New Society 19,* 640–643.

Braham, P., Rattansi, A. and Skellington (1992) *Racism and Anti-racism: Inequalities, Opportunities and Policies.* London: Sage.

Brimblecombe, F.S.W. (1987) *The Needs of Handicapped Young Adults.* Exeter: Institute of Child Health, University of Exeter.

Brown, G., Anderson, A., Shillcock, R. and Yule, G. (1984) *Teaching Talk. Strategies for Production and Assessment.* Cambridge: Cambridge University Press.

Browne, K.D. and Saqi, S. (1988) 'Approaches to screening for child abuse and neglect.' In K. Browne, C. Davies and P. Stratton (eds) *Early Prediction and Prevention of Child Abuse.* Chichester: John Wiley & Sons.

Browne, K.D. and Stevenson, J. (1983) 'A Checklist for Completion by Health Visitors to Identify Children at Risk of Child Abuse.' Report to Surrey County Area Committee on Child Abuse (unpublished) summarised in K.D. Browne and S. Saqi (1988) 'Approaches to screening for child abuse and neglect.' In K. Browne, C. Davies and P. Stratton (eds) *Early Prediction and Prevention of Child Abuse.* Chichester: John Wiley & Sons.

Bruce, N. (1983) 'Social work and education.' In J. Lishman (ed) *Collaboration and Conflict.* Aberdeen: Aberdeen University Press.

Buckingham, K., Bebbington, A., Campbell, S., Dennis, C., Evans, G., Freeman, P., Martin, N. and Olver, L. (1996) *Interim Needs Indicators for Community Health Services.* Canterbury: PSSRU, University of Kent at Canterbury.

Bullard, D.M., Glaser, H.H., Heagarty, M.C. and Privchik, E.C. (1967) 'Failure-to-thrive in the neglected child.' *American Journal of Orthopsychiatry 37,* 680.

Bullock, R., Little, M. and Millham, S. (1998) *Secure Treatment Outcomes: The Care Careers of Very Difficult Adolescents*. Aldershot: Ashgate.

Burman, E. (1994) *Deconstructing Developmental Psychology*. London: Routledge.

Cadman, M. and Chakrabarti, M. (1992) 'Social work in a multi-racial society: A survey of practice in two Scottish local authorities.' In *One Small Step Towards Racial Justice*. London: CCETSW.

Cannan, C. (1992) *Changing Families, Changing Welfare: Family Centres and the Welfare State*. London: Harvester.

Carletta, J., Isard, A., Isard, S., Kowtko, J., Doherty-Sneddon, G. and Anderson, A. (1997) 'The reliability of a dialogue coding scheme.' *Computational Linguistics 23*, 12–31.

Carr-Hill, R.A., Dixon, P., Mannion, R., Rice, N., Rudat, K., Sinclair, R. and Smith P.C. (1997) *A Model for the Determination of Expenditure on Children's Personal Social Services*. York: Centre for Health Economics, University of York.

Carr-Hill, R.A., Rice, N. and Smith, P.C. (1999) 'Determinants of expenditure on Children's Personal Social Services.' *British Journal of Social Work 29*, 5, 679–706.

Carter, C.A., Bottoms, B.L. and Levine, M. (1996) 'Linguistic and socioemotional influences on the accuracy of children's reports.' *Law and Human Behaviour 20*, 579.

Cashmore, J. and De Haas, N. (1992) *The Use of Close-circuit Television for Children Witnesses in the ACT*. Report for the Australian Law Reform Commission and the Australian Capital Magistrates Court. Sydney: Australian Law Commission.

Cassell, J., McNeill, D. and McCullough, K.E. (1994) 'Speech-gesture mismatches: evidence for one underlying representation of linguistic and non-linguistic information.' Paper presented at Human Communication Research Centre seminar, University of Edinburgh.

Central Council for Education and Training of Social Work (CCETSW) (1991) *Rules and Requirements for the Diploma in Social Work*, 2nd (edn). London: CCETSW.

Chakrabarti, M., Thorne, J., Brown, N., Hill, M., Khand, I., Lindsey, M. and Hosie, A. (1998) *Valuing Diversity*. Edinburgh: Scottish Office.

Chapanis, A., Ochsman, R.B., Parrish, R.N. and Weeks, G.D. (1972) 'Studies in interactive communication: the effects of four communication modes on the behaviour of teams during co-operative problem-solving.' *Human Factors 14*, 487–509.

Chatoor, L., Hirsch, R. and Persinger, M. (1997) 'Facilitating internal regulation of eating: a treatment model for infantile anorexia.' *Infants and Young Children 9*, 4, 12–22.

Cheetham, J. (1982) *Social Work and Ethnicity*. London: George Allen & Unwin.

Cheetham, J., Fuller, R., McIvor, G. and Petch, A. (1992) *Evaluating Social Work Effectiveness*. Buckingham: Open University Press.

Cheetham, J. and Kazi, M.A.F. (eds) (1998) *The Working of Social Work*. London: Jessica Kingsley Publishers.

Children (1995 Order) (Amendment). *Children's Services Planning Order (Northern Ireland) (1998)*. Belfast: HMSO.

Children (NI) Order Implementation Officers Group (1996) *Interim Policy and Procedures Handbook on Family Support, Volume One.* Belfast: HMSO.

Children (NI) Order Implementation Officers Group (1998) *Policy and Procedures Handbook.* Belfast: Department of Health and Social Services.

Children (Northern Ireland) Order 1995, No. 755 (N.I.2). Belfast: HMSO.

Children (Scotland) Act 1995. Edinburgh: HMSO.

Children Act 1989. London: HMSO.

Children in Scotland Voluntary Sector Implementation Forum (1998) *Making the Act Work: Views of the Voluntary Sector on the Children (Scotland) Act 1995.* Edinburgh: Children in Scotland.

Children's Rights Development Unit (1994) *UK Agenda for Children.* London: CRDU.

Chronically Sick and Disabled Persons (NI) Act 1978. Belfast: HMSO.

Church, R.B. and Goldin-Meadow, S. (1986) 'The mismatch between gesture and speech as an index of transitional knowledge.' *Cognition 23,* 43–71.

Clarke, A. and Hirst, M. (1989) 'Disability in adulthood: ten year follow-up of young people with disabilities.' *Disability Handicap and Society 4,* 271–281.

Cohen, P. and Bains, H. (eds) (1988) *Multi-Racial Britain.* Basingstoke: Macmillan.

Coie, J.D., Watt, N.F., West, S.G., Hawkins, J.D., Asarnow, J.R., Markman, H.J., Ramey, S.L., Shure, M.B. and Long, B. (1993) 'The science of prevention: a conceptual framework and some directions for a national research program.' *American Psychologist,* October, 1013–1023.

Cole, K. (undated) *The 1991 Local Base and Small Area Statistics.* Manchester: Census Dissemination Unit University of Manchester.

Coleman, R. and Provence, S. (1957) 'Environmental retardation (hospitalism) in infants living in families.' *Paediatrics 19,* 285.

Colton, M. (1988) *Dimensions of Substitute Child Care.* Aldershot: Avebury.

Colton, M., Drury, C. and Williams, M. (1995a) 'Children in need: definition, identification and support.' *British Journal of Social Work 25,* 711–728.

Colton, M., Drury, C. and Williams, M. (1995b) *Children in Need.* Aldershot: Avebury Publishing.

Colton, M., Heath, A. and Aldgate, J. (1995c) 'Factors which influence the educational attainment of children in foster family care.' *Community Alternatives 7,* 1, 15–38.

Commission for Racial Equality (CRE) (1989) *Race Equality in Social Service Departments: A Survey of Equal Opportunities Policies in England, Scotland and Wales.* London: CRE.

Common Purpose, Scottish Conference (1998) Scottish Graduates Conference Report.

Connelly, N. (1989) *Race and Change in Social Service Departments.* London: PSI.

Connor, A. and Black, S. (1994) *Performance Review and Quality in Social Care.* London: Jessica Kingsley Publishers.

Corby, B. and Millar, M. (1997) 'A parents' view of partnership.' In J. Bates, R. Pugh and N. Thompson (eds) *Protecting Children.* Aldershot: Arena.

Craig, G., Hill, M., Manthorpe, J., Tisdall, K., Monaghan, B. and Wheelaghan, S. (2000) 'Picking up the pieces: Local government reorganisation and voluntary sector children's services.' *Children & Society*.

Cree, V. (1995) *From Public Streets to Private Lives*. Aldershot: Avebury.

Cullen, M.A. and Lloyd, G. (1997) *Exclusions from School and Alternatives Vol 2. Alternative Education Provision for Excluded Pupils: A Literature Review*. Edinburgh: Moray House Institute of Education, Heriot-Watt University.

Dartington Social Research Unit (1995) *Matching Needs and Services: The Audit and Planning of Provision for Children Looked After by Local Authorities*. Cheshire: Dartington Social Research Unit.

Davies, C., Morgan, J., Packman, J., Smith, G. and Smith, J. (1994) *A Wider Strategy for Research and Development Relating to Personal Social Services*. London: HMSO.

Davies, G.M. and Noon, E. (1991) *An Evaluation of the Live Link for Child Witnesses*. London: Home Office.

Davies, H., Joshi, H. and Clarke, L. (1997) 'Is it cash that the deprived are short of?' *Journal of the Royal Statistical Society: Series A, 160*, 1, 107–126.

Davies, M. (1994) *The Essential Social Worker: An Introduction to Professional Practice in the 1990s*. Aldershot: Arena.

Dearden, C. and Becker, S. (1998) *Young Carers in the United Kingdom*. London: Carers National Association.

De'Ath, E. (1988) 'The family centre approach.' *Focus on Families, No. 2*. London: Children's Society.

Deloitte and Touche (1997a) *Children Order Data Quality Audit: Report to the Department of Health and Social Service on Stage 2*. Belfast: Deloitte & Touche.

Deloitte and Touche (1997b) *Children Order Data Quality Audit: Stage 3 Report to the Project Board*. Belfast: Deloitte & Touche.

Dent, H.R. and Stephenson, G.M. (1979) 'An experimental study of the effectiveness of different techniques of questioning child witnesses.' *British Journal of Social and Clinical Psychology 18*, 41–51.

Department of Education and Employment (DfEE) (1994) *Code of Practice on the Identification and Assessment of Special Education Needs*. London: HMSO.

Department of Education for Northern Ireland (DENI) (1997) *Code of Practice on the Identification and Assessment of Special Education Needs*. Belfast: HMSO.

Department of Health (1988) *Protecting Children: A Guide for Social Workers Undertaking a Comprehensive Assessment*. London: HMSO.

Department of Health (1991) *Patterns and Outcomes of Placement*. London: Department of Health.

Department of Health (1995) *Child Protection: Messages from Research*. London: Department of Health.

Department of Health (1999) *Working Together to Safeguard Children*. London: Department of Health.

Department of Health and Social Services (NI) (1979) *Report of the Children's and Young Person's Review Group: Legislation and Services for Children and Young People (Black Report)*. Belfast: HMSO.

Department of Health and Social Services (NI) (1995) *Annual Report of the Chief Medical Officer – the Health of the Public in Northern Ireland*. Belfast: HMSO.

Department of Health and Social Services (NI) (1995) *An Introduction to the Children (NI) Order 1995*. Belfast: HMSO.

Department of Health and Social Services (1996a) *Children (NI) Order 1995. Regulations and Guidance: Family Support, Childminding and Daycare, Vol. 2*. Belfast: HMSO.

Department of Health and Social Services (1996b) *Regional Strategy for Health and Social Welfare 1997–2002*, Belfast: DHSS.

Department of Health and Social Services (1996c) *Children Order Guidance and Regulations, Volume 5*. Belfast: DHSS (NI).

Department of Health and Social Services (1997) 'Well into 2000.' Belfast: DHSS.

Department of Health and Social Services and Department of Education (NI) (1994) *Policy on Early Years Provision for Northern Ireland*. Belfast: HMSO.

Department of Health, Social Care Group (????) *Quality Protects. Framework for Action*. London: Department of Health.

Department of Health/Price Waterhouse (1993) *Population Needs Assessment: Good Practice Guide*. London: Department of Health.

Devine, P., Higgins, K. and Pinkerton, J. (1998) *Family Support Perspectives from Practice: Report of the Evaluation of Creggan Day Centre*. Belfast: Centre for Child Care Research, Queen's University of Belfast.

Diamond, I., Simpson, S., Middleton, E., Lunn, D. and Tye, R. (1997) *Estimating with Confidence: Making Small Area Population Estimates in Britain*. Manchester: Centre for Census and Surveys, University of Manchester.

Dingwall, R. (1989) 'Some problems about predicting child abuse and neglect.' In O. Stevenson (ed) *Child Abuse: Professional Practice and Public Policy*. New York: Harvester Wheatsheaf.

Disability Discrimination Act 1995. Belfast: HMSO.

Disabled Persons (NI) Act 1989. Belfast: HMSO.

Doel, M. and Shardlow, S. (eds) (1996) *Social Work in a Changing World: An International Perspective on Practice Learning*. Ashgate: Arena.

Doherty-Sneddon, G. (1995) 'The Development of Conversational and Communication Skills.' Unpublished Ph.D. thesis. University of Glasgow.

Doherty-Sneddon, G., Anderson, A.H., O'Malley, C., Langton, S., Garrod, S. and Bruce, V. (1997) 'Face-to-face and video mediated communication: a comparison of dialogue structure and task performance.' *Journal of Experimental Psychology: Applied 3*, 105–125.

Doherty-Sneddon, G. and Kent, G. (1996) 'Visual signals and the communication abilities of children.' *Journal of Child Psychology and Psychiatry 37*, 949–959.

Doherty-Sneddon, G. and McAuley, S. (in press) 'Influence of video mediation on adult-child interviews: implications for the use of the live link with child witnesses.' *Applied Cognitive Psychology.*

Dominelli, L. (1998) *Anti-Racist Social Work, 2nd Edition.* Basingstoke: Macmillan.

Downey, R. (1995) 'Voluntary bodies warned of danger of contract wars.' *Community Care,* 6–12 April, 3.

Doyle, C. (1997) 'Emotional abuse of children: issues for intervention.' *Child Abuse Review 6,* 330–342.

Drotar, D. (1991) 'The family context of non-organic failure-to-thrive.' *American Journal of Orthopsychiatry 6,* 1, 23–34.

Drotar, D. and Sturm, L. (1988) 'Predication of intellectual development in young children with histories of non-organic failure-to-thrive.' *Journal of Pediatric Psychology 13,* 218–296.

Eastern Area Children and Young People's Committee (1999) *Children Services Plan 1999–2002.* Belfast: Eastern Health and Social Services Board.

Education (NI) Order 1996. Belfast: HMSO.

Education and Libraries (NI) Order 1986. Belfast: HMSO.

Ekman, S. and Friesen, N.V. (1969) 'The repertoires of non-verbal behaviour: categories, origins, usage and coding.' *Semiotica 1,* 49–98.

Essen, J., Lambert, L. and Head, J. (1976) 'School attainment of children who have been in care.' *Child Care, Health and Development 2,* 339–351.

Fabb, J. and Guthrie, T. (1997) *Social Work Law in Scotland.* Edinburgh: Butterworths.

Farmer, E. (1993) 'The impact of child protection interventions: the experiences of children and parents.' In L. Waterhouse (ed) *Child Abuse and Child Abusers.* London: Jessica Kingsley Publishers.

Feyereisen, P. and de Lannoy, J.D. (1991) *Gesture and Speech.* Cambridge: Cambridge University Press.

Finkelhor, D., Moore, D., Hamby, S.L. and Straus, M.A. (1997) 'Sexually abused children in a national survey of parents: methodological issues.' *Child Abuse and Neglect 21,* 1–9.

Fischhoff, J., Whitten, C.F. and Pettit, M.G. (1971) 'A psychiatric study of mothers of infants with growth failure secondary to maternal deprivation.' *Journal of Paediatrics 79,* 209–215.

Fletcher, B. (1993) *Not Just a Name: The Views of Young People in Foster and Residential Care.* London: National Consumer Council/Who Cares? Trust.

Fletcher, B. (1995) '"Looked after" pupils' experience of education and exclusion from school.' In E. Blyth. and S. Hollingsworth (eds) *The Prevention and Management of Exclusion from School: An Inter-agency Conference.* Huddersfield: Centre for Education Welfare Studies, University of Huddersfield.

Fletcher, B. (1998) 'Achieving Success in the Education of Looked After Children.' Seminar paper, February 1998, University of Dundee and BAAF.

Fletcher-Campbell, F. (1998a) *The Education of Children who are Looked After.* Slough: National Foundation for Educational Research.

Fletcher-Campbell, F. (1998b) 'Progress and procrastination.' *Children and Society 12,* 1, 3–11.

Fletcher-Campbell, F. and Hall, C. (1990) *Changing Schools? Changing People? The Education of Children in Care.* Slough: National Foundation for Educational Research.

Flin, R.H., Bull, R., Boon, J. and Knox, A. (1990) *Child Witnesses in Scottish Criminal Prosecutions. Report to the Scottish Home and Health Department.* Glasgow: Glasgow College of Technology.

Flin, R.H., Kearney, B. and Murray, K. (1996) 'Children's evidence: Scottish research and law.' *Criminal Justice and Behaviour 23,* 358–376.

Flynn, M. and Hirst, M. (1992) *This Year, Next Year, Sometime...? Learning Disability and Adulthood.* London and York: National Development Team and Social Policy Research Unit.

Francis, J., Thomson, G. and Mills, S. (1995) *The Quality of the Educational Experience of Children in Care: A Report to Lothian Regional Council Departments of Social Work and Education.* Edinburgh: University of Edinburgh.

Frank, D.A. and Zeisel, S.H. (1988) 'Failure-to-thrive.' *Paediatric Clinics of North America 35,* 1187–1206.

Franklin, B. (ed) (1995) *The Handbook of Children's Rights.* London: Routledge.

Frost, N. (1996) *Negotiated Friendship, HomeStart and the Delivery of Family Support.* Leicester: HomeStart.

Fuller, R. (1996) 'Evaluating social work effectiveness: a pragmatic approach.' In P. Alderson, S. Brill, I. Chalmers, R. Fuller, P. Hinkley-Smith, G. MacDonald, T. Newman, A. Oakley, H. Roberts and H. Ward (eds) *What Works?* Barkingside: Barnardos.

Garnett, L. (1992) *Leaving Care and After: A Follow-up Study to the Placement Outcomes Project.* London: National Children's Bureau.

Garbarino, J. (1999) *Lost Boys: Why Our Sons Turn Violent and How We Can Save Them.* New York: Free Press.

Garrett, P.M. (1999) 'Mapping child-care social work in the final years of the twentieth century: A critical response to the "Looking After Children" system.' *British Journal of Social Work 29,* 27–47.

Geiselman, R.E., Fisher, R., Firstenberg, I., Hutton, L., Sullivan, A. and Prosk, A. (1984) 'Enhancement of eyewitness memory: an empirical evaluation of the cognitive interview.' *Journal of Police Science and Administration 12,* 74–80.

Ghate, D. and Spencer, L. (1995) *The Prevalence of Child Sexual Abuse in Britain.* London: HMSO.

Gibbons, J., Conroy, S. and Bell, C. (1994) *Operating the Child Protection System.* London: HMSO.

Gibbons, J., Thorpe, S. and Wilkinson, P. (1990) *Family Support and Prevention: Studies in Local Areas.* London: HMSO.

Gibbons, J. and Wilding, J. (1995) *Needs, Risks and Family Support Plans: Social Services Departments' Responses To Neglected Children.* Interim Report to Department of Health. Norwich: University of East Anglia.

Gilligan, R. (1997) 'Beyond permanence? "The importance of resilience in child placement practice and planning".' *Adoption & Fostering 21,* 1, 12–20.

Gilligan, R. (1998) 'The importance of schools and teachers in child welfare.' *Child and Family Social Work 3,* 1, 13–25.

Gilligan, R. (1999) 'Working with social networks.' In M. Hill (ed) *Effective Ways of Working with Children and Their Families.* London: Jessica Kingsley Publishers.

Gilroy, P. (1987) *There Ain't no Black in the Union Jack.* London: Hutchison.

Glaser, D. and Prior, V. (1997) 'Is the term child protection applicable to emotional abuse?' *Child Abuse Review 6,* 315–329.

Glucksberg, S., Krauss, R.M. and Weisberg, R. (1966) 'Referential communication in nursery school children: method and some preliminary findings.' *Journal of Experimental Child Psychology 3,* 333–342.

Goerge, R.M., Sommer, T.E., Lee, B.J. and Harris, A.G. (1995) *Use of the Multiple Human Services by Illinois Children and Families: The Use of Administrative Data for Research Purposes.* Chicago: The Chapin Hall Centre for Children at the University of Chicago.

Goerge, R.M., Van Voorhis, J. and Lee, B.J. (1994) 'Illinois's longitudinal and relational child and family database.' *Social Science Computer Review 12,* 3, 351–365.

Goldin-Meadow, S., Wein, D. and Chang, C. (1992) 'Assessing knowledge through gesture: using children's hands to read their mind.' *Cognition And Instruction 9,* 201–219.

Goodman, G.S., Bottoms, B.L., Schwartz, K., Beth, M. and Rudy, L. (1991) 'Children's testimony about a stressful event: Improving children's reports.' *Journal of Narrative and Life History 1,* 69–99.

Goodman, G.S., Tobey, A.E., Batterman-Faunce, J.M., Orcutt, H., Thomas, S., Shapiro, C. and Sachsenmaier, T. (1998) 'Face-to-face confrontation: Effects of closed-circuit technology on children's eyewitness testimony and jurors' decisions.' *Law and Human Behaviour 22,* 165–203.

Grantham-McGregor, S., Powell, C., Walker, S., Chang, S. and Fletcher, P. (1994) 'The long term follow-up of severely malnourished children who participated in an intervention programme.' *Child Development 65,* 428–439.

Green, W.H., Deutsch, S.I. and Campbell, M. (1987). 'Psychosocial dwarfism: psychological and aetiological considerations.' In C.B. Nemesoff and P.T. Loosens (eds) *Handbook of Psychoneuroendocrinology.* New York: Guilford Press.

Hallett, C. and Birchall, E. (1992) *Coordination and Child Protection: A Review of the Literature.* Edinburgh: HMSO.

Hampton, D. (1996) 'Resolving the feeding difficulties associated with non-organic failure to thrive.' *Child Care, Health and Development 22,* 4, 273–284.

Hanks, H. and Hobbs, C. (1993) 'Failure-to-thrive: a model for treatment.' *Bailliere's Clinical Paediatrics 1,* 1, 101–119.

Harbison, J.J.M. (1996) 'Countdown to the Children Order – a departmental perspective.' *Child Care in Practice, Special Children Order Edition,* 2–9.

Hardiker, P. (1999) 'Children still in need indeed: prevention across five decades.' In O. Stevenson (ed) *Child Welfare in the UK.* Oxford: Blackwell.

Hardiker, P., Exton, K. and Barker, M. (1991) *Policies and Practices in Preventative Child Care.* Aldershot: Avebury.

Harding, L.F. (1996) *Perspectives in Child Care Policy.* London: Longman.

Harrington, J. (1608/1920) *The Englishman's Doctor or the School of Salernum.* London. Edited by F.R. Packard and R.H. Garrison, New York, 1920.

Hawthorne-Kirk, R. (1995) 'Social support and early years centres.' In M. Hill, R. Hawthorne-Kirk and D. Part (eds) *Supporting Families.* Edinburgh: HMSO.

Health and Personal Social Services (NI) Order 1991. Belfast: HMSO.

Health and Personal Social Services (NI) Order 1994. Belfast: HMSO.

Hearn, B. and Sinclair, R. (1998) *Children's Services Plans. Analysing Need: Reallocating Resources.* Report to the Department of Health. London: National Children's Bureau.

Heath, A., Colton, M. and Aldgate, J. (1994) 'Failure to escape: a longitudinal study of foster children's educational attainment.' *British Journal of Social Work 24,* 241–260.

Heath, C. and Luff, P. (1991) 'Disembodied conduct: communication through video in a multi-media office environment.' In S.P. Robertson, G.M. Olson and J. Olson (eds) *Human Factors in Computing Systems: Research Through Technology.* CHI 1991 Conference Proceedings. New Orleans: CHI.

Hemenway, D., Solnick, S. and Carter, J. (1994) 'Child rearing violence.' *Child Abuse and Neglect 18,* 12, 1011–1020.

Herbert, M. (1998) *Clinical Child Psychology.* Chichester: Wiley.

Herbert, M. and Iwaniec, D. (1979) 'Behavioural casework and failure-to-thrive.' *Australian Journal of Child and Family Welfare 5,* 19–31.

Heywood, J. (1978) *Children in Care.* London: Routledge & Kegan.

Higgins, K. (1998) 'Researching hidden populations.' In D. Iwaniec and J. Pinkerton (eds) *Making Research Work: Promoting Child Care Policy and Practice.* Chichester: John Wiley and Sons.

Higgins, K., Devine, P. and Pinkerton, J. (1998b) *Family Support Perspectives from Practice: Report of the Evaluation of Ballymena Children's Centre.* Belfast: Centre for Child Care Research, The Queen's University of Belfast.

Higgins, K., Pinkerton, J. and Devine, P. (1998a) *Perspectives from Practice.* Belfast: Centre for Child Care Research.

Higgins, K., Pinkerton, J. and Devine, P (1998b) *Family Support in Northern Ireland: Perspectives from Practice.* Belfast: Centre for Childcare Research.

Higgins, K., Pinkerton, J. and Switzer, V. (1997) *Family Support in Northern Ireland – Starting Points.* Belfast: Centre for Child Care Research.

Higgins, K., Switzer, V., Devine, P., Pinkerton, J. (1998d) *Family Support Perspectives from Practice: Report of the Evaluation of Pomeroy Playgroup.* Belfast: Centre for Child Care Research, The Queen's University of Belfast.

Hill, M. (1990) 'The manifest and latent lessons of child abuse inquiries.' *British Journal of Social Work 20,* 3, 197–213.

Hill, M. (1997) *Understanding Social Policy.* Oxford: Blackwell.

Hill, M. (1998) 'What children and young people say they want from social work services.' *Research, Policy and Planning 15,* 3, 17–27.

Hill, M. (ed) (1999a) *Effective Ways of Working with Children and their Families.* London: Jessica Kingsley Publishers.

Hill, M. (1999b) 'Effective professional intervention in children's lives.' In M. Hill (ed) *Effective Ways of Working with Children and their Families.* London: Jessica Kingsley Publishers.

Hill, M. and Aldgate, J. (eds) (1996) *Child Welfare Services.* London: Jessica Kingsley Publishers.

Hill, M. and Shaw, M. (1998) *Signposts in Adoption.* London: BAAF.

Hill, M. and Tisdall, K. (1997) *Children and Society.* London: Longman.

Hill, M., Lambert, L. and Triseliotis, J. (1989) *Achieving Adoption with Love and Money.* London: National Children's Bureau.

Hill, M., Murray, K. and Rankin, J. (1991) 'The early history of Scottish child welfare.' *Children and Society 5,* 2, 182–195.

Hirst, M. and Baldwin, S. (1994) *Unequal Opportunities: Growing Up Disabled.* London: HMSO.

Hirst, M.A. (1984) *Moving On: Transfer of Young People with Disabilities to Adult Services.* York: Social Policy Research Unit, University of York.

Holman, B. (1988) *Putting Families First.* London: Macmillan.

Home Office with Department of Health (1992) *Memorandum of Good Practice for Video Recorded Interviews with Child Witnesses for Criminal Proceedings.* London: HMSO.

Houston, S. (1996) 'A clarion call to planners, managers and practitioners: don't forget the U.N. Convention.' *Child Care in Practice 3,* 1, 38–41.

Howe, D. (1995) *Attachment Theory for Social Work Practice.* London: Macmillan.

Howe, D. (ed) (1996) *Attachment Theory and Child and Family Social Work.* Aldershot: Avebury.

Howe, D. (1998) *Patterns of Adoption.* Oxford: Blackwell.

Humberside County Council (1995) *The Educational Attainments and Destinations of Young People Looked After by Humberside County Council.* Humberside: Humberside County Council.

Humphreys, C., Atkar, S. and Baldwin, N. (1999) 'Discrimination in child protection work: recurring themes in work with Asian families.' *Child and Family Social Work 4,* 4, 283–291.

Ince, L. (1998) *Making it Alone.* London: BAAF.

Iwaniec, D. (1983) *Social and Psychological Factors in the Aetiology and Management of Children who Fail to Thrive.* Ph.D. thesis. University of Leicester.

Iwaniec, D. (1995) *The Emotionally Abused and Neglected Child: Identification, Assessment and Intervention.* Chichester: Wiley.

Iwaniec, D. (1997) 'An overview of emotional maltreatment and failure-to-thrive.' *Child Abuse Review 6*, 370–388.

Iwaniec, D. and Herbert, M. (1999) 'Multi-dimensional approach to helping emotionally abused and neglected children and abusive parents.' *Children and Society* (13, 365–379).

Iwaniec, D., Herbert, M. and McNeish, A.S. (1985a) 'Social work with failure-to-thrive children and their families – Part I: Psychosocial factors.' *British Journal of Social Work 15*, 3, 243–259.

Iwaniec, D., McNeish, A.S. and Herbert, M. (1985b) 'Social work with failure-to-thrive children and their families – Part II: Behavioural social work intervention.' *British Journal of Social Work 15*, 4, 375–389.

Iwaniec, D. and Pinkerton, J. (eds) (1998) *Making Research Work.* Chichester: Wiley.

Jackson, S. (1987) 'Residential care and education.' *Children and Society 2*, 4, 335–350.

Jackson, S. (1989) 'The education of children in care.' In B. Kahan (ed) *Child Care: Research, Policy and Practice.* London: Hodder and Stoughton.

Jackson, S. (1994) 'Educating children in residential and foster care.' *Oxford Review of Education 20*, 3, 267–279.

Jackson, S. (1998) 'Looking After Children: A new approach or just an exercise in form filling? A response to Knight and Caveney.' *British Journal of Social Work 22*, 1, 45–56.

Jackson, S. and Martin, P.Y. (1998) 'Surviving the care system: education and resilience.' *Journal of Adolescence 21*, 5, 569–584.

James, A., Jenks, C. and Prout, A. (1998) *Theorising Childhood.* London: Falmer Press.

Johnson, N. (1990) *Reconstructing the Welfare State.* Hemel Hempstead: Harvester Wheatsheaf.

Jones, D.P.H. (1992) *Interviewing the Sexually Abused Child: Investigation of Suspected Abuse.* London: Gaskell.

Jones, G. and Wallace, C. (1992) *Youth, Family and Citizenship.* Milton Keynes: Open University Press.

Jones, H., Clark, R., Kufeldt, K. and Norman, M. (1998) 'Looking After Children: assessing outcomes in child care. The experience of implementation.' *Children & Society 12*, 3, 212–222.

Jordan, B. (1997) 'Social work in society.' In M. Davies (ed) *The Blackwell Companion to Social Work.* Oxford: Blackwell.

Kahan, B. (1979) *Growing Up in Care.* Oxford: Blackwell.

Keith, L. and Morris, J. (1995) 'Easy targets: a disability rights perspective on the "children as carers" debate.' *Critical Social Policy 44/5*, 36–57.

Kelly, G. (1998) 'The influence of research on child care policy and practice: the case of "Children who Wait" and the development of the Permanence Movement in the United Kingdom.' In D. Iwaniec and J. Pinkerton (eds) *Making Research Work*. Chichester: Wiley.

Kelly, G. and Pinkerton, J. (1996) 'The Children (NI) Order 1995: Prospects for progress?' In M. Hill and J. Aldgate (eds) *Child Welfare Services: Developments in Law, Policy, Practice and Research*. London: Jessica Kingsley Publishers.

Kendrick, A. (1995a) 'Residential care in the integration of child care services.' Research Findings No 5. Edinburgh: Scottish Office Central Research Unit.

Kendrick, A. (1995b) 'The integration of child care services in Scotland.' *Children & Youth Services Review 17*, 5/6, 619–636.

Kendrick, A., Simpson, M. and Mapstone, E. (1996) *Getting it Together: Changing Services for Children and Young People in Difficulty*. York: York Publishing Ltd.

Kent, R. (1997) *Children's Safeguards Review*. Edinburgh: The Stationery Office, Social Work Services Inspectorate.

Kerslake, A. (1998) 'Computerisation of the Looking After Children records: Issues of implementation.' *Children and Society 12*, 3, 236–237.

Kilbrandon Report. Scottish Home and Health Department and the Scottish Education Department (1964) *Children and Young Persons. Scotland*. Report to the Committee Appointed by the Secretary of State for Scotland. Presented to Parliament April 1964. Cm 2306. Edinburgh: HMSO.

Kleinke, C.L., Staneski, R.A. and Berger, D.E. (1975) 'Evaluation of an interviewer as a function of interviewer gaze, reinforcement of subject gaze, and interviewer attractiveness.' *Journal of Personality and Social Psychology 6*, 7–12.

Knapp, M. (1997) 'Economic evaluations and interventions for children with mental health problems.' *Journal of Child Psychology and Psychiatry 38*, 1, 3–16.

Knapp, M., Bryson, D. and Lewis, J. (1985) *The Objectives of Child Care and their Attainment over a Twelve Month Period for a Cohort of New Admissions*. The Suffolk Cohort Study, Discussion Paper, 373. Canterbury: PSSRU, University of Kent.

Knapp, M. and Lowin (1998) 'Childcare outcome: economic perspectives and issues.' *Children and Society 12*, 169–179.

Knight, T. and Caveney, S. (1998) 'Assessment and Action Records: Will they promote good parenting?' *British Journal of Social Work 22*, 1, 29–44.

Kuzel, A. (1992) 'Theory based sampling.' In B. Crabtree and W. Miller (eds) *Doing Qualitative Research*. Newbury, CA: Sage.

Langlan, L. (1998) 'Radical social work.' In R. Adams, L. Dominelli and M. Payne (eds) *Social Work: Theory Issues and Critical Debates*. Basingstoke: Macmillan.

Leonard, M.F., Rhymes, J.P. and Solnit, A.J. (1966) 'Failure-to-thrive in infants.' *American Journal of Diseases of Children 111*, 600–612.

Lewis, J. (1996) 'Contracting and voluntary agencies.' In D. Billis and M. Harris (eds) *Voluntary Agencies: Challenges of Organisation and Management*. London: Macmillan.

Lloyd, M. and Taylor, C. (1995) 'From Hollis to the Orange Book: Developing a holistic model of social work assessment in the 1990s.' *British Journal of Social Work* 25, 691–710.

Lockhart, F. *et al.* (1996) 'School/Training/Employment Survey.' Strathclyde Regional Council Social Work Department, unpublished.

Lockyer, A. and Stone, F. (eds) (1998) *Juvenile Justice in Scotland.* Edinburgh: Green.

Macdonald, G. and Roberts, H. (1995) *What Works in the Early Years? Effective Interventions for Children and their Families in Health, Social Welfare, Education and Child Protection.* Ilford: Barnardos.

Macdonald, G., Sheldon, B. and Gillespie, J. (1992) 'Contemporary studies of the effectiveness of social work.' *British Journal of Social Work 22,* 6, 615–643.

Maginnis, E. (1993) *An Inter-agency Response to Children with Special Needs – The Lothian Experience – A Scottish Perspective.* Paper presented at the conference 'Exclusions from Schools: Bridging the Gap between Policy and Practice' organised by the National Children's Bureau, 13 July. London: National Children's Bureau.

Malahleka, B. and Woolfe, S. (1991) 'Ethnically sensitive social work: the obstacle race.' *Practice 5,* 1.

Marsh, P. and Crow, G. (1998) *Family Group Conferences in Child Welfare.* Oxford: Blackwell.

Marsh, P. and Peel, M. (1999) *Leaving Care in Partnership: Family Involvement with Care Leavers.* London: Stationery Office.

Marshall, T.F. (1996) 'Can we define the voluntary sector?' In D. Billis and M. Harris (eds) *Voluntary Agencies: Challenges of Organisation and Management.* London: Macmillan.

Mather, M., Humphrey, J. and Robson, J. (1997) 'The statutory medical and health needs of looked after children.' *Adoption & Fostering 21,* 2, 36–40.

McAuley, C. (1999) *The Family Support Outcome Study.* Research Report. Belfast: Northern Health and Social Services Board, Northern Ireland.

McCluskey, J. (1991) 'Ethnic minorities and the social work service in Glasgow.' In A. Bowes and D. Sim (eds) *Demands and Constraints: Ethnic Minorities and Social Services in Scotland.* Edinburgh: SCVO.

McDonald, G. and McDonald, K. (1995) 'Ethical issues in social work research.' In R. Hughman and D. Smith (eds) (1995) *Ethical Issues in Social Work.* London: Routledge.

McDonald, G. and Roberts, H. (1995) *What Works in the Early Years?* Barkingside: Barnardos.

McGee, C. and Westcott, H. (1996) 'System abuse: towards greater understanding from the perspectives of children and parents.' *Child and Family Social Work 1,* 3, 169–80.

McGinty, J. and Fish, J. (1992) *Learning Support for Young People: Transition: Leaving School for Further Education and Work.* Buckingham: Oxford University Press.

McLeod, N. (1996) *Children and Racism.* London: Childline.

McNeill, D. (1985) 'So you think gestures are non verbal?' *Psychological Review 92*, 320–371.

McNeill, D. (1992) *Hand and Mind: What Gestures Reveal About Thought.* Chicago: University of Chicago Press.

McPherson, Lord (1999) *Inquiry into the Murder of Stephen Lawrence.* London: HMSO.

Midgley, J. (1981) *Professional Imperialism: Social Work in the Third World.* London: Heinemann.

Miles, R. and Muirhead, L. (1986) 'Racism in Scotland: A matter for further investigation.' *Scottish Government Year Book.* Edinburgh.

Monaghan, B., Hill, M. and Tisdall, K. (1998) *The Evolving Contribution of the Voluntary Sector to Children's Services Planning.* Interim Report. http://www.gla.ac.uk/Inter/Child/Baring.htm

Monteith, M. (1999) 'Researching the Transition to Adulthood for Disabled Young People: Methodology.' Belfast: Centre for Child Care Research (unpublished paper).

Monteith, M. and Cousins, W. (1999) *Children and Young People with Disabilities in Northern Ireland. Part 3: The Impact of the Children (NI) Order.* Belfast: Centre for Child Care Research.

Monteith, M. and Sneddon, S. (1999) *The Circumstances, Experiences and Aspirations of Young People with Disabilities Making the Transition to Adulthood.* Belfast: Centre for Child Care Research.

Moosa-Mitha, M. (1999) 'The Children Act 1989: a partnership with parents?' In L. Dominelli (ed) *Community Approaches to Child Welfare.* Aldershot: Ashgate.

Morrow, V. and Richards, M. (1996) *Transitions to Adulthood: A Family Matter.* York: York Publishing Services (for Joseph Rowntree Foundation).

Moser, C.A. and Kalton, G. (1971) *Survey Methods in Social Investigations* (2nd edn). Aldershot: Dartmouth Publishing Company.

Moyers, S. (1997) *Report of an Audit of the Looking After Children forms in 1996.* Leicester: University of Leicester.

Muncie, J., Wetherell, M., Dallos, R. and Cochrane, A. (eds) (1999) *Understanding the Family.* London: Sage.

Murray, K. (1995) *Live Television Link: An Evaluation of its Use by Child Witnesses in Scottish Criminal Trials.* The Scottish Office Central Research Unit, Crime and Criminal Justice Research Findings No. 4. Edinburgh: The Scottish Office, HMSO.

Murray, K. and Hill, M. (1991) 'The recent history of Scottish child welfare.' *Children and Society 5*, 3, 266–281.

Newson, E. and Davies, J. (1994) 'Supporting siblings of children with autism and related developmental disorders.' In S. Mather and M. Rutter (eds) *Innovation in Family Support for People with Learning Difficulties.* Chorley: Lisieux Hall.

Oakley, A., Mauthner, M., Rajan, L. and Turner, H. (1995) 'Supporting vulnerable families: an evaluation of Newpin.' *Health Visitor 68*, 5.

Oakley, A. and Roberts, H. (eds) (1996) *Evaluating Social Interventions.* Essex: Barnardos.

Oates, R.K., Peacock, A. and Forest, D. (1984) 'Long-term effects of non-organic failure-to-thrive.' *Paediatrics 75,* 36–40.

Oates, R.K., and Yu, J.S. (1971) 'Children with non-organic failure-to-thrive: a community problem' *Australian Medical Journal 2,* 199.

O'Connaill, B., Whittaker, S. and Wilbur, S. (1993) 'Conversations over video conferences; An evaluation of video mediated interaction.' *Human–Computer Interaction 8,* 389–428.

OECD (1986) *Young People with Handicaps: The Road to Adulthood.* Paris: Centre for Education Research and Innovation (CERI), Organization for Economic Co-operation and Development (OECD).

Office for National Statistics (1994) *Social Trends, 24.* London: HMSO.

Office of Population Census and Survey (1991) *Census.* General Register Office for Scotland: HMSO.

Office for Standards in Education (Ofsted) and Social Services Inspectorate (SSI) (1995) *The Education of Children who are Looked-After by Local Authorities.* London: Ofsted/ SSI.

O'Hagan, K. (1993) *Emotional and Psychological Abuse of Children.* Buckingham: Open University Press.

O'Hagan, K. (1999) 'Culture, cultural identity and cultural sensitivity in child and family social work.' *Child and Family Social Work 4,* 4, 269–282.

Oliver, M. and Sapey, B. (1998) *Social Work with Disabled People.* London: Macmillan.

Olson, J.S., Olson, G.M. and Meader, D.K. (1995) 'What mix of video and audio is useful for remote real-time work.' *Proceedings of Workshop on VMC, CSCW.* Chapel Hill, NC, 22 October 1994. New York: ACM.

O'Malley, C. and Langton, S. (1994) 'Video-mediated communication: strategies for research.' *Proceedings of Workshop on MC,* CSCW. Chapel Hill, NC, 22 October 1994. New York: ACM.

Orme, J. (1998) 'Feminist social work.' In R. Adams, L. Dominelli and M. Payne (eds) *Social Work: Theory Issues and Critical Debates.* Basingstoke: Macmillan.

Osborn, A. and St Claire, L. (1987) 'The ability and behaviour of children who have been in care or separated from their parents.' *Early Child Development and Care 28,* 3, 187–354.

Otteson, J.P. and Otteson, C.R. (1980) 'Effect of teacher's gaze on children's story recall.' *Perceptual Motor Skills 50,* 35–42.

Packman, J. and Jordan, B. (1991) 'The Children Act: looking forward, looking back.' *British Journal of Social Work 21,* 4, 315–328.

Parker, G. (1984) *Into Work: A Review of the Literature About Disabled Young Adults' Preparation for and Movement into Employment.* York: Social Policy Research Unit, University of York.

Parker, R. (1998) 'Reflections on the Assessment of Outcomes in child care.' *Children & Society 12*, 3, 192–201.

Parker, R., Ward, H., Jackson, S., Aldgate, J. and Wedge, P. (1991) *Looking After Children: Assessing Outcomes in Child Care.* London: HMSO.

Parton, N. (1985) *The Politics of Child Abuse.* London: Macmillan.

Parton, N. (1991) *Governing the Family.* London: Macmillan.

Parton, N. (1996) *Social Theory, Social Change and Social Work.* London: Routledge.

Patton, R.G. and Gardner, L.I. (1962) 'Influence of family environment on growth: the syndrome of maternal deprivation.' *Paediatrics 30*, 957–962.

Payne, M. (1997) *Modern Social Work Theory,* (2nd edn). Basingstoke: Macmillan.

Pechman, T. and Deutsch, W. (1982) 'The development of verbal and nonverbal devices for reference.' *Journal of Experimental Child Psychology 34*, 330–341.

Percy, A., Iwaniec, D., Carr-Hill, R., Jamison, J. and Dixon, P. (1998) *Development of Needs Indicators for the Family and Childcare Programme of Care in Northern Ireland: Stage 1 – Scoping Study.* Report to The HSS Executive. Belfast: Health and Social Care Research Unit.

Percy, A. and Mayhew, P. (1997) 'Estimating sexual victimisation in a national crime survey: a new approach.' *Studies on Crime and Crime Prevention 6*, 2, 125–150.

Peyton, L. (1996) 'Strategic planning for children in need.' *Child Care in Practice, Special Children Order Edition,* 23–27.

Phelan, J. (1983) *Family Centres: A Study.* London: Children's Society.

Phillips, M. and Worlock, D. (1996) 'Implementing the Looking After Children system in RBK&C.' *Adoption & Fostering 20*, 4, 42–48.

Pinkerton, J., Higgins. K, and Devine, P. (1998a) *Family Support Perspectives from Practice: Report of the Evaluation of South Belfast Leaving Care Scheme.* Belfast: Centre for Child Care Research, The Queen's University of Belfast.

Pinkerton, J., Higgins, K. and Devine, P. (1998b) *Family Support Perspectives from Practice: Report of the Evaluation of Portadown Child and Family Care Team.* Belfast: Centre for Child Care Research, Queen's University of Belfast.

Pinkerton, J., Higgins, K. and Devine, P. (2000) *Family Support: Linking Project Evaluation to Policy Analysis.* Aldershot: Ashgate.

Pinkerton, J., Higgins, K. and Switzer, V. (1997) *Family Support Perspectives from Practice: Report of the Pilot Evaluation of Simpson Family Resource Centre.* Belfast: Centre for Child Care Research, The Queen's University of Belfast.

Pinkerton, J. and McCrea, R. (1999) *Meeting the Challenge: Young People Leaving Care in Northern Ireland.* Aldershot: Ashgate.

Pinkerton, J. and Stein, M. (1995) 'Responding to the needs of young people leaving state care; law practice and policy in England and Northern Ireland.' *Children and Youth Services Review 17*, 5/6. 683–695.

Pollitt, E. and Eichler, A.W. (1976) 'Behavioural disturbances among failure-to-thrive children.' *American Journal of Diseases of Children 130*, 24–29.

Pollitt, E., Eichler, A.W. and Chan, C.K. (1975) 'Psychosocial development and behaviour of mothers of failure-to-thrive children.' *American Journal of Orthopsychiatry 45*, 525–537.

Powell, G.F., Brasel, J.A. and Blizzard, R.M. (1967) 'Emotional deprivation and growth retardation simulating idiopathic hypopituitarism: I. Clinical evaluation of the syndrome.' *New England Journal of Medicine 276*, 1271–1278.

Ramsay, M. and Percy, A. (1996) *Drug Misuse Declared: Results of the 1994 British Crime Survey.* London: Home Office.

Ramsay, M. and Percy, A. (1997) 'A national survey of drug misuse in Britain: a decade of development.' *Addiction 92*, 8, 931–937.

Raynor, P. and Rudolf, M.C.J. (1996) 'What do we know about children who fail-to-thrive?' *Child Care, Heath and Development 22*, 4, 241–250.

Reif, S., Beler, B., Villa, Y. and Spirer, L. (1995) 'Long-term follow-up and outcome of infants with non-organic failure-to-thrive.' *Israel Journal of Medical Sciences 31*, 483–489.

Rickford, F. (1998) 'Partner or put upon.' *Community Care*, 29 January–4 February, 20–21.

Ritchie, P., Christie, S. and Wilson, E. (1996) *Population Needs Assessment in Community Care – A Handbook for Planners and Practitioners.* Edinburgh: Social Work Service Inspectorate for Scotland.

Roberts, H. and Macdonald, G. (1999) 'Working with families in the Early Years.' In M. Hill (ed) *Effective Ways of Working with Children and Families.* London: Jessica Kingsley Publishers.

Robson, B., Bradford, M. and Deas, I. (1994) *Relative Deprivation in Northern Ireland.* Policy Planning and Research Unit Occasional Paper 28. Belfast: PPRU.

Ross, S.M. (1996) 'Risk of physical abuse to children of spouse abusing parents.' *Child Abuse and Neglect 20*, 589–598.

Rutter, M. (1981) *Maternal Deprivation Reassessed.* Harmondsworth: Penguin.

Rutter, R.R. (1987) *Communicating by Telephone.* Oxford: Pergamon Press.

Rutter, R.R., Stephenson, G.M. and Dewey, M.E. (1981) 'Visual communication and the content and style of conversation.' *British Journal of Social Psychology 20*, 41–52.

Rutter, M., Tizard, J. and Whitmore, R. (1970) *Education, Health and Behaviour.* London: Longman.

Ryan, M. (1994) *The Children Act – Putting it into Practice.* Aldershot: Arena.

Saywitz, K., Geiselman, R.E. and Bornstein, R. (1992) 'Effects of cognitive interviewing on children's recall performance.' *Journal of Applied Psychology 77*, 744–756.

Saywitz, K.J. and Nathanson, R. (1993) 'Children's testimony and their perceptions of stress in and out of the courtroom.' *Child Abuse and Neglect 17*, 613–622.

Scally, M. and Shabbaz, A. (1995) 'Recasting support for children with disabilities.' *Child Care in Practice 2*, 2, 10–21.

Schaffer, H.R. (1990) *Making Decisions about Children.* Oxford: Blackwell.

Scheman, J.D. and Lockard, J.S. (1979) 'Development of gaze aversion in children.' *Child Development 50*, 594–596.

Scott, J. (1999) *Report of an Audit of the Looking After Children Forms in Year 3: 1997/8.* Leicester: University of Leicester.

Scottish Office (1992) *Another Kind of Home: Review of Residential Child Care in Scotland (The Skinner Report).*Edinburgh: HMSO.

Scottish Office (1994a) *Working Together: The Scottish Office, Volunteers and Voluntary Organisations.* Edinburgh: Scottish Office.

Scottish Office (1994b) *Teaching with Care* (Video) Scottish Office Education Department and Quality in Education Centre, University of Strathclyde.

Scottish Office (1997b) *Scotland's Children. Volume 2.* Edinburgh: HMSO.

Scottish Office (1998a) *The Scottish Compact.* Cm 4083. Edinburgh: Scottish Office.

Scottish Office (1998b) *Valuing Diversity.* Edinburgh: HMSO.

Scottish Office, Social Work Services Group (1993) *Scotland's Children: Proposals for Child Care Policy and Law. Cm 2286.* Edinburgh: HMSO.

Scottish Office, Social Work Services Group (1997a) *Scotland's Children. The Children (Scotland) Act 1995 Regulations and Guidance. Volume 1: Support and Protection for Children and their Families.* Edinburgh: Stationery Office.

Scottish Office, Social Work Services Group (1999) *Children (Scotland) Act 1995: Review of Children's Services.* Letter, 11 January.

Sellen, A.J. (1995) 'Remote conversations: the effects of mediating talk with technology.' *Human Computer Interaction 10*, 401–444.

Shakespeare, T. (1998) *The Disability Reader.* London: Cassell.

Shatz, M. (1977) 'The relationship between cognitive processes and the development of communication skills.' In C.B. Keasey (ed) *Current Theory and Research in Motivation.* Nebraska Symposium on Motivation. Lincoln, NB: University of Nebraska Press.

Shaw, C. (1998) *Remember My Messages.* The Who Cares? Trust. London: Stationery Office.

Shaw, I. (1996) *Evaluating in Practice.* Aldershot: Arena.

Shaw, I. (1999) 'Evidence for practice.' In I. Shaw and J. Lishman (eds) *Evaluation and Social Work Practice.* London: Sage.

Shaw, I. and Lishman, J. (eds) (1999) *Evaluation and Social Work Practice.* London: Sage.

Sheppard, M. and Woodcock, J. (1999) 'Need as an operating concept: the case of social work with children and families.' *Child and Family Social Work 4*, 67–76.

Shepperdson, B. (1995) 'Changes in options for school leavers with Down's Syndrome.' *Care in Place 2*, 1, 22–28.

Sinclair, I. and Gibbs, I. (1998) *Children's Homes. A Study of Diversity.* Chichester: Wiley.

Sinclair, R. (1998) 'Developing evidence-based policy and practice in social interventions with children and families.' *International Journal of Social Research Methodology 1*, 2, 169–176.

Sinclair, R. and Carr-Hill, R. (1995) *The Categorisation of Children in Need.* York: Centre for Health Economics, University of York.

Singer, L. and Fagan, J. (1984) 'Cognitive development in the failure-to-thrive infants.' *Journal of Pediatric Psychology 9*, 363–383.

Singh, S. (1997) 'Assessing Asian families in Scotland.' *Adoption & Fostering 21*, 3, 35–39.

Skellington, R. and Morris, P. (1992) *'Race' in Britain Today.* London: Sage.

Skuse, D. (1989). 'Emotional abuse and delay in growth.' In R. Meadow (ed) *ABC of Child Abuse.* London: British Medical Association.

Skuse, D., Albanese, A., Stanhope, R, Gilmore, J. and Voss, L. (1996) 'A new stress-related syndrome of growth failure and hyperphagia in children associated with reversibility of growth-hormone insufficiency.' *Lancet 348(9024)*, 353–358.

Skuse, D., Wolke, D. and Reilly, S. (1992) 'Failure-to-thrive: clinical and developmental aspects.' In H. Remschmidt and M.H. Schmidt (eds) *Developmental Psychopathology.* Lewiston, NY: Hogrefe and Huber.

Smith, R., O'Shea, T., O'Malley, C., Scanlon, E. and Taylor, J. (1991) 'Preliminary experiments with a distributed, multi-media, problem-solving environment.' In J. Bowers and S. Benford (eds) *Studies in Computer-supported Co-operative Work: Theory, Practice and Design.* Amsterdam: Elsevier.

Smith, T. (1987) 'Family centres: prevention, partnership or community alternative?' In J.A. Macfarlane (ed) *Progress in Child Health, Vol. 3.* London: Churchill Livingstone.

Smith, T. (1996) *Family Centres and Bringing Up Young Children.* London: HMSO.

Social Information Systems (SIS) (1994) *Defining, Managing and Monitoring Children in Need.* Cheshire: Social Information Systems Ltd.

Social Information Systems (1995) *Children in Need in Northern Ireland.* Cheshire: Social Information Systems Ltd.

Social Information Systems, Association of Directors of Social Services, and Social Services Inspectorate (Wales) (1994) *Defining, Managing and Monitoring Children in Need in Wales: A Joint Overview for the New Local Authorities.* Produced for the Children in Need Working Group. Cheshire: Social Information Systems Ltd.

Social Services Inspectorate (1996) *Children's Services Plans: An Analysis of Children's Services Plans 1993/94.* Wetherby: Department of Health.

Social Services Inspectorate (1994) *The Challenge of Partnership in Child Protection: Practice Guide.* London: HMSO.

Social Services Inspectorate (1997) *Responding to Families in Need: Inspection of Assessment, Planning and Decision-making in Family Support Services.* Wetherby: Department of Health.

Social Services Inspectorate (1998) *Partners in Planning: Approaches to Planning Services for Children and their Families.* Wetherby: Department of Health.

Social Work Services Group (SWSG) (1997) *Scotland's Children. The Children (Scotland) Act 1995 Regulations and Guidance, Volume 2: Children Looked After by Local Authorities.* Edinburgh: Stationery Office.

Spitz, R.A. (1945) 'Hospitalism: an inquiry into the genesis of psychiatric conditions in early childhood.' *Psychoanalytic Study of the Child 1*, 53–74.

Statham, J. (1994) *Child Care in the Community*. London: Save the Children.

Stein, M. (1990) *Living Out of Care*. Ilford: Barnardos.

Stein, M. and Carey, K. (1986) *Leaving Care*. Oxford: Basil Blackwell.

Stevens, A. and Raftery, J. (1994) *Health Care Needs Assessment: The Epidemiological Based Needs Assessment Reviews*. Oxford: Radcliffe Medical.

Stevenson, O. (ed) (1999) *Child Welfare in the UK*. Oxford: Blackwell.

Straus, M.A., Hamby, S.L., Finkelhor, D., Moore, D.W. and Runyan, D. (1998) 'Identification of child maltreatment with the Parent–Child Conflict Tactics Scale: development and psychometric data for a national sample of American parents.' *Child Abuse and Neglect 22*, 249–270.

Sutton, P. (1995) *Crossing the Boundaries. A Discussion of Children's Services Plans*. London: National Children's Bureau.

Sweeting, H. (forthcoming) 'One family, whose perspective?' *Journal of Adolescence*.

Talbot, N.B., Sobel, E.H., Burke, B.S., Lindeman, E. and Kaufman, S.B. (1947) 'Dwarfism in healthy children: its possible relation to emotional, nutritional and endocrine disturbances.' *New England Journal of Medicine 263*, 783–793.

Taylor, M., Langan, J. and Hoggett, P. (1995) *Encouraging Diversity: Voluntary and Private Organisations in Community Care*. Aldershot: Arena, Ashgate.

Thoburn, J. (1998) *Children in Need: A Review of Family Support in Three Local Authorities*. London: HMSO.

Thoburn, J., Lewis, A. and Shemmings, D. (1995) *Paternalism or Partnership: Family Involvement in the Child Protection Process*. London: HMSO.

Thoburn, J., Nourfurd, L. and Rashid, S. (1999) *Permanent Family Placement for Minority Ethnic Children*. Norwich: UEA.

Thoburn, J., Wilding, J. and Watson, J. (1997) 'Family support plans for neglected children referred to Social Services Departments.' *Family Support Network Newsletter 10*, 3–5.

Thompson, N. (1997) *Anti-Discriminatory Practice*, (2nd edn). Basingstoke: Macmillan.

Tisdall, K., Lavery, R. and McCrystal, P. (1998) *Child Care Law: A Comparative Review of New Legislation in Northern Ireland and Scotland*. Belfast: Centre for Child Care Research, The Queen's University of Belfast.

Tizard, B. (1977) *Adoption: A Second Chance*. London: Open Books.

Tobey, A.E., Goodman, G.S., Batterman-Faunce, J.M., Orcutt, H.K. and Sachsenmaier, T. (1995) 'Balancing the rights of children and defendants: Effects of closed-circuit television on children's accuracy and jurors' perceptions.' In M.S. Zaragoza and J.R. Graham (eds) *Memory and Testimony in the Child Witness Applied Psychology Individual, Social, and Community Issues*. Thousand Oaks, CA: Sage Publications.

Trinder, L. (1996) 'Social work research: the state of the art or science.' *Child and Family Social Work 1*, 233–242.

Triseliotis, J. (1999) 'Is permanency through adoption in decline?' *Adoption & foStering* 22, 4, 41–49.

Triseliotis, J., Borland, M., Hill, M. and Lambert, L. (1997) *Teenagers and the Social Work Services.* London: HMSO.

Triseliotis, J. and Russell, J. (1984) *Hard to Place.* London: Heinemann.

Tunstill, J. (1996) 'Family support: past, present and future challenges.' *Child and Family Social Work 1*, 3, 151–158.

Tunstill, J. (1998) *The Conceptual and Technical Challenges of Evaluating Family Support: Some Reflections following Two National Studies on Section 17 of the Children Act (1989).* Proceedings from the Family Support Evaluation Network Conference, October. Occasional Paper. Belfast: The Queen's University of Belfast.

Tunstill, J., Aldgate, J., Wilson, M. and Sutton, P. (1996) 'Crossing the organisational divide.' *Health and Social Care in the Community 4*, 1, 41–49.

Turvey, K. (1995) *Needs Based Planning: Use of Information from Individual Assessments to Develop Population Estimates of Need and Use of Resources.* PSSRU Discussion Paper 1136. Canterbury: University of Kent.

Tutt, N. and Giller, H. (1995) *Children in Need – A Set of Operational Indicators.* Belfast: DHSS.

Utting, W. (1989) 'Foreword.' In B. Kahan *Child Care Research, Policy and Practice.* London: Hodder and Stoughton.

Utting, W. (1991) *Children in the Public Care: A Review of Residential Child Care.* London: HMSO.

Utting, W. (1997) *People Like Us. The Report of the Review of the Safeguards for Children Living Away from Home.* London: Stationery Office.

Van der Eyken, W. (1982) *HomeStart: A Four Year Evaluation.* Leicester: HomeStart.

Vygotsky, L. (1962) *Thought and Language.* Cambridge, MA: MIT Press. First published 1934.

Walker, A. (1982) *Unqualified and Unemployed: Handicapped Young People and the Labour Market.* London: Macmillan Press.

Walker, T. (1994) 'Educating children in the public care: a strategic approach.' *Oxford Review of Education 20*, 3, 329–347.

Ward, H. (ed) (1995) *Looking After Children: Research into Practice.* London: HMSO.

Ward, H. (1996) 'Constructing and implementing measures to assess the outcomes of looking after children away from home.' In M. Hill and J. Aldgate (eds) *Child Welfare Services.* London: Jessica Kingsley Publishers.

Ward, H. (1998) 'Using a child development model to assess the outcomes for social work intervention with families.' *Children and Society 12*, 3, 202–209.

Warner, N. (1992) *The Report of the Committee of Inquiry into the Selection, Development and Management of Staff in Children's Homes.* London: HMSO.

Webb, D. (1996) 'Regulation for Radicals: The state, CCETSW and the Academy.' In N. Parton (1996) *Social Theory, Social Change and Social Work.* London: Routledge.

Webster-Stratton, C. and Herbert, M. (1994) *Troubled Families: Problem Children.* Chichester: Wiley.

Wellings, K., Field, J., Johnston, A.M. and Wadsworth, J. (1994) *Sexual Behaviour in Britain: The National Survey of Sexual Attitudes and Lifestyles.* London: Penguin.

Westcott, H., Davies, G. and Clifford, B. (1991a) 'The credibility of child witnesses seen on closed-circuit television.' *Adoption & foStering 15,* 14–19.

Westcott, H., Davies, G. and Clifford, B.R. (1991b) 'Adults' perceptions of children's videotaped truthful and deceptive statements.' *Children & Society 5,* 123–135.

Western Area Children and Young People's Committee (1999) *Children Services Plan.* Omagh: Western Health and Social Services Board.

Wheelaghan, S., Hill, M., Borland, M., Lambert, L. and Triseliotis, J. (1999) *Looking After Children in Scotland.* Edinburgh: Scottish Office.

Whitten, C.F. (1976) 'Can treatment be effectively investigated?' *American Journal of Diseases of Children 130,* 15.

Wickens, T.D. (1993) 'Quantitative methods for estimating the size of a drug-using population.' *The Journal of Drug Issues 23,* 2, 185–216.

Widdowson, E.M. (1951) 'Mental contentment and physical growth.' *Lancet 260,* 1316–1318.

Widom, C.S. and Morris, S. (1997) 'Accuracy of recollections of childhood victimisation: Part 2. Childhood sexual abuse.' *Psychological Assessment 9,* 34–46.

Widom, C.S. and Shepard, R.L. (1996) 'Accuracy of recollections of childhood victimisation: Part 1. Childhood physical abuse.' *Psychological Assessment 8,* 412–421.

Wilding, J. and Thoburn, J. (1997) 'Family support plans for neglected and emotionally maltreated children.' *Child Abuse Review 6,* 5, 343–356.

Williams, E. (1977) 'Experimental comparisons of face-to-face and video mediated communication.' *Psychological Bulletin 84,* 963–976.

Wilson, M. (1996) 'Children (NI) Order 1995 – implications for working with children with a disability and their families.' *Child Care in Practice 2,* 3, 81–85.

Wynne, M. (1996) 'What is failure to thrive?' Introduction to Special Edition. *Child Care, Health and Development 22,* 4, 212–213.

Subject Index

Author Index